Legal Concepts for
Facility Managers

LIVERPOOL JMU LIBRARY

3   1111   01514   3439

Legal Concepts for Facility Managers

Linda Thomas-Mobley

Former Associate Chair, School of Building Construction,
College of Architecture

Dean, Former Chair of the Construction Management Department

This edition first published 2014
© 2014 by John Wiley & Sons Limited

Registered office
John Wiley & Sons, Ltd, The Atrium, Southern Gate, Chichester, West Sussex,
PO19 8SQ, United Kingdom.

Editorial offices:
9600 Garsington Road, Oxford, OX4 2DQ, United Kingdom.
The Atrium, Southern Gate, Chichester, West Sussex, PO19 8SQ, United Kingdom.

For details of our global editorial offices, for customer services and for information about how to apply for permission to reuse the copyright material in this book please see our website at www.wiley.com/wiley-blackwell.

The right of the author to be identified as the author of this work has been asserted in accordance with the UK Copyright, Designs and Patents Act 1988.

All rights reserved. No part of this publication may be reproduced, stored in a retrieval system, or transmitted, in any form or by any means, electronic, mechanical, photocopying, recording or otherwise, except as permitted by the UK Copyright, Designs and Patents Act 1988, without the prior permission of the publisher.

Designations used by companies to distinguish their products are often claimed as trademarks. All brand names and product names used in this book are trade names, service marks, trademarks or registered trademarks of their respective owners. The publisher is not associated with any product or vendor mentioned in this book.

Limit of Liability/Disclaimer of Warranty: While the publisher and author(s) have used their best efforts in preparing this book, they make no representations or warranties with respect to the accuracy or completeness of the contents of this book and specifically disclaim any implied warranties of merchantability or fitness for a particular purpose. It is sold on the understanding that the publisher is not engaged in rendering professional services and neither the publisher nor the author shall be liable for damages arising herefrom. If professional advice or other expert assistance is required, the services of a competent professional should be sought.

Library of Congress Cataloging-in-Publication Data

Thomas-Mobley, Linda
    Legal concepts for facility managers / Linda Thomas-Mobley.
         pages cm
    Includes bibliographical references and index.
    ISBN 978-0-470-67474-1 (pbk.)
    1. Facility management – Law and legislation – United States.   I. Title.
    KF905.F34T48 2014
    349.73024′6582 – dc23
                                                            2013026693

A catalogue record for this book is available from the British Library.

Wiley also publishes its books in a variety of electronic formats. Some content that appears in print may not be available in electronic books.

Cover image: © Shutterstock/zayats-and-zayats
Cover design by Andy Meaden, Meaden Creative

Set in 10/13pt HelveticaNeue by Laserwords Private Limited, Chennai, India
Printed and bound in Malaysia by Vivar Printing Sdn Bhd

1   2014

To Joyce and Alvin Thomas, I would like to publicly acknowledge your interminable support, you taught me to look at the world as it is, and face life head-on with my eyes wide-open, thanks for making me resilient.

Contents

About the Author

Linda Thomas-Mobley is Dean and former Chair of the Construction Management Department at the NewSchool of Architecture and Design in San Diego, California. She formerly served as Associate Chair of the School of Building and Construction at the Georgia Institute of Technology. She is a veteran academic with professional experience as a Construction Manager, Facility Manager and an attorney at law. As a professor teaching graduate and undergraduate students how to navigate the US legal system and avoid exposure to liability, she discovered the need for an illustrated legal textbook for built environment professionals. She holds a Juris Doctorate in law, a BS and MS in Civil Engineering and a PhD.

Acknowledgments

To my love, Michael, you poor soul; thanks for taking care of me, keeping me safe and accompanying me along this unfamiliar journey. To my daughter, Morgan; thanks for your encouragement, never forget who you are, where you come from and how to balance your checkbook. And to my sister, Carroll; thanks for always setting the bar just beyond my reach.

Thanks to all of my friends and colleagues at the NewSchool of Architecture and Design, your encouragement helped me make it through many a long night.

Finally, I am forever indebted to Lucy Campbell for her cheerful disposition and stern reminders to keep writing.

Preface

In the state of nature. . . all men are born equal, but they cannot continue in this equality. Society makes them lose it, and they recover it only by the protection of the law.
Charles de Montesquieu, French lawyer and philosopher (1689–1755).

Studying the law is thought by many to consist of memorizing a fixed set of rules, often called "black letter law". Black letter law refers to the basic rules of law accepted by most judges in most areas. Knowledge of these rules is important but simply knowing applicable rules does not do justice to the study of law. For example, merely knowing that thou shall not kill is inadequate. What exactly is "killing"? Also, if someone kills according our definition, shall we punish the killer by killing her? Would we then be killed? The act may be the result of war or in defense of a spouse, or in the case of capital punishment, even authorized by the state. Simply memorizing black letter law prevents one from fully understanding, disguising the beauty of its logic, and how legal theory evolves over time.

For example, Hammurabi, a First Dynasty king of the city-state of Babylon in 1792 BCE, is best known for proclaiming a new code of Babylonian law called the Code of Hammurabi. Many consider this code one of the first written laws in the world[1]. Paraphrasing Hammurabi's Code, if a builder constructs a house and it falls and kills the owner, the builder is to be slain[2]. Memorizing this rule is useless for modern built environment disputes, but understanding that the builder has a special duty to build a structure that does not fall and kill the owner, is a legal principle that has survived. The deeper we investigate the study of law the sooner we learn that "there is no abstract rule of law outside of any specific fact situation"[3]. That means the answer to the often-asked question, "Can I get sued if. . . ?" is always "yes"; because anyone with the requisite filing fee following the court's procedures can sue. It also means the answer to the follow up question, "Will I be held liable if. . . ?" is a resounding "maybe", because it all depends on the specific facts.

This text is not written to impress my peers but to help non-lawyers understand the legal system and determine where the built environment professional fits into the larger picture. Those who have studied the law may find some

---

[1] Breasted (2003)
[2] King (2007)
[3] Mentschikoff and Stotzky (1981)

sections elementary, but I expect you will find the application of the law to the practice of facility management and examples used instructional. As a former Construction Manager, Facility Manager and practicing attorney, I've written this text not only for students studying facility management but for all who intend to work in the built environment industry. This text focuses on the application of law to the role of the Facility Manager and thereby fills a much-needed gap in instructional literature. Many US undergraduate and graduate facility management programs teach legal issues in the context of construction or business law. However, prior to this text, courses on legal issues for Facility Managers tended to utilize construction law texts and either supplement them with additional case studies and legal topics or simply ignore the subject altogether. It is my intention to address this oversight. I hope to fill the gap experienced by those studying facility management or working in the industry who seek an understanding of legal concepts beyond construction issues. The instructor, either lawyer or non-lawyer, is now equipped with a resource for explaining legal concepts from the viewpoint of the built environment professional managing the facility.

As with any text expressly written for non-legal professionals, the objective is to both enlighten the reader and help keep her free from unnecessary court proceedings. Although the average cost of a trial in the USA is almost impossible to predict, any day a Facility Manager can spend managing facilities rather than sitting in a courtroom is a good day. It is my hope that this text will also demonstrate that the US legal system is not one organism; rather it is a web of integrated organisms.

Currently, standard higher education courses require the student to spend three hours working each week for every one credit awarded. Additionally many accrediting bodies and the US Department of Education are requiring schools to show evidence that this directive is followed. This book was designed with such a formula in mind, and it is estimated that the average student will require six hours each week, reading and preparing for a three-credit class in Facility Management Law. With the exception of cases reported throughout the book, students will find the reading comparable to most undergraduate textbooks.

For reference and explanation of specific legal terms used, it is recommended that the student have access to a legal dictionary. Legal dictionaries, such as *Black's Law Dictionary*, published by West, contain well-written definitions of concepts you will learn about in this textbook.

The text is organized in three main parts, Part I focuses on an introduction to the US legal system and form of government. Part II introduces the major areas of law. Finally, Part III applies concepts and knowledge gained from Part I and II to modern built environment problems.

Instructional goals for this book include the following:

1. Demystify the US legal system.
2. Link the US legal system to the practice of facility management.
3. Help students acquire and retain legal information.
4. Create "law-literate" citizens.

The specific learning objectives, or what students will be able demonstrate after a course using this textbook include:

- Understand how the US legal system operates.
- Describe what is legally required from a Facility Manager.
- Analyze legal issues faced by Facility Managers.
- Evaluate the legal risks involved in the management of the built environment.
- Illustrate how to mitigate risks faced by the typical Facility Manager.

Additional learning outcomes for specific chapters will be presented at the beginning of each chapter in hopes of helping the student to focus.

Finally, relevant chapters will end with discussion questions to help students recall salient information and are intended to be used as homework assignments or prompts for classroom discussions.

Now let's get on with learning about the law!

Ut humiliter opinor

Part I

Fundamentals

Introduction

This section serves as an introduction to the US legal system and its unique form of government. The chapters are written to assume that the student has no background in the subject and makes an attempt to define what "law" means. As you will quickly discover, defining the law is difficult because it is more concept or theory than specific rules.

Understanding the three main functions that include regulator, facilitator and dispute resolver is also considered. Finally, appreciating legal theory is difficult without basic knowledge of the US Government and the operation of its three branches.

1

American Jurisprudence

We the People of the United States, in Order to form a more perfect Union, establish Justice, insure domestic Tranquility, provide for the common defence [sic], promote the general Welfare, and secure the Blessings of Liberty to ourselves and our Posterity, do ordain and establish this Constitution for the United States of America.

Constitution of The United States of America

1.1 Introduction

Using the famous preamble to the United States Constitution is fitting to begin this chapter, and this entire text, for several reasons. The first and most important reason is because the Constitution is the supreme law of the land in the USA, and all laws must be in accord with this charter. Another reason for using the preamble is because it shows the intent of the founding fathers. All of the words not usually capitalized in the middle of a sentence, such as People, Justice and Tranquility, indicate a higher level of importance placed on these concepts by the founders. Finally, the British spelling of the word "defence" is used instead of the US English spelling of defense. This spelling hints at the origins of US Law that lie in Great Britain.

In Chapter 1, we will consider the basic theory behind US Law. This basic theory or philosophy of law is known as *jurisprudence*. These theories are typically debated in US law schools at the commencement of a student's course of study. They form the foundation for understanding why judges apply laws in a particular way. The process used by judges applying law to a case is one component of a larger skill set used by judges and attorneys, referred to

Legal Concepts for Facility Managers, First Edition. Linda Thomas-Mobley.
© 2014 John Wiley & Sons, Ltd. Published 2014 by John Wiley & Sons, Ltd.

as *legal reasoning*. Although deceptively simple sounding, the student is urged not to underestimate the importance of understanding legal reasoning and the resulting legal argument. Briefly, legal reasoning involves understanding what specific issue is at hand; knowing what legal theory governs this type of issue; knowing which facts are relevant to this legal theory and applying the legal theory to the facts.

At the end of this chapter the following student learning outcomes are expected:

- Discuss the concept of "law".
- Recognize the specific functions it serves.
- Describe how law is made.
- Explain how law is implemented.
- Define the components of the US Legal System.
- Explain the formal dispute resolution process.

1.2 Definition

Defining law as it is used in the US legal system is so problematic that even our best efforts fall short. In one aspect the law is a set of rules used to maintain peace and order in society. It is also a state-recognized notion or principle such that failure to follow it can bring about punishment. Additionally, it is a set of community standards necessary for us to recognize acceptable behavior.

To get around this problem, textbook authors describe what the law does, or how the law is applied. In light of the goal of this textbook, we shall follow suit and describe the law's main functions, what the law and those who practice law hope to accomplish, and how it is applied to the built environment.

1.3 Functions

Figure 1.1 depicts the three major functions of the law. In studying US law, we see that, for the law to have existed over hundreds of years, it must serve some function useful to society. These functions can be as varied as the individuals who rely on the law. However, three functions tend to be of the most significance; namely the functions of regulator, facilitator and dispute resolver. In its regulatory function, the law controls behavior so that society can function smoothly. As a facilitator, the law is a catalyst for action by deciding whether a question is best decided by a court, another body of government such as the legislature, or not subjected to judicial review at all. Finally, the function most familiar to us all is the law's dispute resolution function, useful in settling various types of disagreements without violence.

Figure 1.1 The three major functions of US law.

The law as regulator serves to keep individuals within the accepted customs of society, thereby ensuring a smoothly functioning civilization. Without this function another system for maintaining accepted customs would be necessary. If you have ever been a part of the formation of a new club or informal social group, you have experienced the need for this regulatory function.

For example, in social media environments there are written or expressed customs and unwritten customs generally expected of members. A written custom, for example, may be that each individual may only have one account and can only post messages that are non-offensive. An unwritten custom may be the preference for short, pointed statements and the use of initialisms such as "LOL" that are understood by most members without the need for explanation. The software designer easily regulates these customs by writing computer code that limits the number of accounts at registration and controls the number of characters a user can use in a post. In this instance, the software designer, using the "law" of computer code is serving as a regulator. As in many instances across society, this regulatory function speaks to the members' sense of fairness and seeks to control excesses that may undermine the entire purpose of the community.

In the greater society, regulatory laws are plentiful and include controls on many areas of industry, from laws against insider trading, to laws controlling fire retardant standards in children's sleepwear. The regulation function promotes an ordered society where citizens can predict the consequences of their actions. If an entrepreneur can predict the consequences of her decisions, she is able to easily assess risks and being able to assess risks allows for economic stability.

Much more subtle is the law's function as a facilitator. Since the legal system in the USA is an actual system of governmental bodies and not just one entity, it requires a facilitator to assign roles and decide which of those bodies should speak to a decision. The different branches of government perform specific and unique duties. This structure allows for the equal division of power and control among three branches of government: judicial, executive and legislative. Additionally, deciding whether or not a matter should be taken up in a state or a federal court is the job of the facilitating function of the law.

Though this function is subtle, parties resolving a dispute within the rules set up by the law serving as facilitator can fully rely on decisions made by the courts. This function will be further explained in Chapter 2 when we discuss state and federal jurisdiction, and the role these play in legal decisions and legal strategy.

The law's dispute resolution function is easily understood in the context of courts making judgments for or against a party involved in a disagreement with another. This major function serves society by attempting to settle disputes in a peaceful manner. It allows people with distinct interests the opportunity to assert claims and resolve differences peacefully. This function is closest to the idea of the law as a series of rules, called the *black letter rule of law*. Even in the law's dispute resolution function, the regulating and facilitating functions also operate in the background.

While this short summary provides an overview of what the law is used for, it is important to remember that the functions of the law are as varied as the individuals who rely upon it. The other functions of the law will be discussed when appropriate in the hopes of demonstrating the earlier assertion made. That is, the law is not simply a list of rules to be used for dispute resolution.

1.4 Sources of law

In the instance of US laws, the source of law has a direct relationship to how the law impacts Facility Managers. The creation of law is a by-product of governing citizens. This is why it is often said that the USA is a nation of laws since the act of governing can also be an act of making law. In the US federal system, power is shared between the federal and state governments. This arrangement gives local entities some autonomy to deal with parochial issues while also protecting numerically minority populations from domination by the majority. Allowing a state like Rhode Island to control its driving age laws for its own citizens gives an amount of independence to the smaller state. Teenagers living in rural areas may require the ability to drive earlier than teenagers living in New York City. Not subjecting citizens in Rhode Island to the driving age laws of a city in New York State protects this independence.

In this system there is recognition that a central government is still necessary to govern certain issues on behalf of all citizens. It would be a confusing situation if, for example, each state independently controlled currency, foreign relations and defense of the nation. In contrast, issues such as building codes and sales tax are better controlled at the state level.

1.4.1 United States Constitution

The creation of any organization requires a basic set of rules to provide a framework for operation. This concept applies to all systems including the system of the US Government. The governing charters for the USA include the Declaration of Independence, the Constitution and the Bill of Rights. The US Constitution regulates power among the federal government and government branches, federal government and the states, and all governments and the people.

This basic framework – this Constitution of the United States – also comprises the primary law in the USA. It and its amendments enumerate the basic rights of the citizens of the United States, and detail the three chief branches of the Federal Government and their jurisdictions. Figure 1.2 illustrates the Legislative, Executive and Judicial branches, how they relate to the Constitution and each other, and which government officials are connected to the various branches.

In addition to being a major source of US law, the constitution is also important for understanding the structure of the government, its basic goals and how these goals are achieved.

However historically noteworthy, constitutional law does not play a significant role in the day-to-day operations of the built environment. Notable exceptions to this blanket statement include issues involving public contracts and timeliness of the application of certain human rights. In addition, each state has its own constitution, which directs the separation of powers among the state legislative, state executive and state judicial branches of government, and the protection of state citizens from the abuse of power by citizens of other states.

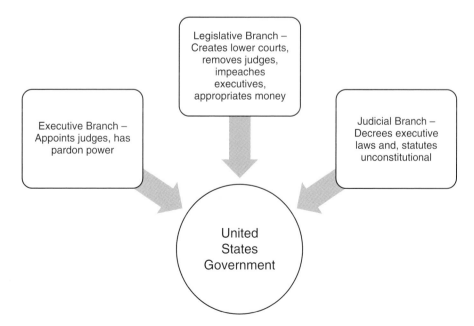

Figure 1.2   Branches of US Government.

1.4.2 Statutory law

Because of growth, there is sometimes the need for expanding and updating the Constitution. This modification to our laws can be accomplished by several means, one of which is enacting legislation by a representative congress elected by the people. In addition to modifying the law by amending the Constitution, congress also enacts legislation. The word "legislation" is used interchangeably with Statutory Law. Proposed new ideas or bills that are approved according to the rules set by the Constitution become statutory law and are also identified as statutes. Figure 1.3 depicts a high level flowchart of the path an idea takes to become a law in the federal legislative process. Other levels of government have their own processes but many are similar to the federal process.

Each year, legislation proposed by congress has, and continues to add to, rules in the constitution. This expands the total number of laws and creates an additional source of law, called "statutes", in the US system. There are many more statutes than there are distinct laws in the constitution. Both the constitution's rules and the rules contained in statutes have the weight of law and are applied by the courts in dispute resolution.

Even though legislation is used to expand the constitution, these laws are limited by the US government's system of checks and balances. Judges, to make sure they comply with the rules of the constitution, check statutes. This check prevents Congress from making a law that runs counter to the constitution's spirit and intent. Unsurprisingly, whether or not a statute runs counter to the constitution can be hotly debated. The federal and state courts weigh in on this debate and decide on the constitutionality of statutes. If examined closely, this check by the court seems almost circular (see Figure 1.4). Courts determine if a statute enacted by the legislature to expand the constitution is, in fact, constitutional.

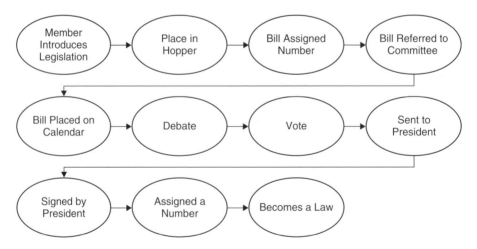

Figure 1.3 Pathway from idea to law.

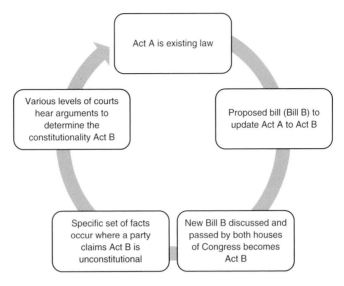

Figure 1.4 Illustration of court's constitutionality check.

The power to deem a statute unconstitutional can potentially permit the courts to control the political desires of the citizens by allowing the courts to decide that action taken by duly elected representatives, in the form of a statute, is unconstitutional. One only has to look as far as the recent court decision in *National Federation of Independent Business v. Sibelius*, decided in 2012. In this case the Supreme Court of the United States upheld major provisions of the Patient Protection and Affordable Care Act (PPACA) and the Health Care and Education Reconciliation Act (HCERA), even though there were a considerable number of elected officials arguing that requiring citizens to buy private insurance was unconstitutional. If the people elect a representative in Congress who passes a statute, which is in turn deemed unconstitutional by a court of non-elected judges, what power does Congress genuinely have?

Protection for Congress to curb a court's power exists for this very reason. These protections include the executive appointment of key judges, and a rule stating that a court can only get to the question of constitutionality of a statute if, and only if, there is an identifiable party involved in a real dispute against another identifiable party, and the specific court has jurisdiction. This means that if a citizen simply disagrees with a statutory law and desires to use the court system to theoretically decide on its constitutionality, this may be considered an improper use of the court system. There are times, however, when the courts make exceptions and rule on the constitutionality of a statute under specific circumstances. These circumstances will be discussed later in Chapter 3. In most cases, there must be a valid dispute with parties who stand to win or lose something of value to have a full hearing requiring the court to make a decision. This legal concept of requiring a real dispute is an example of the law's facilitating function and also stops the system from being clogged up with theoretical questions. This concept is discussed later in Chapter 3.

With its authority to restrict the power of the courts, Congress's power does not go unfettered. The executive branch, consisting of the president (in the federal system), governors and some mayors (in the state systems), serves as a check on potential statutes through the power to veto legislation. Figure 1.5 illustrates this web of checks by the three branches of government as applied to the legislative process.

1.4.3 Executive orders

Additional sources with the weight of law include the chief executive's power to issue executive orders to those under their control. Historically, executive orders were issued for simple administrative matters and usually internal operations of federal agencies. Recently, presidents have used executive orders to carry out legislative policies and programs. These orders do not need the approval of Congress, making the use of them highly controversial.

There are many examples of presidents using the executive order authority. President Roosevelt issued an executive order to mandate the confinement of Japanese-Americans to internment camps following the bombing of Pearl Harbor. (Exec, Order No. 9066). President Jimmy Carter used the power to stop the US Attorney General's investigations and indictment of Vietnam War draft evaders (Exec. Order No. 11 967). President Bill Clinton used executive order power to order the reserve military into active duty to augment operations in Bosnia. (Exec. Order No. 12 982).

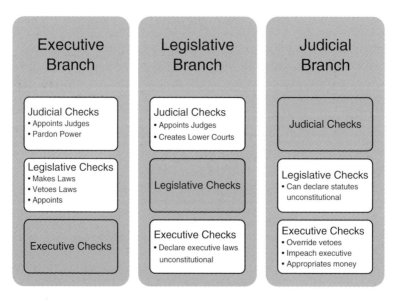

Figure 1.5   Checks by three branches of government.

In the past, Congress has taken action to counter executive orders, including passing legislation in conflict with the order, and refusing to approve funding necessary to carry out the order. As with any legislation, the president can veto this counteractive legislation, but with two-thirds majority vote the president's veto can be overridden. Because of the high requirement of a two-thirds majority vote, some believe that currently an executive order is nearly impossible to override (Koh 1990).

In the built environment industry several executive orders issued over the years impact upon the Facility Manager. For example, Executive Order (EO) 13423 requires federal agencies to implement plans to reduce their greenhouse gas emissions. Also, and a bit more controversial, EO 13502 encourages federal agencies to use union-only project labor agreements (PLAs) on construction projects, exceeding $25 million. A PLA is a union collective bargaining agreement that all contractors must sign to work on a construction project. The text of all current Executive Orders appears in the daily Federal Register when the Executive Order is signed by the President and received by the Office of the Federal Register. The text of Executive Orders beginning with Executive Order 7316 of March 13, 1936, also appears in the sequential editions of Title 3 of the Code of Federal Regulations (CFR). Additional information can be found in an index called Executive Order Disposition Tables, which are compiled and maintained by the Office of the Federal Register Editors.

1.4.4 Administrative law

A sometimes controversial but important source of law is the law of government agencies, known as *administrative law*. Focus of administrative law usually includes making rules and regulations and enforcement of a specific regulatory area, such as the environment. Considered the fastest growing source of US law, administrative law governs the activities of the administrative agencies of government, such as the Department of Education, the Environmental Protection Agency and others. Administrative law is different from legislation because directors appointed by the chief executive, not representatives elected by the people, lead agencies. This source of law exists at the federal, state and local levels.

Administrative law is considered a branch of public law and was created in response to the increasing complexities of modern society. Law was developed in response to perplexing questions such as, how can a politician keep the public from nuclear harm without detailed knowledge of the nuclear industry? How can Congress devise regulations that are both fair to the financial interests of industry and safe for the citizenry? Congress thought experts in those industries best regulated the special activities of industries. They created Agency Law to serve this purpose.

The guiding policy for these agencies is the actual legislation creating the agency. Therefore, these agencies are created by the legislature and the same body oversees their activities. To keep checks and balances in place, the chief executive is usually the person who appoints the top agency officials with the consent of Congress, and any action taken to enforce the agency regulations is subject to judicial review. It is interesting to note that the Constitution created Congress, which created a statute, which created an agency that created the administrative law.

Agencies issuing regulation of significant interest to the built environment industry include: the Occupational Safety and Health Administration (OSHA), the Environmental Protection Agency, and local agencies controlling land use and construction quality.

1.4.5 Common law

Common law is at the same time a rule and a legal reasoning process. Taking the time to appreciate what common law is and how it is made will help you understand the process of legal reasoning. Common law is also referred to as "judge-made law" and considered to be a different source of law from constitutional law and statutory law. Understanding common law requires an understanding of how it came to be. Judges make law when they apply legal principles, or current laws to actual cases. By reading a judge's written decision, you can follow the logical steps taken by the judge to get from a generic rule to applying that rule to a specific set of facts in a case. This process made by judges is essentially legal reasoning and defined as the use of established law on a given set of facts. The established law, and how the court in a particular situation applies it, is also one working definition of common law. Therefore, common law is the work of the trial court judge in addition to being a distinct set of rules. These decisions, written by a judge in law books called *reporters*, explain exactly how a court interpreted the law giving reasons for its decision.

In the instance of common law, for us to know what the law is in a particular situation, we must know how judges decided similar disputes in the past. This is why we say US courts follow precedent. Precedent is a decision by a judge that has occurred in an earlier case. This decision is considered authority for identical situations that come after the initial decision is provided. Understanding prior cases, rationale and decisions is important because future judges will decide similar cases in the same way. Precedent then, is a rule of law established for the first time by a court and thereafter referred to in deciding similar cases.

Using precedent is required under an important legal theory called *stare decisis* , which is a policy followed by judges to stand by previous cases or precedents. This allows the US system stability and serves to protect a settled point of law. Generally when a judge has once laid down a principle of law as applicable to a certain set of facts, other judges will adhere to that principle and apply it to future cases where the facts are the same. This use of precedent under the policy of stare decisis is why we often refer to the judge's decision more definitively as a "decision by the court" and not a specific person. So in the future, even if the same judge is not hearing a similar case, since the judge acts for the government, prior decisions are considered already decided by the court and must be followed. Referring to the judge's decision as a "decision by the court" also implies impartiality and the notion that what the court has settled is the rule of law.

It is hopefully obvious that court decisions, in addition to the amendments of the US Constitution, Statutory Law written by Congress, Executive Orders and Agency laws, are all distinct sources of law. What may not be obvious is that these sources are also constantly being updated creating new laws. In sum, the sources of US law include: common law, the constitution, statutes, executive orders and administrative law.

1.5 Chapter summary

Understanding the definition of law presented in this chapter should help further the argument that law is not simply a list of rules to be followed. The labyrinthine structure of the US Government and how it operates is as important in understanding the law as an understanding of the principles set out by the US Constitution. One way of learning the law is by sorting it into categories. Law can be categorized in several ways such as: source of law, application of law and knowledge of its specific function. Knowing the operation of government helps in learning the law also. All of these connections should help the student to better understand the expression by James Harrington made more famous by John Adams that the USA is a nation of "laws and not of men".

1.6 Questions

1. Using your own words, how would you define the word *jurisprudence*?
2. How is common law made?
3. How is administrative law connected to the US Constitution?
4. Who makes administrative law and under what authority?
5. Why is there a need for both common law and statutory law? Explain your answer.
6. Are executive orders "legal"? Explain your answer.
7. Which branches "make" law?

8. Why would the US Constitution insist on checking the power of the three different branches?
9. How is the executive power to issue executive orders checked by the courts?
10. Using your school's resources, find a copy of a constitution from another country. Summarize the commonalities and differences with the US Constitution. Reflect on your findings.

References

Koh, H. *The National Security Constitution: Sharing Power after the Iran-Contra Affair* (Yale Fastback Series). Yale University Press, 1990.

2

Law in Operation

It was the boast of Augustus that he found Rome of brick and left it of marble. But how much nobler will be the sovereign's boast when he shall have it to say that he found law . . . a sealed book and left it a living letter; found it the patrimony of the rich and left it the inheritance of the poor; found it the two-edged sword of craft and oppression and left it the staff of honesty and the shield of innocence.

Henry Brougham (1778–1868)

2.1 Introduction

Henry Peter Brougham is credited for discovering the resort town of Cannes, holding the longest record for non-stop speaking in the British House of Commons (six hours), and being a prominent fighter of the British slave trade, but the above quote is one of his most famous contributions. It speaks of the evolving quality of the Roman law as a result of the efforts of Augustus. Today, in most common law systems like the US, law continues to evolve with hopes of becoming the "staff of honesty and the shield of innocence". In this chapter, you will add to your knowledge of the law through a more detailed discussion on the US court system. For the Facility Manager, this is helpful because it will help you to hone your ability to predict consequences of your actions, thereby avoiding exposure to liability. Knowing how a court will decide under specific facts allows the Facility Manager not only to avoid exposure to liability, but also to make better decisions in her day-to-day work.

Legal Concepts for Facility Managers, First Edition. Linda Thomas-Mobley.
© 2014 John Wiley & Sons, Ltd. Published 2014 by John Wiley & Sons, Ltd.

Integral to understanding how the US legal system operates is an understanding of the use of common terminology. As you learned in Chapter 1, referring to a "law" could mean an administrative rule, a statute or a provision in the constitution. In this chapter you will learn that the law in question may not be a law that could help a court resolve a dispute at all. Law may refer to rules or areas of law called *procedural law* that provide the framework for using the court system. There are rules that attorneys follow when accessing the courts that have the full weight of other laws, which apply to the substance of a dispute. This chapter introduces procedural law and this is explained in more depth in Chapter 3.

When attorneys refer to "the court" they could be using a familiar or unfamiliar definition of the word. The *court* may refer to the courthouse, which is the physical space a party goes to have the judge settle a current dispute. Or it can refer to the judge, who made the decision in a specific case; for example, "the court held that embezzlement is unlawful". Furthermore, the court may refer to a trial court or another recognized tribunal such as an *appellate court*. Generally, when talking about decisions made by the court, we refer to the appellate level court, not the trial level. If you read this chapter carefully, making sure to understand the examples given, you will understand the differences between these courts and their functions by the end of this chapter.

Other terms of art used in the legal field are more easily explained through examples used in this chapter. You are encouraged to pay special attention to the difference between a trial and litigation, the definitions of plaintiff and defendant, and the various documents used in the practice of law such as motions, complaints and answers. In addition to understanding common terminology, one of the major concepts in this chapter is the notion of "jurisdiction"; not only what the word means, but what types of jurisdiction exist and how one would know if they should be in a trial, appellate, federal or state court. A fundamental question asked prior to any litigation is "who has proper jurisdiction?"

At the end of this chapter, the student should be able to:

- Discuss how a dispute travels through the legal system.
- Define the term *jurisdiction*.
- List the major types of court.
- Describe the difference between federal and state courts.
- Define federal jurisdiction.
- Define subject matter jurisdiction.
- Describe diversity jurisdiction.
- Define discovery.
- Describe the effect of procedural law on the practice of law.
- Describe the process used to extract the rule of law in an appeal.

2.2 A brief background on US courts

To put the study of law into context, understanding the background on US Courts and how the USA has evolved into the litigious society we see today, a brief background is warranted. The historical give-and-take between the functions of the court, as represented by the judge and the functions as represented by a jury, is in constant flux; a slowly moving pendulum swinging in perpetuity. Since the Seventh Amendment to the US Constitution codifies a right to trial by jury, the extent and power of these rules and regulations must be understood by more than those who practice law, especially in the context of the ever-changing and more complex scientific world the Facility Manager finds herself in.

As necessary background for understanding the US court system, a brief explanation of the USA with regard to government organization is warranted.

Although the details of how the state and federal governments interact will be explained, understanding the fundamental nature of federalism is necessary. Ingrained in the idea of a United States of America is the laudable notion of an organized federal society consisting of several member states united under a common flag. This unification is accomplished through a federal constitution and is organized in such a way that the country is a republic, or a non-monarch-ruled country. The conglomeration of stand-alone states is designed to exploit both individual and collective resources. A federation allows states to be sovereign entities with the authority to act on their own interests while delicately balancing the whole, sharing authority with a centralized unit, and having the goal of maintaining unity and representing the states to foreign countries. Thus, the USA is a federal republic. This federal republic has two administratively separate systems; federal and state. The courts can have separate or overlapping jurisdictions, depending on the circumstances. Because of the different nature of the interests governed by the federal and state systems, differing rules and procedures have developed over time, causing seemingly subtle differences in the operation of the two systems. One such difference lies in rules regulating how evidence is admitted during trials in the separate systems. These differences can be exploited and lead to cases in which parties have the option to carefully choose the forum that is best for their cause. This is informally called *forum shopping*.

During colonial times, US courts were generally based on the complex British legal system. Each colony had its own structure and trial procedure, and powerful justices of the peace performed tasks that were both legal and administrative. Many judges served as triers of fact or fact-finders, performing the task of finding the specifics that supported their predetermined verdict. Different colonies also had different structures with regard to the jury tradition;

furthermore, over time, the concept of a jury went in and out of favor and was constantly changing. In some colonies, colonial judges controlled every aspect of trial evidence, which led to testimony being admitted in the court without challenge to its relevance or truth.

American colonists eventually distrusted the legal system, since the British government appointed some judges with this unfettered power.

As the pendulum swung away from influential judges, the newly empowered juries emerged and gained a disproportionate amount of control. One pre-Revolutionary War case alleged that John Peter Zenger committed seditious libel. The jury in the case wholly rejected the judge's instructions and made its own decision. In some colonies at differing times, judges seemed to lose complete control over a verdict. By the time of the American Revolution, the predominant method of trying cases included presenting evidence to a jury. This increased importance of the jury was seen as revolutionary, causing colonists to fight for the right to a trial by jury.

2.2.1 Restoring the balance of power

By the nineteenth century, an attempt to balance the country's legal system and to assure necessary liability predictability for citizens was made. It was decided that judges, as knowledgeable members of the legal profession, should decide questions of law and that juries should decide matters of fact (Jhaveri 1999). This arrangement provided more certainty with regard to the law so businesses were able to predict, with a fair amount of certainty, behavior that would be free from legal liability.

In this streamlined version of the new US legal structure, judges were able to develop personal guidelines that helped them filter evidence to the jury. This process was viewed as a necessary one, since using irrelevant evidence would slow court proceedings down and hinder fact-finding. Over time, rules of thumb regarding the admissibility of evidence were developed to aid judges in keeping misleading, irrelevant evidence from jurors. Judicial evidence filtering was one way that a trial judge could assess the relevance or prejudicial nature of witness testimony. If the judge deemed evidence relevant and truthful, a jury was allowed to consider it. If the evidence was not helpful, not truthful or prejudicial, the judge could cause the evidence to be struck from the record or do allow it into the evidence the jury considered when making its decision.

One important subset of this filtering function is the judge's instrumental role in allowing expert-witness testimony. Expert testimony is any testimony requiring specialized training that a layperson would not generally have. The actual testimony is an informed opinion that is based on a review of the facts and specialized knowledge.

2.3 Functions of the US legal system

The legal system in the USA resembles a web of integrated organisms con-sisting of the executive, legislative and judicial branches of government, along with state and federal courts. The judicial, executive and legislative branches of government all contribute to the interpretation and making of law regardless of the jurisdiction. For a Facility Manager to navigate the legal system, basic understanding of the government: its organization, functions and limitations is required. Figure 2.1 illustrates how the Senate and House of Representatives make up the US Congress: also known as the *federal legislature*.

A chief executive officer leads the executive branch of government: the President at the federal level, Governor at the state level and Mayor or other chief executive officer at the local level. This chief executive officer has a major impact on the legal system by issuing orders, appointing the judiciary and possibly vetoing legislation.

Since ensuring the wellbeing of citizens is the major task of government, at all levels, legislators represent their constituents by making laws as needed to ensure proper operation of the government for the health, safety and welfare of those represented.

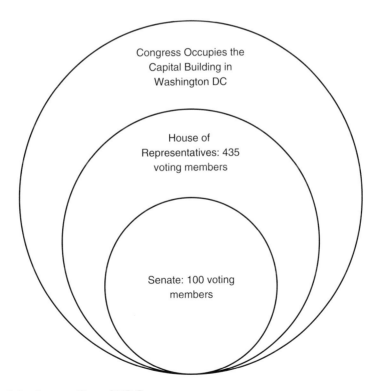

Figure 2.1   Composition of US Congress.

The judicial branch, comprised of the courts at all levels, is charged with implementing and interpreting the law. It tends to be the body most Facility Managers will encounter when a dispute arises and is therefore the one we will concentrate on here. Like the other two, the judicial branch has federal and state counterparts, but the arrangement within each level is also consequential. Article III of the US Constitution is relatively short compared to Articles I and II that set forth the framework for the other two branches of government. It is hard to imagine that the authors of the Constitution only created one court, the Supreme Court of the United States, when outlining where the judicial power would be vested. But they did provide for flexibility so that additional courts could be created as Congress deemed necessary. Over time, Congress has seen fit to create several other courts.

The four main functions of the US courts include enforcement, interpretation, invalidation and law making. These four functions allow the court to help the parties resolve disputes and enjoy constitutionally granted freedoms. The four functions can be illustrated within the context of copyright issues. The Copyright Act gives a copyright holder the exclusive right to reproduce the owner's work. If this right is violated, the owner can file a suit; this copyright infringement suit is an example of the court being called to enforce a statute. According to the Copyright Act, the employer owns the copyright of work created by an employee as a part of her employment, but the Copyright Act does not define the term "employee". How can an owner know if she actually owns the rights to copyrightable work produced by someone she pays? How do we fairly resolve the definition of employee in this context? The legal system can help with these questions once and for all with a decision from the highest court in the land, the US Supreme Court. If an owner has her copyright ownership case reviewed by the Supreme Court, and the issue of the definition of an employee is disputed, once the court rules, the term employee will be defined for similar situations once and for all. This definition of the term "employee" is an example of the court interpreting a statute serving the valuable function for all citizens who have copyright ownership questions.

Since the US Constitution is the supreme law of the United States, unconstitutional laws are defined as laws that conflict with one or more tenets of the Constitution and must be changed. If there were a provision in the Copyright Act that excluded copyright ownership from men born to women from Ohio, a possible violation of the constitution would have to be sorted out by the courts. This is an example of the invalidation function of the court. Finally, function number four, that of creating law, is familiar to the student because this function was illustrated and used to define common law. Many times, common law is created by judges to fill in the areas not covered by statutes or regulations. In our copyright example, a question as to whether a virtual citizen of a virtual city created entirely on-line and not existing in the real world can be a copyright owner may arise. As the world changes and new realities emerge, the courts will have plenty opportunities for law making, particularly when the legislature or chief executive office have not drafted or passed laws addressing the issues.

What if the copyright issue does not involve one's status as an employee but more directly questions whether or not an architect, for example, owns the copyright to her work? Fortunately for design professionals, statutory law already exists in the form of the Architectural Works Copyright Protection Act (AWCPA). Copyright in work performed by architects is covered under 17 U.S.C. § 102(a)(8). Under 17 U.S.C. § 102(a)(5), designers are afforded some protection of pictorial, graphic and sculptural works. In order to obtain protection as an "architectural work" under 17 U.S.C. § 102(a)(8), the work must include a design of a building, not simply non-building structures like bridges and walkways. Also, architects are automatically given copyright protection beginning at the time of creation so no formal registration of the work is necessary, but there are precautions designers should take themselves in addition to protections provided by the law. If the architect takes the trouble to register her design she saves a few steps in the event her design is used without permission and she has to assert her copyright ownership. If the work is not formally registered, it is still protected but before a designer can bring a lawsuit for copyright infringement, she must register the work. If this registration is done as a matter of good business practice and a copyright question arises, the architect will not have to bring evidence to prove that the design is her own. Furthermore, if she registers her design within three years, she can get extra benefits such as attorney's fees. Depending on the situation, this amount can be significant.

2.3.1 Dispute resolution

There are several avenues to resolve common disputes that arise in the built environment in addition to court litigation. It is paramount that the Facility Manager be aware of these widely used methods in hopes of avoiding unnecessary lawsuits. One major reason to avoid courtroom litigation is cost, especially in the USA. Regardless of the amount paid in legal fees and time diverted from principle duties, the job of the Facility Manager is to add value by responsibly managing capital assets, not decrease value through unnecessary litigation costs. An even more insidious element of courtroom litigation is the hidden laws that exist. Laws such as Civil or Criminal Procedure and Evidence, known as *procedural law*, have a large effect on the outcome of the case, yet have nothing to do with the actual facts being disputed. A more detailed explanation of these procedural laws is covered later, but understand that they play a major role in the resolution of a dispute.

Although beyond the scope of this text, the Facility Manager should know that these procedural laws constitute the "rules of the game" and just like most sports, not following the rules will disqualify a participant, even if she is an excellent athlete. Unless you've actually been party to a lawsuit that continued on to the trial stage, it is difficult for most people to understand that procedural laws cause a distortion from reality during trial. Matters that seem to be most important to the Facility Manager may be trivial to the attorney representing you, and seemingly unimportant facts can mean the difference between prevailing on a claim and having to pay additional costs above the disputed amount.

In addition to significant unwanted costs and procedural law, both parties require representation and will therefore ultimately experience a loss of control because of the intricate nature of court systems. In almost all cases, finding an alternative form of dispute resolution is best.

2.3.2 Types of courts

There are several types of courts. The federal and state systems consist of two levels of courts, generically called *trial* and *appellate* level courts. Cases are tried in the traditional sense in trial courts, while appellate courts review the decisions of the trial courts. It bears repeating that these trial courts are physical spaces where the parties go before a judge who renders a decision. This decision can be reviewed by an appellate court, which is also a physical space with three or more judges that allows the parties to explain additional points of law. Most depictions of courtrooms do not show the appellate courtrooms. In these courts the judge's bench is replaced by a longer bench with three or more judges hearing the dispute. An appellate court's decision on an issue is binding on other trial courts in the appellate court's jurisdiction. This means that a state's highest appellate court decisions represent settled or binding law in the state, and the Supreme Court of the United States' decisions represent settled law for the country. When states have intermediate appellate courts, the decisions of these courts are only binding in the court's jurisdiction. Thus, court decisions serve as precedent for all those subject to that appellate court's jurisdiction. Figure 2.2 illustrates the US court system showing the federal system alongside the state system, and special courts created by the constitution or statute.

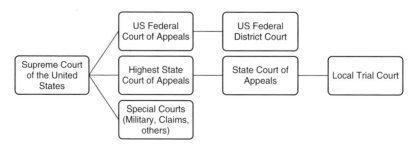

Figure 2.2   Federal and state court systems.

There are 12 US Federal Courts of Appeal. These 12 courts represent the 92 judicial districts (or jurisdictions), which correspond to different geographical areas of the country. Each of the 92 districts has at least one trial level court. The federal courts of appeal preside over their specific geographical areas called *circuits*. The 12 circuits, along with the location of the appellate court for that geographical area and the list of states in specific circuits, include:

Federal Circuit (Appellate court located in Washington, DC)

- DC Circuit
- District of Columbia

1st Circuit (Appellate court located in Boston, MA)

- Maine
- Massachusetts
- New Hampshire
- Puerto Rico
- Rhode Island

2nd Circuit (Appellate court located in New York, NY)

- Connecticut
- New York
- Vermont

3rd Circuit (Appellate court located in Philadelphia, PA)

- Delaware
- New Jersey
- Pennsylvania
- US Virgin Islands

4th Circuit (Appellate court located in Richmond, VA)

- Maryland
- North Carolina
- South Carolina
- Virginia
- West Virginia

5th Circuit (Appellate court located in New Orleans, LA)

- Louisiana
- Mississippi
- Texas

6th Circuit (Appellate court located in Cincinnati, OH)

- Kentucky

- Michigan
- Ohio
- Tennessee

7th Circuit (Appellate court located in Chicago, IL)

- Illinois
- Indiana
- Wisconsin

8th Circuit (Appellate court located in St. Louis, MO)

- Arkansas
- Iowa
- Minnesota
- Missouri
- Nebraska
- North Dakota
- South Dakota

9th Circuit (Appellate court located in San Francisco, CA)

- Alaska
- Arizona
- California
- Guam
- Hawaii
- Idaho
- Montana
- Nevada
- Northern Mariana Islands
- Oregon
- Washington

10th Circuit (Appellate court located in Denver, CO)

- Colorado
- Kansas
- New Mexico
- Oklahoma
- Utah
- Wyoming

11th Circuit (Appellate court located in Atlanta, GA)

- Alabama
- Florida
- Georgia

Continuing with our copyright example, one of the federal courts of appeal held that the grant of a nonexclusive copyright license can be implied from the copyright owner's conduct. This decision is binding on all federal trial level courts located in the jurisdiction of this federal appellate court. Thus, the trial level federal courts in this jurisdiction are not free to decide that a nonexclusive copyright license cannot be implied from conduct. It should be noted that a lower court's decision is not binding on a higher court. In fact, appellate courts frequently reverse decisions made by trial courts to correct the trial courts' errors of law. Because the United States Supreme Court is the highest court in the land, the Supreme Court's decisions are binding on all courts in the United States. At the state level, the state constitution and laws of each state establish their own state courts. A state may have one or two levels of appellate courts, the highest of which are often called *state supreme courts*, would be the state's court of last resort. State supreme court decisions are appealed to the US Supreme Court.

2.3.3 Jurisdiction

It would be easy to imagine the chaos that would exist if every litigant was able to file a lawsuit in all courts state and federal. Not all types of cases, nor all litigants, are free to have their disputes heard by all courts in the legal system. To keep matters organized, all courts follow a set of procedures that mandate the types of cases they are allowed to hear. As mentioned before these procedures are so powerful, they are granted the full weight of a law and referred to as *procedural law*. These laws, granting power to specific courts to hear certain matters, govern the courts' jurisdiction. Jurisdiction is the power of a court to hear a particular case. This power may be based on geographical location or type of dispute.

For example, if there is a payment dispute between a builder and a subcontractor both residing in California, and the dispute reaches trial, the California state trial level court will hear the case. Compare this to a slightly different scenario with the exact same payment dispute and same parties, builder and subcontractor, but in this instance the subcontractor resides in New York State. This specific dispute requires the trial to be held in a federal court so that the case can be heard in a "neutral" setting. At one time, with a smaller US population, states would favor their own citizens over those from another state; this requirement that disputes be held in a neutral setting addressed this situation. An understanding of what jurisdiction the state courts have compared to the jurisdiction of the federal courts goes a long way toward understanding the law and how it is applied. A deeper understanding is gained by careful study of procedural law, a course taken by all first year law students preparing to practice in the USA.

Federal court jurisdiction

To afford the states an opportunity to limit the power of the federal government, jurisdiction of the federal courts is regulated. For any specific federal court to have jurisdiction, the dispute and its litigants must meet two benchmarks. The first benchmark is called *subject matter jurisdiction*. Subject matter jurisdiction is a court's authority, granted by procedural law, to hear the type of dispute in question. The second benchmark that must be met is *personal jurisdiction*, which refers to the authority over the person or persons involved. For example, the lack of subject matter jurisdiction occurs if the US Bankruptcy Court is asked to hear a dispute regarding an automobile accident, since the subject matter for this court should be claims of bankruptcy. Using our example of the payment dispute between contractor and subcontractor, if both parties reside in the USA, the federal trial court probably does not have personal jurisdiction to hear the dispute. There are examples of exceptions. One significant exception involving the built environment is the exception granted when both parties agree to have their disputes settled in a US federal court; this agreement could be accomplished through careful contract language.

Subject matter jurisdiction can be further explained by outlining the specific criteria used by attorneys to gauge proper federal subject matter jurisdiction. These criteria include looking for a "federal question" or "diversity of citizenship", or some other reserved miscellaneous subject matter such as bankruptcy. Please note only one of these criteria needs to be present for overall subject matter jurisdiction to be met.

Federal question jurisdiction exists in cases involving the federal constitution, federal statutes or federal treaties. If there is no federal question, then disputes may be heard in federal court only if the parties are from different states; this is called diversity jurisdiction. Diversity jurisdiction requires two things; a minimum dollar amount in dispute and the parties must be residents of different states. The set dollar amount is called the *amount in controversy*. Understandably, this amount has risen over time to keep pace with inflation. At the time the US courts were created, Article III of the US Constitution required the amount to be $500. In 1877 this amount was raised to $2000; in 1911 to $3000, in 1958 to $10 000; in 1988 to $50 000 and then in 1996 to $75 000. The latest required amount can be found in title 28 of the United States Code, Section 1332. One way of organizing the jurisdictional requirements is depicted in Figure 2.3.

Federal question or diversity jurisdiction is the main avenue to a federal court, but there are others. A suit by or against the US Government will automatically be heard in a federal court irrespective of the amount in controversy. Also, certain types of case, such as those related to patents, bankruptcy, admiralty (maritime cases), trademarks and copyrights, and other miscellaneous national issues, are heard in a federal court.

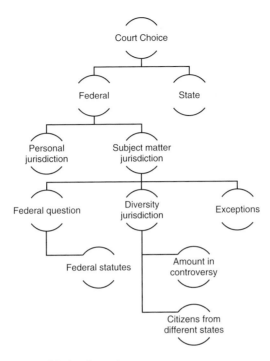

Figure 2.3 Jurisdiction of federal courts.

It should be noted that court jurisdictional definitions and procedural law carry numerous exceptions, which have evolved over time. Thus, law in the form of procedural rules is just as important and intricate as other rules of law that govern issues actually being disputed, or non-procedural law, called *substantive law*.

In addition to jurisdiction over the persons and the subject matter, there are issues of federal districts that also govern jurisdiction. The districts are divided regionally, respecting state lines as discussed at the beginning of this section. A depiction of how federal district jurisdiction operates is shown in Figure 2.4.

Lifecycle of a lawsuit
Understanding the general process a lawsuit usually follows as it travels through the legal system is helpful to all. Although there are an infinite number of ways one can initiate or be drawn into a lawsuit, for the sake of an explanation, the process will be divided into four phases. These phases are: commencement, pre-trial motions, trial and post-trial motions.

Commencement
The party beginning the process is called the plaintiff who is responsible for preparing the *complaint*. The complaint document identifies the parties in dispute, outlines facts, describes any harm suffered and lists what the

LIVERPOOL JOHN MOORES UNIVERSITY
LEARNING SERVICES

Trial Courts

Makes and interprets law for disputes heard

Decisions are usually not written

Examples: state trial courts, federal district courts

Appellate Courts

Makes and interprets law for locations in its jurisdiction

Decisions are written and recorded

Examples: state intermediate appellate courts, state supreme courts, federal circuit courts of appeal

Supreme Court of the United States

Makes and interprets laws for all of the USA

Decisions are written and recorded

Example: Supreme Court of the United States

Figure 2.4   Federal court levels.

party requests the court to decide. Procedural law of various jurisdictions dictates how this document should be drafted and what should be included in a complaint. The time starts for a lawsuit the day the plaintiff submits her completed complaint document to the clerk at the courthouse. Timing in lawsuits is important because there are several procedural laws limiting the amount of time a party has to respond to the court or another party. It is the responsibility of the plaintiff to make sure the parties named in her complaint receive a copy of the complaint document.

About 30–45 days after the complaint document is submitted to a clerk at the courthouse having jurisdiction, another document is prepared by the other party, the defendant, and filed with the clerk. This document is referred to as the defendant's *answer*. In the answer document, the defendant has the opportunity to state what they believe are the facts surrounding the dispute. Answers usually include explanations to counter assertions made in the complaint in an attempt to show that the defendant not responsible for the plaintiff's injuries. Additionally, if the defendant thinks she may have a complaint of her own, called a *counter claim*, she typically describes this in her answer so that all matters in dispute can be decided in the most efficient manner.

Counterclaims are lawsuits within a lawsuit in which the defendant files a claim against the plaintiff. This beginning phase is helpful to the court and used to identify the issues in dispute, the parties allegedly responsible and remedies being requested. There are other documents that may be filed by both parties during this phase. For example, amendments, which may include individuals not listed in the plaintiff's original complaint, are used to make sure all parties with potential responsibility but not listed earlier, are made known to the court.

Pre-Trial

Overlapping the commencement phase is the pre-trial phase. After the complaints and answers are filed, strategic actions are made by the parties to gain an advantage for their argument. These strategic actions are accomplished through a motion with the court. Motions are oral or written requests made by the parties to the judge for a specific decision called an *order*. For example, the defendant may agree with everything stated in the plaintiff's complaint and then file a motion to dismiss the case if they believe no legal claim has been made. Another common motion requests the court make a decision based on the facts contained in the complaint and answer without any testimony. The requester of this motion, known as a *summary judgment motion*, is made by the party believing they will prevail without need for further information.

If the lawsuit continues without being dismissed by the court, the parties begin the process of requesting information from each other. This give and take of information, such as business files, oral statements, photographs, doctor's reports and other types of evidence, is called *discovery*. Discovery occurs in the commencement phase and helps parties to analyze all evidence produced by the other side. This allows the attorneys to determine the strength of the client's case. During the first and second phases, commencement and pre-trial, many disputes are settled prior to the third phase allowing parties to escape the rest of the pre-trial and trial process.

Trial

The third phase of a lawsuit is the actual trial, beginning with conferences with the judge, where the parties attempt to settle the dispute again. This trial phase also overlaps with the pre-trial phase because parties can file pre-trial motions and use other strategies including supervised meetings right up to the time the jury makes a decision. These supervised meetings are intended to guide the parties toward a resolution. It is thought that the presence of a judge will incentivize the parties to come to an agreement without going forward with a trial. If unsuccessful, the trial then proceeds with each side presenting persuasive evidence in the form of documents and witness testimony. The concluding activity in the trial phase is a decision by the judge or a jury.

There are two basic standards the jury must use to determine which side prevails in a trial. For cases that do not involve crimes, the jury must find that the plaintiff showed a "preponderance of the evidence", which suggests that the defendant is liable. If a preponderance of the evidence does not show the plaintiff is liable, the jury will find the defendant "not liable". But what is a *preponderance of the evidence*? This standard means that when the jury considers all of the plaintiff's evidence, the plaintiff has shown that the defendant more likely than not caused the damages asserted. If you think of the scales of justice with a small amount of sand on both plates, when the plaintiff's side has one more grain of sand than the defendant's side, the preponderance of the evidence standard has been met. A different standard is used in criminal trials. This standard is the *beyond a reasonable doubt* standard, and is much higher, as it should be since the defendant in a criminal trial is either found guilty or not guilty. If found guilty this means that the jury believed the evidence presented against the defendant showed, without a doubt, that she was guilty. This would mean that a majority of the sand is on one side of the scale.

Post-Trial

After a decision has been made, the fourth phase, post-trial, begins. Using the mechanism of the written motion, the losing party usually has the right to one appeal within a certain period of time. If an appeal is filed and the appellate court gives permission to proceed with arguments, appellate briefs are written, oral arguments made to a panel of three to nine judges, and then a decision by the entire panel of judges is made.

Appellate court arguments are made by the representing attorneys without a jury. The attorneys are also limited to the evidence brought out during the trial. The appellate arguments made by both parties is restricted to the evidence presented at the trial court, which is called the *court below*, to make sure all parties try to settle disputes at the lowest court level. All courts that make decisions that can be appealed are referred to as the "court below" by the appellate courts. On rare occasions, appellate decisions may themselves be appealed until the parties reach the highest court in the USA, the Supreme Court of the United States (SCOTUS). Parties do not have a right to be heard by the SCOTUS. Through a separate strategic and procedural law governed process, SCOTUS, through its nine justices, makes the decision to hear a specific case brought before it. If the case will be heard by the Supreme Court, this is called *granting certiorari*. Certiorari is a writ issued by the SCOTUS to a lower court agreeing review the lower court's judgment.

Please note that the process described as the litigation process is not the same as the trial process. The litigation process is more than just the trial proceedings; it includes all of the motions and posturing that comes before a trial and after. Although this description is simplified it is hoped this will illustrate the various phases of a lawsuit. The US legal system is much more complex but if you remember the following:

- The system consists of the three branches of government;
- The court system has two types of courts, trial and appellate; and
- Two systems of court, federal and state; and finally
- Even though the federal and state courts are parallel, the highest court of the land is the Supreme Court of the United States.

Your understanding will help you to avoid unnecessary litigation and exposure to risk.

2.4 Chapter summary

By now it should be apparent to that the law has many functions but one of its most important is in dispute resolution. You should also understand the rationale for jurisdiction and how the federal and state court systems are generally organized.

The four phases of a law suit, although not separate and distinct as the previous model implies, is a good technique to understand the difference between litigation and trail. Chapter 3 will help to complete an introduction to the US legal system by describing the people involved and where the sources of law are physically located.

2.5 Questions

1. Creatively illustrate the path a dispute travels from filing the complaint until the judge issues the decision.
2. Using news sources and an Internet search, determine the average cost of litigation in your area. Is this amount reasonable or unreasonable? Why?
3. What is the reason for the discovery process?
4. Explain what is meant by the term "jurisdiction".
5. Describe what must be present for diversity jurisdiction to exist.
6. Which court is more "important": federal or state? Explain your answer.
7. Explain why it is important for the Facility Manager to understand the litigation process.
8. If a party wants to appeal a decision made by a state supreme court, where should she go?
9. Why is evidence limited during an appeal?
10. Using information sources available in your library, draw a diagram illustrating your state court system.

References

Jhaveri, K. *Judicial Gate Keeping in the United States: A Historical Perspective*. Cambridge MA: Harvard Law School, 1999.

3

Legal Concepts

> *Laws are like sausages. It's better not to see them being made.*
> **Otto von Bismarck (1815–1898)**

3.1 Introduction

At this point in the text, it should be obvious why Bismarck's humorous quote may be true. This chapter is intended to give the student additional information on various legal concepts that will be useful in Parts II and III. Additional details and the reasons behind relevant legal processes are addressed. Understanding who does what and why, will go a long way in helping the Facility Manager to understand how the legal system in the USA operates, and more importantly, how she can focus on adding value to the assets she manages.

At the end of Chapter 3 the following student learning outcomes are expected:

- List the major parties involved in litigation.
- Define the term *civil procedure*.
- Describe the various functions of an attorney at law.
- Describe how the local community is involved in court disputes.
- Describe how the legal system is involved in court disputes.
- Describe the purpose of case law reporters.
- Define the types of cases recorded in case law reporters.
- Briefly describe the goal of legal research.
- Describe common sections in a written appellate decision.
- Define the legal concept of "standing to sue".

Legal Concepts for Facility Managers, First Edition. Linda Thomas-Mobley.
© 2014 John Wiley & Sons, Ltd. Published 2014 by John Wiley & Sons, Ltd.

- Describe the purpose of the rules of evidence.
- Describe the difference between substantive law and procedural law.
- Define *stare decisis*.

It is also important for Facility Managers to understand how courts resolve disputes and where to find access to information about previously decided cases. It should be emphasized that the "court" referenced in previous decisions is not the court that immediately comes to mind. When we refer to the *court* in the USA, one assumes we are referring to the trial court where citizens go to settle a dispute in front of a judge and possibly a jury. In Chapter 2 you have been introduced to the concept that there are many types of courts and the trial court is just one. How the courts function independently and in concert with each other is discussed in further detail in this chapter.

3.2 Who are the players?

The US legal system is an integral part of the operation of government and provides a systematic framework for dispute resolution. However, the work of the legal system is still accomplished by people playing different roles, with different jobs and different points of view. Figure 3.1 represents a few of the typical players normally involved in a legal dispute.

Usually involved in a dispute are: the two parties at odds; a neutral decision maker; a neutral court official making sure things run smoothly; and other individuals providing additional facts to aid the decision-maker. Sometimes the decision-maker is the jury and, sometimes, it is only the judge who ends

Figure 3.1   Players in the US legal system.

up making a decision. What names we give the parties in a lawsuit depends on the type of dispute. For example, in some disputes there is a plaintiff and a defendant, in others there is a prosecutor instead of a plaintiff.

Also, the type of dispute will govern the specific procedures to be used. If one is involved in a criminal action, the rules of Criminal Procedure govern the procedures followed in the courtroom. Under these procedures, the parties to a lawsuit would be the state and the defendant, and the defendant has a constitutional right to a jury of her peers. In the US system, even though there are private citizens who are victims of crime, the party bringing a criminal lawsuit against a defendant is always the government. The "government" in criminal cases also refers to the municipality, city, county, state or commonwealth, not only the federal government. Compare these labels to the ones used in civil cases, with procedures governed by the Rules of Civil Procedure. The parties to civil lawsuits are called *plaintiffs*, the injured party bringing the suit, and defendant. In civil disputes, the party bringing the dispute to the court by filing a complaint to begin the process is called the plaintiff. Plaintiffs may be individuals or entities that state there is a dispute they want the legal system to resolve.

Since state laws vary slightly from state to state, so do the Rules of Criminal and Civil Procedure, because they are also laws. You will similarly find a slight difference between procedures in federal and state courts. What is not different among the various procedural rules is that they all seek to establish a predictable and orderly structure working to exercise impartial justice. Further information about the rules of criminal and civil procedure will be discussed shortly.

The list of individuals involved in disputes goes far beyond simply the parties to the dispute and their attorneys. Participants include those directly involved in the dispute, witnesses, experts to help the court understand a dispute better, those representing the legal system and other members of the community.

In criminal cases, an attorney general, who formally initiates a lawsuit against the criminal defendant, usually represents the government entity that is either the USA or an individual state. These attorneys general are the main legal advisors to the government. In some states, the attorney general may also have the responsibility for enforcement of the law. All attorneys, while in the role of representing the government, especially in criminal prosecutions, are called attorneys general or something similar, even if they are only acting in this capacity temporarily. The government entity, as the client of the attorney general, is sometimes referred to as the state, the commonwealth, the USA or other names of the sovereign entity bringing criminal cases before a court. Several different labels, depending on the state or jurisdiction, refer to the title of attorney general. Other names for this function include prosecutor, prosecuting attorney, city attorney, state attorney and state prosecutor.

In both criminal and civil cases, the individual responding to the lawsuit is called the defendant. The defendants are ostensibly guilty of some violation or liable for some injury and must appear in person to answer charges and give testimony in the form of oral, written or another media for the purpose of telling their side of the story. In addition to the defendant, government entity and attorney general, other attorneys at law are involved either serving as the advocate representing the accused, or assisting either side as additional counsel. The attorney representing the defendant can be a private attorney, who has been given permission to practice in the particular court and jurisdiction; or a government appointed attorney, paid for by the government to represent those who would otherwise not be able to pay for representation. Depending on the jurisdiction, this government or court-appointed attorney is provided based upon varying definitions of a defendant's inability to pay.

Local community members may also participate depending on their personal involvement in the dispute. Community members with knowledge of facts in the case may serve as witnesses, providing information helpful to the resolution of the case. Disinterested community members also serve in the roles of expert witnesses if needed, or jurors to help the court decide on seemingly contradictory facts presented by the parties.

A jury is a sworn body of individuals called by the state to render an impartial finding of fact on a question, called a verdict. This question is officially submitted to the jury by the judge; also, the judge may request that a jury set a penalty or judgment once a guilty verdict has been found. Juries are composed of jurors, who are by definition, lay-finders of fact, not professionals. The selection of members of the jury can be accomplished in several ways. As long as the process is fair and impartial, methods used are left to the jurisdiction. The goal is to convene a pool of potential jury members randomly selected from the community. From this pool, a panel of jurors is randomly assigned to a courtroom where the prospective members are randomly selected to sit in the jury box, then are questioned in court by the judge and/or attorneys. This process is called *voir dire*. The term *voir dire* originally referred to an oath taken by jurors to tell the truth. The main duty of the jury, once chosen, is to decide on the facts: this function makes them the *trier of fact*. People serving as triers of fact are necessary because in disputes there are usually competing versions of the facts and determining which version is most likely is a necessary step in rendering a decision. Not all cases have juries acting as a trier of fact; sometimes the judge takes this role. When the trier of fact is a judge, the trial is referred to as a bench trial.

In the USA, civil disputes are generally operated using bench trials unless a party requests a jury. A criminal case in which the judge serves as the trier of fact will only occur if the constitutional right to a jury trial is waived by the defendant. Also, in most states the criminal defendant alone has the ability to waive the right to a jury.

A very important participant in all cases is the judge. This expert in the law and court procedure is charged with upholding a fair and impartial hearing. The judge's monitoring of the process to ensure impartiality affords the parties a forum to settle disputes without bias. It also gives society faith in the legal system, creating stability and respect for the law of the land.

Other community members may participate as victim's advocates, independent children's advocates or journalists, depending on the nature of the case and interest of the public. Additional representatives of the legal system include courtroom personnel, such as clerks and bailiffs. Depending on the state or jurisdiction, others may represent the legal system behind the scenes, all working toward maintaining order in the process and ensuring the safety of participants. By no means is this list of participants exhaustive, but those directly involved with the dispute, attorneys for each side, and community members participating in the process carry the bulk of the responsibility.

3.3 Statutes

In addition to the rules imbedded in the text of the constitution, federal and state statutes exist as formal written enactments of legislative authority governing a state, city or county. Statutes are laws made by legislative bodies, as opposed to case law that is decided by courts or regulations that are issued by government agencies. Most law is made via the legislative process originating as Acts of Congress and signed into law by the chief executive.

Federal statutes are compiled in the Code of Laws of the United States of America. This collection of laws is referred to as the Code of Laws of the United States, United States Code and the US Code. The US Code contains 51 titles and is published every six years by the Office of the Law Revision Counsel of the House of Representatives, with supplements published annually according to Title 1 of the US Code. State statutes are also codified serving as a primary source of state laws in the same way federal statutes are a primary source of federal law.

The US Code is organized into titles that are intended to be logical categories of legislation. These titles are sometimes divided into subtitles, parts, subparts, chapters and subchapters. As a further division the codes are organized into sections, using the symbol § to represent the word "section", these sections are also divided further into subsections, paragraphs, subparagraphs, clauses, sub clauses, items and sub items (Bellis 2008).

3.4 Administrative laws

As was previously mentioned, administrative laws, developed by federal agencies, also constitute a source of law. These regulations, having the force of law are located in the Code of Federal Regulations. United States federal agencies are given the power to clarify, establish and enforce laws within their specific areas of delegated power. This is accomplished through rule-making by the administrative agencies. Since the executive, legislative and judicial branches of the government cannot always directly perform all of their administrative responsibilities, authority over matters requiring specialized knowledge is delegated to an agency, board or commission. Examples of administrative bodies monitoring activities include financial security markets and aviation.

The category of administrative law includes: all rules giving authority to administrative agencies; procedures used by the agencies in employing the rules; how agency decisions are validated and how these decisions are reviewed by the courts.

3.5 Executive orders

In US law, the executive order is a regulation given with the full force of law, issued by the head of the executive branch of government as introduced in Chapter 2, The term is usually applied to orders issued by the President of the United States, but may also be issued at the state level by a governor or at the local level by the city's mayor (Contrubis 1999).

Executive orders issued by presidents have been around since 1789. Their primary use is in helping agencies of the executive branch manage operations. At various times throughout history, executive orders have been criticized for exceeding executive authority. In other countries, similar orders are known as decrees or orders in council. A list of all recorded presidential executive orders can be found in the United States Federal Register. This important repository of laws will be further detailed at the end of this section.

3.6 Common law

Common law is case law, developed over time by judges making decisions. It is an alternate source for law in addition to law from statute and executive orders. You will often hear attorneys refer to the US system as a common law system. This means that the US legal system gives great weight to prior decisions and follows the principle that courts must treat similar facts similarly. The collective prior decisions, which are binding on future similar cases, make up the common law.

There are occasions where the common law seems to be in conflict, or the parties to litigation disagree on what the settled law should be. In this instance the judge looks to similar decisions from other courts. If a court in the same jurisdiction has decided a comparable case in the past, the court is required to follow the prior decision; this requirement is called *stare decisis*. *Stare decisis* is more than a simple term; it is an idea, a legal concept. This is explained further at the end of this chapter.

In the instance where the judge determines that the case being decided is different from all cases decided in the past, the dispute will be deemed a *matter of first impression*. Matters of first impression create opportunities for a judge to make a new law. This new law, the reasoning behind the decision and the types of cases it should be applied to in the future, is outlined in a summary called the decision of the court, or court's decision. Valuable ideas and legal reasoning are also contained in the court's written decision, these decisions help attorneys predict what a court will do in a future situation, even if the facts are very different.

It should be noted that the majority of detailed information about federal or state court decisions is actually found in an appellate records, not trial transcripts. Only a few trial court level decisions are formally documented to be used as common law, so the making of common law generally requires the parties to have their dispute heard by an appellate court.

Decisions for or against plaintiffs are decided by the trial court judge and are rarely referred to unless a set of facts is particularly noteworthy. It is the cases that are not easy to decide, or where there are questions as to the proper application of a law, that get appealed. The decisions from appellate judges serve as laws for future cases. Legal researchers try to compile all of the appellate decisions made by courts in their jurisdiction when a similar set of facts arises in a future dispute.

Cases heard on a second appeal are even more infrequent and tend to be the cases that law students study in an effort to learn legal reasoning and legal concepts. Cases decided by the supreme court of a state or the Supreme Court of the United States are considered definitive law unless later overruled. Thus, it is the legal researcher's duty to not only find what courts have decided about a particular set of facts, but to also find out whether that decision has been overruled or still stands.

3.7 Appeals

An appeal is a process for requesting a formal review of an official decision by a judge. Generally, there two types of appeals the first type is called an "on the record" appeal and the second type is called a "*de novo* appeal". *De novo*, is translated from the Latin word for afresh, or, "beginning again".

The more common type of appeal is the on the record appeal. In this type, one party challenges the decision made by the trial judge asserting that the judge misapplied the law, made an error regarding the facts, acted beyond her jurisdiction, was biased, abused her powers, allowed evidence that was improper or failed to allow proper evidence. Either party can file an appeal. Once the decision is made to file an appeal the parties are no longer referred to as plaintiff and defendant. Typically the party bringing the appeal is called the *petitioner* and the other party is called the *respondent*. At the appeal hearing, both parties are represented by attorneys who argue a very limited amount of the case to a panel of three to nine judges. The arguments are limited to the reason given for the appeal, such as factual errors or improper evidence. This very narrow scope often confuses readers, but many judges' opinions are written so as to inform the reader of all relevant facts in addition to the rationale for the decision made. There is no jury or trier of fact in appellate proceedings and the facts in the record that were brought out during the trial are assumed to be true.

Since, common law is recorded not as a list of rules but as decisions of the appellate courts and the Supreme Court of the United States, it is often confusing to non-lawyers seeking a definitive statement of the law. This is amplified because trial court transcripts, where the law is actually applied by the trial judge, are not collected for others to read unless those cases are appealed. One way to think about common law is that it is more like legal theory than actual rules. Thus, legal concepts that describe how a court is likely to decide upon a certain set of facts is actually more of what "the law" is than a declarative statement in a rulebook.

Appellate cases are recorded and published in volumes, aptly called *reporters*. It should be noted that trial level cases that preceded the appeal and reached the verdict phase might have publicly available transcripts. However, the judge's decision and the legal reasoning used to reach that decision are generally not transcribed or written for others to read. It is the smaller percentage of cases, which are appealed, that end up in the reporters for the public to learn from or use in future similar cases.

Since there are more than one court of appeals there are more than one series of reporters. Each appellate court has its own series of reporters that give basic details and other information on a dispute that is brought before it. The compilation of the common law is found in reporters, available on-line and in law libraries.

3.8 Recording the common law

The appellate decisions published by the courts contain standard information designed to be useful for future parties. They outline how the court decided on a specific set of facts and what legal reasoning was used to make that decision. Generally, the reporter is organized chronologically according to when the decision was published. Jurisdictions with a higher number of appeals have a larger series of volumes to contain the cases. Each case in the volume is a complete "story" capturing the history of the dispute, what the trial court decided, how and why the case was appealed, what arguments the claimant and respondent offered, which law the appellate court applied to its decision, if any and the legal reasoning for this decision. In some cases, a judge who sees the case in a different light, or wants to argue a different interpretation of the law, may write an alternative narrative. When the narrative argues for a different result, it is called a dissenting opinion.

Appellate decisions can be difficult to read because they span history and can include unfamiliar language or legal jargon. One of the reporter series called the *Federal Reporter*, published by the Thomson Reuters Westlaw company, dates back to cases decided in 1880. Antiquated language, or situations that are no longer common, such as horse thievery, are referenced giving the modern reader difficulty. Furthermore, discussions about points of procedural law often cite legal concepts and terms unfamiliar to non-lawyers. However, if one continues reading the case and puts forth the effort required to understand the basic facts surrounding the identity of the parties involved, what transpired and how the case was or was not resolved, then a suitable understanding of what happened can be obtained.

In reading case law reporters, attorneys initially try to determine who is suing whom for what and under what legal theory. The answer to the question of "Who?" is not defined by the litigant's name, but her official relationship to the other party. For example, understanding that a Mrs Smith sued a Mrs Thomas is not as helpful as knowing that a tenant of an apartment building sued her landlord. Knowing how these parties are officially connected helps the attorney determine if the appellate case she is reading could be applicable to her own landlord/tenant case. This knowledge also helps her understand which area of law, such as property or contracts, would most likely govern any decisions made. You will learn more about property and contract law in Part II.

The answer to the question: "for what?" is found by determining what compensation was sought by the plaintiff at the trial level, and the answer to: "under what legal theory?", usually found in the section outlining the judge's decision, gives the reader a more detailed understanding of what the plaintiff had to prove to the trial court to prevail.

From the written case report or judge's opinion one can also obtain facts that brought forth the dispute. Not all of the facts, only the relevant facts. For instance, if the dispute is about breaching a contract to lease property, we would not need to know what color jacket the landlord wore when she signed the contract but we should know the terms of the lease. The definition of relevant facts changes with the type of case, the relief sought, state or federal law governing the parties and which specific legal theory is in question. This information from the written case report is summarized and referred to as the *issue at hand*, or simply the *issue*.

Using legal precedent from previous similar cases, the court may make a decision in favor of one of the parties but often the appellate court will not decide on the issue at all, if the court reasons that the trial court followed proper procedure and interpreted the law correctly, the trial court decision will be upheld.

To illustrate this, let us consider the case of the City of Chicago, (and other parties) versus the Environmental Defense Fund (and other parties). Many times more than one party may be a part of a lawsuit, for ease of discussion here the names of the other parties are eliminated. In the legal community, "other listed parties" are referred to using the Latin term *Et Alii*, abbreviated to *et al*. Reference to this case can be abbreviated by using the following nomenclature or citation: *City of Chicago, et al. v. Environmental Defense Fund et al. 511 US 328 (1994)*. This citation means that the case is published in the United States Reporter Volume 511, published in 1994, which contains cases decided by the US Supreme Court. We also know from the citation that the case begins on page 328.

An brief summary at the beginning of the written opinion states that the respondent is the Environmental Defense Fund (EDF) who sued the city of Chicago and its mayor, alleging that they were violating the Resource Conservation and Recovery Act of 1976 (RCRA) and implementing regulations of the Environmental Protection Agency (EPA) by using landfills not licensed to accept hazardous wastes. The District Court granted them a quick decision prior to any trial called a *summary judgment*. The appellate court decision also states that the Court of Appeals disagreed and reversed the decision. An appeal to the United States Supreme Court was made. The decision by the United States Supreme Court is the written outlining the basic facts of the dispute. From a short summary the reader can determine the following:

- Who is suing whom? The Environmental Defense Fund, an organization, sued the City of Chicago and its mayor.
- For what? The city is allegedly using landfills not licensed to accept hazardous wastes as disposal sites for the toxic municipal waste combustion.

A further reading of the judge's opinion will help one find out what the issue was on appeal, how the case was decided and what rationale the judge used to come to this decision. To extract the rest of the information from this court's decision is neither absolute nor easy. Interpreting judge's decisions from opinions is what lawyers and judges do for a living and the subject of much argument among themselves. This example was just used to illustrate how the judge's narrative decision must be broken down and interpreted by an attorney in order for her to determine the law. You are encouraged to search the Internet for a copy of the judge's decision using the legal citation previously.

As already mentioned, appeals are trial disputes reheard in a higher court. In states with two appellate courts the next higher court from the trial level will be an intermediate appellate court, not be the state's highest court or the US Supreme Court. In the appellate example previously, the opinion mentions how the case was appealed from another appellate court to the Supreme Court of the United States.

If the initial case is a federal case, heard at the trial level, the first appeal will be to a Circuit Court of Appeals and the Supreme Court of the United States will hear the second and final appeal.

Parties do not have an automatic right to be heard by the Supreme Court of the United States. The various laws of criminal and civil procedure determine what jurisdiction the appellate courts have, and regulates that the Supreme Court of the United States can decide not to hear a case or agree to hear a case, a decision to hear a case is made when a majority of the justices vote yes, this is called *granting certiorari*.

Regardless of the level of the appellate court, most legal case reporters are used to extract who is suing whom for what, what was decided and what rationale did the judge use to make her decision. The more complicated or impactful an appellate case is, the more likely there will be a longer written opinion by the court and a longer history of how the case ended up in an appellate court. This brief explanation of the appellate process and how the common law is recorded will help you to understand the framework of common law and that this law is located in many books that are on the shelves of public and private law libraries. Moving forward, many of these case reporters will be available on the Internet and entrance to a law library will not be necessary to conduct legal research.

3.9 The United States Constitution

Applied by judges in all US courts, the US Constitution is the highest law of the land and anchors the US legal system in the law. The document is organized into subareas called articles. The first three articles describe the government. Rights given to all citizens are at the end of the main document in the first 10 amendments. These basic rights are referred to in the Bill of Rights.

Reading the Constitution not only provides definitive statements regarding the law, it also gives the reader an idea of the founding fathers' vision for the new country. The Constitution and its amendments also illustrate the earlier point that the law is not a static set of rules. For example, in the text of the original Constitution it states:

Representatives and direct Taxes shall be apportioned among the several States which may be included within this Union, according to their respective Numbers, which shall be determined by adding to the whole Number of free Persons, including those bound to Service for a Term of Years, and excluding Indians not taxed, three fifths of all other Persons.

This is called the *The Three-Fifths Compromise* and can be found in Article 1, Section 2, and Paragraph 3 of the Constitution.

The concept of counting citizens of a state as three-fifths of a person for purposes of determining the number of congressional representatives is no longer valid. This law has been modified by an amendment to the constitution. In total, 27 amendments have been approved since the original signing of the Constitution. Procedures for amending the United States Constitution are also contained in Article V of the original text.

Each state additionally has its own constitution; many are longer than the federal constitution. These documents outline the relationship between the citizens of a state and its state government.

The federal and state constitutions are all found in several books, usually called codes and located in law libraries. Some versions of the codes also include notes about application and additional information connecting case law to the text. Versions with these notes are called annotated codes.

3.10 Legal research

Legal research is the process used to determine how the courts might decide on a specific set of facts in a specific jurisdiction or whether any statutes, administrative law or constitution speaks to an issue in question. In its basic sense, legal research is understanding how laws are made, knowing where legal information can be found and locating applicable law for a specific situation.

As you are aware, in a common law country like the United States, finding applicable law is not as simple as defining a category and looking up the definition and rules about punishment for the offense in some big library or book called *The Law*. To find the written statements and explanations on law applied in the United States, one has to look to the sources of law such as statutes, administrative rulings and previous cases recorded as common law. However, the ultimate source of law is always the US Constitution. If any statute or common law decision is counter to the constitution, that law will be overruled eventually.

Since one philosophy of US law is "no harm, no foul": meaning if no harm, injury or breach of duty occurs, there is no case to bring. Whatever harm has occurred will help the researcher decide which sources to investigate. The location of the harm will help narrow down which reporters or which statutes to look at, and over time an attorney will learn a specific area of the law and be able to predict how a court will decide a dispute.

Assume some harm has occurred and the attorney determines the common law is a good place to start. How does a lawyer, or anyone else, find what the courts have done in a similar situation? The answer "legal research" is simple, but the process is not. Legal research is,

> . . . the process of identifying and retrieving information necessary to support legal decision-making. In its broadest sense, legal research includes each step of a course of action that begins with an analysis of the facts of a problem and concludes with the application and communication of the results of the investigation. (Jacobstein and Mersky 2002)

There is no universal method to legal research. The steps used to conduct legal research vary according to the legal system, in the USA the general method is similar to other types of research with some extra steps. Legal research steps include:

- Finding primary sources of law, or primary authority, in a given jurisdiction. Primary sources of law are the US Constitution, statutes, case law or regulation;
- Searching for articles written by lawyers and others attempting to explain primary sources. Examples of secondary sources include: law school journals known as law reviews, legal dictionaries, legal treatises and legal encyclopedias. This step helps the researcher understand how others have interpreted the primary sources and offers additional information about legal theory;
- Checking to make sure all of the primary sources are up-to-date and still in use, this process of making sure the law is up to date includes a process called "shepardizing", which tells the researcher if the cases found have been overturned or are still considered valid law, and what other court decisions relied on the case being checked.

The verb *shepardizing* comes from the most common source for determining this information is the *Shepard's Citation Resource*. The print and electronic resources available are so numerous and complicated law schools require beginning students to take an entire class devoted to nothing but legal research.

3.11 Useful legal theory

As earlier stated, the goal of this first part of the text is to help the student in the built environment understand basic legal theory. In order to maintain brevity, various legal concepts developed over time were omitted. This section is designed to help the student of facilities management understand these concepts and appreciate how they operate in the US legal system.

Every attempt will be made to limit extraneous concepts and only cover topics necessary for the built environment professional. References will be given for those interested in fully understanding the theory.

3.11.1 Stare decisis *and material facts*

The Latin term *stare decisis* translates as "stand by decided matters". In practice it means to *let the prior decision stand*. This is one of the basic legal concepts in US law. It acts as the glue holding past decisions to future decisions. *Stare decisis* leads to stability in the courts, but interestingly enough it also allows for flexibility. *Stare decisis* reasons that similar future cases should be decided in the same way as preceding cases. The more similar the facts, the more likely the court outcome will be similar. Modifications to decisions can occur, but only when the facts of a new case differ enough to warrant a new decision. *Stare decisis* allows members of society to be able to predict how the court will legally respond to specific conduct.

Material facts are the facts that are important to a case. Herein lies an important concept of legal reasoning; that clear-cut answers to what the court will do in any situation depends upon the facts, and different facts may lead to different outcomes. So, if a person driving a car is speeding and causes an accident resulting in loss of life, the result of a trial should find the person guilty of a crime. According to *stare decisis* all subsequent similar cases should be similarly decided. But, suppose the person was a law enforcement official driving a police car? Then even adhering to the concept of *stare decisis* the person may not be guilty of a crime. With changes in material facts the outcome may also change.

If the person in the first case were a dentist and in the second case a law enforcement officer, the facts may be considered materially different. What if in both cases the driver was a law enforcement officer? What if in both cases the car driven was privately owned? Would the court be able to decide the case without additional facts? To fully understand the concept of *stare decisis* and how it operates one must also understand this concept of materiality. For additional information about *stare decisis* and how it looms large in US law, see *The Evolution of Precedent*, Nicola Gannaioli and Andrei Shleifer. (LC control no.: 2005617842, LCCN permalink: http://lccn.loc.gov/2005617842.)

3.11.2 *Issues of justiciability*

Justiciability (May and Ides 2007), answers the question of whether a court can exercise its authority over a specific legal matter brought before it. Justiciability is more than merely a question of jurisdiction. Because the US system was founded on the coordination of government entities that control the power of each other, the court must only exercise its authority when allowed by the US Constitution. Justiciability refers to a dispute that has the ability to be decided in court. This seems simple and obvious, but it is not.

The US legal system is designed for courts to only decide on actual disputes with injured parties with few exceptions. Therefore for justiciability to exist, each case that reaches a judge should have several elements:

- The plaintiff should have standing (the actual party who is injured) to sue;
- There should be an injury;
- There should be a remedy for the alleged injury;
- The defendant(s) should be legally responsible for the injury;
- There should be an issue in disagreement; and
- The court should have jurisdiction over the parties.

Thus when attorneys advocate for their clients, not only are they concerned with the actual facts and the issue in dispute, but also if the claim is legally justiciable. Motions filed back and forth between the plaintiff and defendant disputing justiciability can include disputing the plaintiff's right to sue; if there actually is an injury; if the defendant is truly responsible for the injury and if the court has jurisdiction over the litigants and the subject matter. Additional issues such as whether additional parties should be added to the lawsuit, which laws apply, how much up-front evidence the plaintiff should produce and other items, are all decided prior to the issue that caused the dispute in the first place. This is one reason why it may take years after a lawsuit is filed for it to finally be heard in court. All of this pre-trial litigation is also why the majority of lawsuits filed never reach the trial stage. If you consider that parties have one automatic right to appeal and that there could be additional appeals all the way to the Supreme Court, you can see why some parties give up without a fight. Oftentimes, they run out of money for representation or decide the issue is no longer important. It should be apparent to the prudent facility manager that alternative dispute resolution can save, time, money and sheer aggravation.

Over time, certain rules of thumb have evolved clarifying certain areas, such as when courts will use their authority and when they will not. These concepts involve the use of the court for advisory opinions, issues of ripeness, issues of mootness, political questions and standing. These concepts are explained next.

3.11.3 Advisory opinions

An advisory opinion is an opinion issued by a judge that is not considered law, but merely advises on the interpretation of a law. The United States

Supreme Court has determined that the requirement an actual dispute must exist, found in Article Three of the United States Constitution, disallows courts from delivering consultative opinions. Therefore, prior to a court hearing a case, the parties must show that they have a tangible interest at stake in the matter. Courts have lowered the threshold for advisory opinions in modern times. It is not hard to see why controlling the number of trials just for advice is important.

3.11.4 Ripeness

Ripeness refers to the readiness of a case for litigation; the dispute must not be hypothetical, there must be some threatened injury to the plaintiff. Challenging a law, just for the sake of a challenge, is not done unless there is an overwhelming reason and some real injury could possibly result if something is not done. This challenge is sometimes made when new regulations that could be unconstitutional come about. The Supreme Court of the United States issued guidelines for whether or not a case is ripe in the case of Abbott Laboratories (Abbot Laboratories v. Gardner 1967). The judge in this case stated that the doctrine of ripeness is used to prevent the courts from getting into complicated, abstract disputes over administrative policies prior to an administrative decision being made. "The problem is best seen in a twofold aspect, requiring us to evaluate both the fitness of the issues for judicial decision and the hardship to the parties of withholding court consideration." (Abbot Laboratories v. Gardner 1967). Students often confuse ripeness with the doctrine against giving advisory opinions. Both are principles of *justiciability*. But ripeness questions an injury has not occurred but is imminent, and with the advisory opinion the case is simply an abstract argument in the hypothetical.

3.11.5 Mootness

Another justiciability principle is *mootness*. Mootness refers to a legal question of which the answer will have no effect. It is said that a matter is moot if it has been deprived of concrete consequence or rendered purely theoretical.

The US Constitution requires the courts to decide on matters of interpreting the Constitution and states that courts do not have a role if an issue has no specific connection to interpreting the constitution. If there is nothing for the court to interpret or decide, an issue should be decided through the democratic process. These issues are known as *political disputes*. A good test to tell if an issue would be seen as a political question is to take note of the skills necessary to make the decision. If the decision requires general knowledge and no legal expertise, it just might be a political question. Of course, depending on the issue there can be strong debate over whether or not a dispute is a political question.

3.11.6 *Standing*

Having *standing* means the party bringing the lawsuit has, either directly or indirectly, been injured. This concept is crucial and must be present prior to filing a case in court. Requiring that a potential plaintiff has standing to sue restricts any party unrelated to the situation from bringing an action against a potential defendant. If you tried to sue for damages associated with the broken leg of a complete stranger on the other side of the world, you would not get very far. You would not have standing to sue.

To illustrate the justiciability principle of standing a case called Lujan (Lujan v. Defenders of Wildlife 1992) is often used. Lujan involved a national environmental organization's challenge to a government regulation declaring that federal agencies had no duty to consult with the Department of the Interior about the impact their projects in foreign countries might have on endangered populations of animals.

In this case the court stated the standard it used to decide on the issue of standing by stating:

> Over the years, our cases have established that the irreducible constitutional minimum of standing contains three elements. First, the plaintiff must have suffered an "injury in fact" – an invasion of a legally-protected interest which is (a) concrete and particularized, and (b) "actual or imminent, not 'conjectural' or 'hypothetical'. Second, there must be a . . . connection between the injury and the conduct complained of – the injury has to be "fairly . . . trace[able] to the . . . action of the defendant, and not . . . th[e] result [of] the independent action of some third party not before the court." Third, it must be "likely," as opposed to merely "speculative," that the injury will be "redressed by a favorable decision." (Lujan v. Defenders of Wildlife 1992).

The plaintiff, the Defenders of Wildlife Organization, argued that the process increased the likelihood that endangered species would be extinct sooner. The Court found the organization lacked standing.

3.12 Legislation

Legislation is an important source of US law. Federal statutes are published in two basic formats; public and private laws, and codified law. Public and private laws are published in the format that is signed by both houses of the United States Congress and the President. Codes are called *current law* because a code section consists of the original law that created the section and later amendments integrated together. Federal statutes organized as the United States Code are divided into 50 subject titles with a multi-volume index, which also includes a Popular Name Table. Since the US Code is just a compilation of statutes, it does not contain laws issued by executive branch agencies, decisions of the federal courts, treaties, or laws enacted by state or local governments. Executive branch laws are found in the Code of Federal Regulations and the Federal Register.

When citing the United States Code, students should include the title number and the section number. For example, the citation 20 USC 112 indicates that the information can be found in Title 20 and Section 112 of the United States Code.

The laws of the United States and other jurisdictions can be found in either official or unofficial repositories. Unofficial sources are often private publishers who compile similar areas of law in one convenient location, thereby adding value to attorneys and others conducting legal research.

Officially, the Office of the Federal Register (OFR) provides access to the official text of: Federal Laws, Presidential Documents; Administrative Regulations and Notices; Descriptions of Federal Organizations, Programs and Activities. The Administrative Committee of the Federal Register (ACFR) oversees the work of the OFR and the Federal Register publications system. Their mission is to inform US citizens about the law and document the actions of federal agencies. States also have varying administrative systems for documenting the actions of state legislatures and state courts.

One particularly useful resource for finding the law is the Law Library of Congress. Their collection of sources is the largest and most comprehensive of its kind in the world. The collection covers all periods of law from ancient times to the current day. Although the Law Library of Congress is a repository for the complete record of US law, international jurisdictions are also represented. Information about congressional bills, resolutions, state and federal legal documents, law newspapers, and records of the US Supreme Court and US Courts of Appeals can be accessed. The Law Library of Congress can be accessed via the Internet at www.loc.gov/law (Library of Congress 2013).

3.13 Procedural and substantive laws

As you know, there are many ways to describe the law and several choices for its organization. One way to classify the US law is by purpose. It is known that laws serve to keep the peace in society, but some laws also keep the peace within the legal system. These two different types of peacekeeping laws are known as *substantive* and *procedural*. Substantive law controls subjects that are known to most such as *criminal law*, *property law* and *real estate law*. These laws set forth duties and potential punishments. *Procedural laws*, on the other hand are quite hidden from most of us, but can make the difference between a successful or unfavorable outcome.

The two main types of procedural laws are *Civil* or *Criminal Procedure Laws* and *Evidence Laws*. There are other areas of law controlling the behavior of those practicing law, but these two are the main culprits.

3.13.1 Civil and Criminal Procedure Law

Civil and Criminal Procedure is important because it rises above the level of mere rules. These rules carry the full force of the law and if they are not followed, lawsuits can be dismissed and potential criminals can be released. These rules serve the purpose of the constitutional mandate that everyone should receive due process. The term *due process* refers to a fair and deliberate process to protect basic rights given to all citizens.

The Federal Rules of Civil Procedure (abbreviated to Fed.Civ.P in citations) govern procedure for all civil lawsuits tried in United States federal courts. The United States Supreme Court updates the civil procedures via enactments. Congress has seven months to veto any new rules, if not vetoed, the rules become part of the Federal Rules of Civil Procedure. Although states may determine their own rules, most states have adopted rules that are based on the federal rules. The most up-to-date version of the federal rules, along with the Federal Rules of Criminal Procedure and others, can be found on the US Courts website at www.uscourts.gov (United States Court).

Criminal or Civil Procedure governs the rules of litigation and are a compilation of best practices for efficient operation of the litigation process. For those contemplating court involvement in dispute settlements, Procedural Laws are very useful because they outline what should be done to go forward with a lawsuit and when certain steps should be completed. For example, Federal Rule of Civil Procedure Rule Three, "Commencing an Action", states, "A civil action is commenced by filing a complaint with the court." Rule Four, "Summons", indicates that a civil complaint should contain the:

> . . . name [of] the court and the parties; be directed to the defendant; state the name and address of the plaintiff's attorney or – if unrepresented – of the plaintiff; state the time within which the defendant must appear and defend; notify the defendant that a failure to appear and defend will result in a default judgment against the defendant for the relief demanded in the complaint; be signed by the clerk.

Compare this to the Federal Rules of Criminal Procedure's Rule Three, which states:

> The complaint is a written statement of the essential facts constituting the offense charged. Except as provided in Rule 4.1, it must be made under oath before a magistrate judge or, if none is reasonably available, before a state or local judicial officer.

These rules differ depending upon where the dispute is heard, for example, in a local state court or a federal court. Depending on the level of the court (trial or appeal), various procedures must also be followed for clarity, organization and standardization. These laws help all of the parties receive fair and efficient service from the courts. Other court procedural rules, such as Federal Rules of Appellate Procedure, also state the circumstances under which someone can file an appeal, who the appeal should filed with, how long they have to file an appeal and what to do about paying judgments while waiting for an appeal to be heard.

3.13.2 Federal Rules of Evidence

The Federal Rules of Evidence are also rules with the full weight of the law governing the parties' actions in a dispute. In contrast to Civil and Criminal Procedure, these laws control what type of information will be considered to resolve the case in civil or criminal matters. The rules prevent the consideration of distrustful evidence, and serve as gatekeepers for testimony, documents, media or other information. This helps the jurors or the triers of fact because only fully vetted evidence deemed important by the court will be considered to resolve the case. The Federal Rules of Evidence has three main objectives. To set the standard for determining when evidence is applicable, to make sure only evidence that is relevant is admitted and to help the judge determine if excluding seemingly relevant evidence may have an unfairly detrimental effect. Relevant evidence, for example, the fact that a defendant is a prostitute may be more detrimental than it is useful in some cases, is prohibited under Federal Rules of Evidence Rule 403, "Excluding Relevant Evidence for Prejudice, Confusion, Waste of Time, or Other Reasons", which states that the "court may exclude relevant evidence if its probative value is substantially outweighed by a danger of one or more of the following: unfair prejudice, confusing the issues, misleading the jury, undue delay, wasting time, or needlessly presenting cumulative evidence." It should be kept in mind that the evidence admitted by the judge is the only evidence to be considered by the jury or trier of fact. Since all parties must follow the rules of evidence, the goal is that only relevant, verifiable information will be taken into account.

Evidence presented to the judge or jury is carefully scrutinized so that both sides have an equal chance to present or dispute a proposed fact. Arguing the laws of evidence can be an exciting basis for a courtroom quarrel, particularly when a piece of evidence regarded as helpful is denied consideration because of some irregularity.

One example of the Rules of Evidence in use occurs when a plaintiff or defendant wants to use a document to help prove a particular point during trial. When evidence presented is thought untruthful or not verifiable the attorneys on the opposing side may object to it being admitted for consideration. All evidence admitted for consideration by the trier of fact is recorded in a trial record. One is likely to see a television lawyer trying a case stand up during the questioning of her client and state "Objection, Your Honor. . . ". Though often over-dramatized, this is one avenue attorneys use to urge the judge to disallow evidence that cannot be validated.

The scope of the Federal Rules of Evidence can be subdivided in to three categories: prohibition against unverifiable self-serving statements, prohibition against statements that are prejudicial to one party without helping the trier of fact and any exceptions to these rules. Over time the legal system has determined there may be instances where there is no alternative way to get important information.

Understanding the rules of evidence for the non-lawyer is easy once the rationale behind the rules is understood. By the time parties reach the point when they cannot settle a dispute amongst themselves, some period of time has passed and an emotional investment has been made in their side of the dispute. Like the proverbial exaggerated tale told by the fisherman about the size of fish caught, details may have grown increasingly favorable to the party espousing them. It is a very human tendency to remember events in a light most favorable to us. Details that conflict with our side of the story tend to fade and of course our minds fill in the blanks with details that agree with our internal narrative.

The impact of all the procedural laws, along with the substantive laws, has a major effect on how a case is presented to a trier of fact and eventually can determine how a dispute is decided. As illustrated in Figure 3.2, the small square representing the area of overlap should coincide with the relevant facts and law and, therefore, the correct decision.

Figure 3.2   Overlapping of procedural laws and substantive laws.

Hearsay Rule

One famous evidence rule is the rule against hearsay testimony. Hearsay is defined as an out of court statement given to the court as true. The problem with using hearsay testimony is that if the statement was made out of court, it is difficult for the jury to know if the statement was true or just taken out of context. Rules that allow hearsay to be admitted fall under a specific subset of the evidence laws, and must be explained and analyzed in order to determine if one of the acceptable exceptions exists.

Exceptions to the rule against hearsay include admitting the following:

- Records made during the normal course of business.
- Some public records and reports.
- Evidence of a judgment of conviction at trial.
- Evidence of the absence of a business record or entry.
- Spontaneous statements.
- Family records concerning family history.
- Judgments of a court concerning personal history, family history, general history or boundaries, where those matters were essential to the judgment.
- Academic publications used to question an expert witness.
- Commercial publications.
- Vital statics certificates like birth records.
- Past memories recorded.
- Recorded documents affecting interests in land.
- Records of religious organizations concerning personal or family history.
- Records of vital statistics.
- Reputation concerning boundaries or general history.
- Reputation concerning family history.
- Reputation of a person's character.
- Statements about the speaker's present sense impressions.
- Statements about the speaker's then existing mental, emotional or physical condition.
- Statements in authentic (at least 20 years old) ancient documents.
- Statements in other documents purporting to affect interests in land and relevant to the purpose of the document.
- Statements made by the speaker for the purpose of medical diagnosis or treatment.
- Statements of the absence of a public record or entry.
- The blanket rule, which requires the evidence to be admitted if it meets certain standards made by the rules.

Another major function of the Rules of Evidence is to protect constitutional rights, such as the right to confront the defendant's accuser, a jury by one's peers or to be considered innocent until proven guilty. Above all else the right to be considered innocent until proven guilty can be used as the basis for many exceptions to the rule against hearsay.

So how does an attorney or her client know if evidence will be admitted or not? She will not know for sure until the judge makes a ruling on admissibility. All she can do before offering an item into evidence is take an educated guess and try to find other cases where similar evidence was admitted. Judges endeavor to rule on evidence interpretations in such a way to maintain a fair and impartial hearing.

Federal and state rules
There are Federal Rules of Evidence as described earlier and also various state rules of evidence. Both are similar in that they help the legal system treat all evidence equally to ensure a fair and orderly trial. The Federal Rules of Evidence have developed over time through best practices in trials, much in the same way as common law.

3.14 Chapter summary

This chapter is crammed with information most professional adults should know in order to navigate the business world in the twenty-first century. Abbreviating courses in Civics and Legal Theory into a few chapters is difficult because there were some concepts that had to be left out. You are encouraged to use online resources to fill in your understanding when necessary.

For understanding the structure of US Government, the many components of the US legal system, common law creation and the difference between procedural and substantive law is a great place to start. It is hoped that, provided with this background information, an explanation of selected laws in Part II and application of these laws in Part III can now be comprehended at a deeper level, and will allow the student to practice critical reading and thinking while learning how to limit legal exposure.

3.15 Questions

1. How are legal research and reasoning connected to the doctrine of *stare decisis*?
2. In general, where would you find an appellate case that was decided by the supreme court of Idaho?
3. How important are judges' opinions in appellate cases?
4. Why is procedural law necessary?

5. Would a law against murder be considered a procedural or substantive law? Explain your answer.
6. Who are the most likely participants in a civil lawsuit?
7. How will someone in the future know how a case was decided on a specific set of facts?
8. How does a legal researcher know if a judge's decision is still relevant law?
9. Which is more important, the correct jurisdiction or having standing to sue?
10. Using a quick Internet search, find and summarize one Rule of Evidence and describe why it is an important rule.

References

Bellis, M. *Saturory Structure and Legilative Drafting Conventions: A Primer for Judges*. Publication, United States House of Representatives, Washington DC: Federal Judicial Center, 2008.

Contrubis, J. Executive Orders and Proclamations. *#95-722A*, Washington DC: CRS Report for Congress, 1999.

Jacobstein, J. and R. Mersky. *Fundamentals of Legal Research*. 8th Edition, Foundation Press, 2002.

Library of Congress. *Library of Congress*. January 5, 2013. www.loc.gov/law/ (accessed January 5, 2013).

May, C. and A. Ides. *Constitutional Law: National Power and Federalism*. New York: Aspen, 2007.

Summary of Part I

It is through the power of judicial review that the constitution, common law, statute and administrative law, is applied and given life. Legislation can affect the built environment process from the planning stages through to the resolution of disputes at the culmination of a project. Specific legislation impacting the facility management industry is discussed in Part III. For now, it is sufficient for you to remember that statutes enacted by all levels of government have a significant impact on how a Facility Manager conducts business and are distinct from the rights afforded under the constitution. Finally, all types of laws exist at the federal, state, county and city levels, and there are many, many ways you will find yourself interacting with the law and legal principles.

Legal Concepts for Facility Managers, First Edition. Linda Thomas-Mobley.
© 2014 John Wiley & Sons, Ltd. Published 2014 by John Wiley & Sons, Ltd.

Part II

Facility Management and the Law

Introduction

The law as applied to the Facility Manager falls under the general realm of professional liability law. The Facility Manager, along with the architect and Construction Manager, are considered experts in their respective fields. These professionals are considered to be in possession of greater knowledge about the built environment than the general public. The position of a professional includes an extra burden of owing a special duty of care to others. The most common extra duty associated with being a professional Facility Manager is the duty to protect the public's health and safety. Facility Managers are required operate in a manner so that any risk of harm to others is contemplated and lessened if possible. In short, the Facility Manager must act in a way to lessen the risk of harm to the public associated with the built environment.

The task of helping the Facility Manager to understand exactly what the legal system expects of a professional is difficult to summarize without a substantive law framework. In Part II we introduce such a framework that includes the basic classifications of substantive law as a beginning of the explanation. The basic areas of the law, presented in order from oldest to more current include: *Property Law*, *Contract Law*, *Criminal Law*, *Tort Law*, *Labor Law* and *Environmental Law*.

4

Property Law I: Rights

Property is the right or lawful power, which a person has to a thing.
***On the History of Property,* James Wilson (1742–1798)**

4.1 Introduction

As a signer of the Declaration of Independence, James Wilson is considered a Founding Father of the United States. He was elected twice to the Continental Congress and had a major influence during the drafting the United States Constitution. Wilson is one of only six persons to sign both the Declaration of Independence and the Constitution. George Washington appointed him as one of the six original justices to the Supreme Court of the United States. Although few in number, his writings reveal that he favored a systematic view of the law. Wilson was no stranger to the built environment but unfortunately his life was tragically marked by land-development conspiracies. James Wilson remains somewhat unknown mostly because of his difficulties from the development conspiracies; he holds the distinction of being the only Justice of the Supreme Court ever imprisoned for debt. The paradox of Wilson's apparent respect for the law, yet not-so-legal behavior, is only fitting for the first chapter on property law. This is because the simple notion of an idea as basic as "property" is also paradoxical to the complexity of the study of property law.

Property law can be divided among three realms. The first realm is *definitional*, which includes what types of authority over property is recognized by the law, the second is the realm of *transference*, what constitutes a proper transfer of property from one owner to another, and the third realm is one of *obligation*, the duty the owner has in using the property.

Legal Concepts for Facility Managers, First Edition. Linda Thomas-Mobley.
© 2014 John Wiley & Sons, Ltd. Published 2014 by John Wiley & Sons, Ltd.

Occasionally the Facility Manager will be involved with the transfer of property, but will not likely be responsible for the ensuring the legality of the transfer. Legal transfer of personal property or real estate is not within the scope of this text and assistance from real estate agents and attorneys is highly recommended when the need arises. This chapter, dealing with the first definitional realm, offers a brief explanation on the law of property and the specific authority an individual has over portable and fixed, tangible assets.

The control of specific property lies on a continuum and can range from full ownership to temporary use. The type of property right an individual possesses defines the level of allowable property use. Property rights are also called "estates", which can be confusing due to the more common definition of the term. Having a right to use a certain piece of property means that someone has an estate in this property.

The Facility Manager needs to be familiar with the various types of ownership so that when representing an employer, the proper obligation that is required is upheld. Chapter 5 will continue with basic property law and consider the various responsibilities legally required by owners and users of property.

At the conclusion of Chapter 4 the following learning outcomes are expected:

- Define "property".
- Explain the legal term "estate".
- Distinguish between personal property and real property.
- Define various classes of real property ownership.
- Explain obligations commonly found in a lease.

4.2 What is property?

In its most basic sense, property is something that can be owned. The thing that has the ability to be owned can have physical presence or not. A baseball is something that can be owned in the same way a song can be owned. Both are considered property in the legal sense. A further distinction is made in defining property as either personal or real. Personal property is portable and can be moved by the owner while real property is immovable. Personal property is also referred to as "personality". Theoretically, most any item can be moved and how fixed to the earth an item has to be to qualify as real property is not always clear, but a good rule of thumb to use is that real property is usually land, and all items meant to be permanently attached to that land and personal property are everything else. For example, real property may include a plot of land, any trees growing on the land and a structure built on the land. Even though trees can be cut down and structures can be physically moved from one plot to another, if the items are attached permanently to the land, they are considered real property.

In addition to defining items that can be owned, the law also broadly defines the owner. The owner of the object can be a single person, a group of people, a corporation or a government entity. This distinction is necessary because rights and responsibilities regarding property are tied to the type of owner in many instances. For example, property can be classified as private or public, depending on the owner.

Finally the word "ownership" is also defined in terms of the law. The type of legal ownership one has can range from the right to occupy a room, in the case of a tenant, to the right to sell the entire structure for a building owner. The various rights associated with the various types of ownership are often referred to a "bundle of rights". Figure 4.1 illustrates some of the rights an owner of land may have. The most comprehensive ownership right exists with the person who has the right to sell exclusive use of the property.

For the Facility Manager who tends to be responsible for all types of property, this area of the law can be confusing because corresponding areas of law governing rights may overlap. For instance, in a case involving removing a work computer from an office without permission, Criminal Law and Property Law overlap giving the rightful computer's owner more than one avenue for resolution. This chapter considers the law based in property.

4.3 Property law

The law of property regulates the acquisition, use and disposition of property. There are several sub topics under each of these areas. Acquisition of property can be obtained through purchase, mortgage, taking, war, gifts or other avenues. Use of property may be under license, lease or full ownership, and disposition can be via selling, granting through a will or destruction. Understanding how the law has evolved in acquisition, use and disposition requires an understanding of historical customs regarding the origins of ownership, historical land boundaries and treaties among historic empires, including the formation of current nations, territories and other transfers. Legalities surrounding the

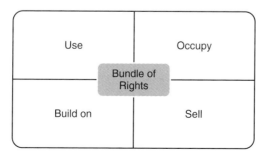

Figure 4.1   A land owner's bundle of rights.

proper acquisition and disposition of property, especially real property, are best done by attorneys, but knowledge of the law surrounding the use of property is helpful to the Facility Manager. It is the law involving types of property use that will be our focus.

4.4 Personal property for Facility Managers

Personal property can be divided into two major categories: tangible personal property, which includes items such as goods, animals and other physical items; and intangible personal property, such as the right to a copyright or invention patent.

Possessing personal property is regarded as exercising power over something to the exclusion of all others. It is a basic property right that entitles the owner to continue peaceful possession against everyone except someone having a more comprehensive ownership right, or a bigger bundle of rights. This more comprehensive ownership right is referred to as a "superior right". The right to recover personal property that has been wrongfully taken, and a legal right to recover damages against others wrongfully interfering with this right, are examples of superior rights. Lost property is defined as the situation where an owner has involuntarily parted with personal property and is ignorant of its location. Compare lost property to "mislaid property" that the owner intentionally places somewhere but forgets where it is, and "abandoned property" in which the owner has intentionally relinquished all rights. These distinctions carry specific legal rights. For example, lost or mislaid property continues to be owned by the person who lost or mislaid it. If someone else finds lost goods, the finder is entitled to possession against everyone with the exception of the true owner. Several other scenarios involving losing control over personal property exist, but one way to understand the rights of property owners is to realize that in the USA, the intent of the law is to do whatever is necessary to return an article to its rightful owner.

The superior right of a finder of personal property has exceptions that can impact the day-to-day operations of a Facility Manager. When an employee finds personal property during the scope of her employment, the right to the property is awarded to the employer rather than to the employee-finder.

Facility Managers also run into personal property situations involving *bailments*. A bailment is the rightful, temporary possession of goods by an individual other than the true owner. Simply, a bailment occurs when one leaves her personal property in the possession of another. The individual who entrusts her property into the hands of another is called the *bailor*, the person who holds such property is the *bailee*. Bailments are created when a designated purpose upon which the parties have agreed exists. This agreement is actually a contract, even though written terms may not exist. The parties voluntarily bind themselves to act according to specific terms. The bailee receives only control or possession of the property, and the bailor retains the ownership interests therein. While a bailment exists, the bailee has an interest in the property that is superior to all others, including the bailor, unless she violates some term of the agreement. When the purpose for which the property has been delivered has been accomplished, the property will be returned to the bailor or otherwise disposed of, according to her instructions.

A typical bailment that may involve a Facility Manager occurs in buildings equipped with garages for valet parking. By leaving the car and car keys with the valet service person, a bailment has been formed and certain duties are then expected of the car owner and the garage owner (Barlow 2003). The bailee is legally obligated to care for the bailed property and redeliver it to the bailor. If the car is lost, stolen or damaged while in the care of the garage owner, the bailee's liability depends on several dynamics, such as which person benefits from the bailment; how the bailed property became lost or damaged, and any contractual limitations on the bailee's liability. The question of who is benefitted by the bailment depends on whether the purpose of the bailment is to benefit the bailor, the bailee or both. If the garage owner is just holding the car without payment for the sole benefit of the car owner, the level of care is insignificant. In this case the liability of the garage owner only occurs if she was exceptionally careless. On the other hand, if the bailment is for the sole benefit of the garage owner and the car owner receives no compensation from the garage owner, then the garage owner is required to exercise a reasonable amount of care for the car. The reasonable amount of care that other garage owners would exercise in a similar setting is referred to as *ordinary care*. In most situations, a mutual benefit occurs; this requires the garage owner to exercise ordinary care for the property. It should be noted that if the keys are not left with the garage and the parking is free, a bailment has not occurred since the garage owner will not have control over the car.

Bailments can also occur inside of an office building. For example, the Facility Manager hired an electrical contractor to repair the elevators, and because of an unexpected situation the contractor is forced to leave the building before finishing work. If the Facility Manager agrees to keep the electrician's tools in a locked office until he returns, a bailment has been created.

4.5 Property ownership

Under the law the definition of property ownership has a broader meaning than what is commonly thought of as ownership. The simple example of purchasing a ball from the store for its full price will make you an owner. But what if you then lease the ball to your brother for 10 cents per minute, who is the owner now? What ownership rights do you have that your brother lacks?

With regard to property ownership in the USA, the definition of ownership can be referred to as a property interest, but an individual can have an interest in property while not being the owner. This is because an interest in property can be a smaller bundle of rights than an ownership of property. For example, your brother has an interest in the ball he is renting from you, in fact he has paid for his interest but it is not the same type of property interest that you enjoy as a full owner.

There are three types of property interests; ownership, possession and title. An ownership interest includes all rights to a property, as mentioned before, it is the right to exclusively use, possess and dispose of property among other rights. Ownership can be shared, in which case no one person as exclusive property rights, but all owners of the property can decide collectively how the property will be used. Forms of joint property ownership will be covered shortly, but for now, think of an ownership interest in property as the largest bundle of property rights. Figure 4.2 illustrates the full bundle of rights.

Compare ownership to possession, which gives the possessor something less than ownership. Possession simply means the exercise of control over the property; the possessor does not have to be the owner or even have the legal right to possess the property in this case.

Finally consider *title*, it is used in US property law to mean "legal ownership" of the property as opposed to "beneficial ownership" of the property. Title, or "legal ownership" is not the same as full ownership as defined previously. The titleholder may have legal ownership but may not benefit from the property. The owner has both title and beneficial use of the property. For example, a trustee may have legal title to land but not be the true owner. The trustee can

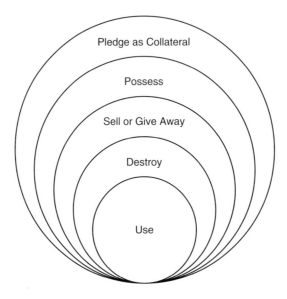

Figure 4.2   Bundle of property rights.

be holding the title for many reasons and still not have beneficial ownership. The person who is the true owner, the person who is receiving income or proceeds from the property, holds beneficial ownership, which is also called equitable title. In the case of a home with a mortgage, the person living in the home and gaining benefit from the property holds equitable title, and is thus the true owner gaining benefit from the property but the mortgage company may be holding title until the loan is paid off.

Property ownership questions can be confusing and apply to all types of property; personal, real estate, tangible and non-tangible. The key is to understand that the status of ownership needs to be known so that a determination of legal rights or legal liabilities can be understood. Ownership, or something less like a possessor of property, will determine what legal duty is owed to others.

Personal property rights vary depending on what level of ownership one has in the property. Similarly, real property rights vary, as we shall see in the next section.

4.5.1 Forms of real property ownership

There are three major forms of real property ownership. *Direct individual* ownership, where one person owns the property allows that person the exclusive right to exercise her rights. *Direct concurrent* ownership occurs when two or more people own the property. This type of ownership allows the parties to hold the property as tenants in common, joint tenants or tenants by the entirety. Tenants in common have an individual, whole ownership interest in the property. For example, each party has the right to sell her ownership interest. A tenancy by the entirety is a joint ownership between married persons; neither tenant has the right to sell without out the consent of the other. When a tenant by the entirety dies, the surviving spouse acquires full ownership of the property. With joint tenants, an individual owner can sell her property, but if that occurs, the tenancy automatically changes to a tenancy in common. Finally, *indirect* ownership occurs when the property is indirectly owned by one or more individuals via a legal entity, like a general partnership or a limited liability company. Figure 4.3 illustrates the relationship among the types of direct, indirect and joint ownership.

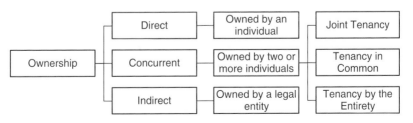

Figure 4.3   Definition of direct, indirect and joint ownership.

4.6 Rights to real property

In real property the rights held by the owner vary according to the level of ownership. The rights or interest a person has in real property is called an "estate". Instead of describing this area as real property rights law, it can simply be referred to as *real estate law*.

There are two main categories of estates; *freehold* and *nonfreehold*. Freehold estates provide a higher level of rights to nonfreehold estates. Freehold estate gives ownership rights for an indefinite period of time. Rights to real property that are indefinite leases are not freehold estates. The right to indefinite use of the property is said to be free and clear and not subjected to lease terms.

Two types of freehold estates exist: a *fee simple* estate, which is the maximum number of rights and privileges and; a *life* estate, possession of the property only during the life of a specified person.

> *Fee simple*: a fee simple estate provides the most legal rights and powers available. It confers the maximum legal ownership with the largest amount of rights and privileges recognized by law. The term of a fee simple estate is infinite. It can be sold or given away in whole or in part and upon the owner's death the fee simple estate may pass to the heirs named in the will, or as regulated by state law if the owner dies without a will.
>
> As discussed earlier, with this idea that property rights are a bundle of separate rights, the owner of a fee simple estate can sell or give some of the rights in the property away but still remain in fee simple ownership. As an example, consider the case where an owner leases the property to a tenant. Both have legal rights to the property but the owner retains fee simple interest to regain possession of the property when the lease expires.
>
> *Life estate*: the duration of a life estate is measured by the life of a person and ends when the life of the estate holder ends. The owner may possess the property for as long as she lives and also may give that right in the property to another for as long as her interest in the estate exists. Life estates provide interesting situations if the estate holder decides to transfer the property.
>
> For example, if Linda has a life estate in beach front property and decides to convey this right to Michael for his life. If Linda dies before Michael, then Michael's right to possess the property ends. This is because Linda cannot give away more than she owns. Her bundle of rights in the beachfront property expires at her death so she cannot give Michael any rights beyond this timeframe. If the conveyance to Michael involved a sale, he is advised to investigate what type of ownership Linda actually possesses before purchasing the property. Figure 4.4 illustrates this concept that a life estate is similar to a fee simple estate but with fewer property rights.

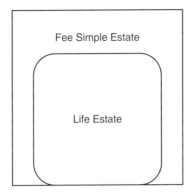

Figure 4.4   Composition of the life estate.

4.6.1 Nonfreehold estates

Nonfreehold estates, also called *leaseholds* involve a duty by the tenant to make periodic payments for the use of the land, usually in the form of rent. Generally, nonfreehold estates are classified as an *estate for years*, a *periodic tenancy'*, *tenancy at will* or a *tenancy at sufferance*. These estates constitute the core of the landlord/tenant relationship.

An *estate for years* has a specific beginning date and a definite end. Commercial leases fall in this category. The tenancy may be for any period of time, from years down to days, as long as the period is known by both parties at the beginning of the term. Automatically, when the end date arrives and the term of the tenancy expires, the right to possess the property reverts to the landlord.

An estate that continues for the successive periods of time, unless either party terminates it by proper notice, is called a *periodic tenancy*. Periodic tenancies usually last from year to year but other term lengths are possible as long as the parties agree at the beginning. What makes the periodic tenancy different from an estate for years is the automatic renewal of the term. The landlord or tenants both have the right to terminate the lease with notice, but without any notice the term just renews itself.

A *tenancy at will* is an estate that can be terminated by either the landlord or the tenant but, unlike an estate for years or a periodic tenancy, there is no specified duration. As in the periodic tenancy, the landlord or the tenant has the right to terminate the lease, but unlike a periodic tenancy no formal notice of a prescribed length of time is required to terminate a tenancy at will. Some jurisdictions have modified tenancy at will requiring parties to give notice, but the original nonfreehold estate of tenancy at will was similar to employment at will, requiring no specific notice to end the term from either party.

Tenancy at sufferance, occurs when a tenant does not move at the end of her lease, this tenant is said to be "holding over". This type of nonfreehold estate exists when a person who originally had a legal right to possess the property wrongfully continues to stay, even after the lease expires. The landlord has one of two choices in this case; she can either evict the tenant or hold the tenant to another term. If the landlord does not hold the tenant over for a new term, the tenant has no right to possess the property in this circumstance. However, if the landlord asserts her right to hold the tenant to another term, the length of the new term is usually equal to the length of the previous term.

4.6.2 Leases

A lease is an agreement between a landlord and a tenant governing the terms of their relationship and the transfer of property from the landlord to the tenant. A lease is both a conveyance and a contract. A conveyance is a transfer of real property creating certain rights (an estate) in the property. A lease is also a contract for periodic payments giving the tenant the right to occupy the property, containing promises made by the landlord and tenant to each other. The key terms in the lease agreement addresses the amount of rent, the term of occupancy and use of the property. Additional provisions in a typical lease agreement have evolved over time in an effort to avoid major disputes.

Regardless of the property size, the following checklist shown in Figure 4.5 can be used to check for completeness.

4.7 Legal duties of the parties

The mention earlier that the lease is both a conveyance and a contract is significant to the Facility Manager. Historically, when property was conveyed,

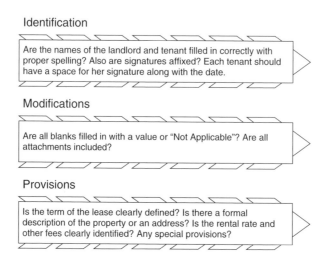

Figure 4.5   Real estate lease components.

the duties of that landlord were complete. The landlord was not required to repair the premises or render any services to the tenant. If the building was destroyed in a tsunami, the tenant was still liable for rent and other obligations per the conveyance. Through additional contract terms that have evolved over time, current leases have changed the landlord/tenant relationship. Laws have changed and so have the basic duties owed by the landlord and tenant.

At the most basic level, the modern tenant is obligated to pay the rent, care for the leased property, return the premises in good condition and meet other terms of the lease. The landlord, on the other hand, has obligations to:

- Disclose concealed dangerous conditions.
- Inspect and repair public use premises.
- Maintain common areas under landlord's control.
- Warrant that the property is habitable and fit for the use advertised.
- Insure that the tenant has possession of the property leased.
- Insure that the tenant has quiet enjoyment of the property leased.
- Meet other terms of the lease.

The Facility Manager needs to be concerned with the legal duties of the landlord and tenant because in many cases she represents one of the two parties.

Practical application of these obligations is further illustrated in Part III with case studies.

4.8 Chapter summary

Property law is a very basic but old area of law and thus can be quite confusing due to antiquated legal reasoning. Over time, the definitions of property and the rights associated with control over the property have evolved to accommodate modern society's needs. Understanding that obligations change when ownership rights change is the key to successfully managing both personal and real assets.

4.9 Questions

1. What is a lease?
2. What is a major distinguishing factor between personal and real property?
3. In your opinion, which is the most useful remedy for the landlord when rent is not paid? Explain your answer.

4. Is it fair that a landlord has the duty to repair property under a lease? Explain your answer.
5. In the typical residential lease scenario, how is an "offer" made?
6. In your own words, define property rights.
7. Explain why the metaphor "a bundle of rights" is used in property law.
8. Summarize two different types of property ownership.
9. Of the two types of property ownership explained in Q 9, which is more desirable? Explain your answer.
10. In your own words, describe what is required in a lease.

References

Barlow, B. *Personal Property in a Nutshell*. St Paul, MN: Westlaw, 2003.

5

Property Law II: Responsibilities

> *Our land is more valuable than your money. As long as the sun shines and the waters flow, this land will be here to give life to men and animals; therefore, we cannot sell this land. It was put here for us by the Great Spirit and we cannot sell it because it does not belong to us.*
>
> **Anonymous, Blackfoot Chief (c. 1880)**

5.1 Introduction

The notion that land is more valuable than money, as quoted above, and that it cannot be sold is not often espoused in our modern understanding of property. The story school children are taught, about the indigenous peoples selling the island of Manhattan in New York City for trinkets, takes on a different meaning if you consider this understanding – the land does not belong to anyone. Consider a deal involving the sale of the Sun for $100 000. Which side would be considered the better bargainer if the deal materialized? The "owner" of the Sun or the owner of the $100 000? What if, one day at high noon, the sky turned completely black and you were told that a deal was made to sell the Sun, so from here on out you will live your life in uninterrupted darkness? Just because we cannot contemplate today how anyone can own the Sun does not mean it is impossible, or taking $100 000 in the deal was stupid. With this view, contemplate whether the Manhattan sale was a foolish deal after all. Whether or not the indigenous people were actually cheated out of a valuable asset depends on the definition of property and what it means to own land.

As defined under US law, property ownership comes with rights, as discussed in Chapter 4, and responsibilities, which are the subject of this chapter. These

Legal Concepts for Facility Managers, First Edition. Linda Thomas-Mobley.
© 2014 John Wiley & Sons, Ltd. Published 2014 by John Wiley & Sons, Ltd.

responsibilities of property ownership fall into the third realm of property law, as discussed in the previous chapter, the realm of owner obligations.

In this chapter we concern ourselves with the various levels of responsibility an owner or controller of property has with regards to the user. Here, we will concentrate on real property responsibilities, since this is typically the case for the Facility Manager. As an agent acting on behalf of the property owner, understanding how the level of owner obligation relates to the type of property user is most beneficial.

Student learning outcomes for Chapter 5 include the following:

- Explain the concept of premises liability.
- Define trespass.
- Define an invitee and how it relates to owner responsibilities.
- Describe the rationale for the American with Disabilities Act and other laws mandating accessibility.
- Describe the evolution of the federal environmental laws.
- Describe the relationship between state and federal environmental laws.
- Define the legal term "pre-emption".
- Identify potentially responsible parties.
- List the major federal environmental statues impacting the built environment.
- Describe the process of determining whether a material is considered a hazardous waste.

5.2 Legal duty of care

This section highlights the responsibilities those involved in a lease agreement have to each other. As stated earlier, the main duty of the tenant is to pay the rent and care for the leased property. Other contractual terms may be outlined in the lease contract but they may differ depending on the type of property leased, economic climate and whether or not one of the parties is a federal, state or local government agency. In all cases, however, the tenant promises to respect the owner's property and make on-time payments.

Landlords, on the other hand, have a greater number of obligations to the tenant since they are the ones engaged in the business of leasing property. The law places this extra burden on the landlord, assuming that those in the business of leasing property are in a superior position since they tend to be the property owners, more familiar with the property details. Furthermore, the landlord is usually responsible for the lease terms and thus enjoys a business advantage with regards to choosing and understanding the myriad of lease provisions.

Traditionally, under common law the landlord had no general obligation to repair the leased premises. In addition, the landlord had no obligation to persons injured on or off the land for defects that existed in the leased premises at the commencement of the lease term, or that arose during the tenancy. Exceptions to this common law include the duty of the landlord to disclose concealed dangerous conditions, inspect and repair the property prior to turning the premises over to the tenant and maintain common areas.

Over time, additional duties considered standard for the landlord have developed; these include ensuring that the premises is fit for human occupancy, ensuring the tenant has exclusive possession and ensuring the quiet enjoyment of the premises.

Understanding these requirements of the landlord involve more than a general understanding of the meanings of the words used. These duties are expressed as legal terms of art and need additional explanation for the student to get the full picture.

When the law requires that the landlord must disclose concealed dangerous conditions, this means that the landlord is labile to the tenant and other third parties if they become injured by the dangerous condition, if the landlord did not disclose that concealed dangerous condition. If, however, the conditions are not concealed, and so open and obvious that any reasonable person would discover them, then the requirement for disclosure from the landlord does not exist and resulting injury would not be considered the fault of the landlord.

Inspecting and repairing of a property by the landlord extends to hazardous disrepair of property leased for a purpose that includes admission of the public. Most all office buildings, multifamily housing buildings and government buildings are open to the public who must be protected by the landlord. It should be noted that this risk of harm from disrepair cannot be shifted to the tenant until after the tenant takes possession. After the tenant possesses the property, the landlord is not liable for the tenant's negligence in maintaining the premises if they were turned over to the tenant in good condition. If the building has common areas, as is the case in most apartment buildings, the duty of the landlord to maintain those common areas remains with the landlord and does not shift to the tenant at possession. This makes sense because in most cases, the common areas are in the control of the landlord and not intended for the exclusive use of the tenant.

The additional duties that have developed over time require a deeper under-standing of legal terminology. The duty that the premises must be "fit for human occupancy" is called the "warranty of habitability" and a "warranty of fitness" in property leases. The word *warranty* essentially means that something is guaranteed by one of the parties, in this case, the landlord. The warranty of habitability is the duty of the landlord of residential property to deliver property that is considered "liveable" when the lease term begins and to maintain the premises in a habitable condition while the tenant pays rent. This warranty is implied to be in existence, and not written in the lease. Compare this to a warranty of fitness that is a promise that the premises will be suitable for the purposes anticipated by the tenant. This type of warranty is broader and potentially problematic. What does it mean for a property to be fit for intergalactic travel? Because of the broad nature of the warranty of fitness, the details of this warranty must be explicitly stated in the lease, especially commercial leases. It is also known as a *Covenant of Fitness*.

The covenant of possession requires that the tenant has exclusive possession and control of the leased premises. Under this concept, a landlord cannot enter a tenant's property unless the landlord reserves specific entry rights in the lease. Landlords usually exercise this prerogative by reserving the right to come onto the property to accomplish repairs and other duties. Finally, the duty of the landlord to ensure that the tenant has quiet enjoyment of the premises is not concerned with loud noises. Under US law, quiet enjoyment means that tenants will have peaceful possession of the property, free of interference from the acts or claims of the landlord, or certain third parties claiming rights through the landlord. Tenants are protected from being thrown into the street if a dispute between the landlord and a third party claiming a right to the property exists. This quiet enjoyment is also a covenant that is usually implied in the lease.

5.3 Americans with Disabilities Act

The Americans with Disabilities Act of 1990 (ADA) is a statute enacted by congress and later amended with changes effective from January 1, 2009. The ADA is a civil rights statute that prohibits discrimination based on disability. It has similar protections against discrimination to Americans with disabilities as the Civil Rights Act of 1964, which made discrimination based on race, religion, sex, national origin and other characteristics, illegal.

A qualified individual with a disability is defined under the ADA as a person who has a physical or mental impairment that substantially limits one or more major life activities, a person who has a history or record of such impairment or a person who is perceived by others as having such impairment. Additionally, discrimination may not take place in job application procedures, hiring, firing, advancement, compensation, job training or other terms, conditions and privileges of employment. Because the ADA does not specifically name all of the impairments that are covered, the determination of whether the impairment substantially limits an activity and if the activity is considered a "major life activity" is made by the court on a case by case basis. Some impairment is excluded, such as disabilities like substance abuse and visual impairment correctable by prescription lenses.

The ADA prohibits discrimination on the basis of disability in employment, state and local government, public accommodations, commercial facilities, transportation and telecommunications. It also applies to the United States Congress. To be protected by the ADA, one must have a disability or have a relationship or association with an individual with a disability.

The ADA applies employers with 15 or more employees, including state and local governments. It also applies to employment agencies, labor organizations and federal sector employees. The public accommodations provisions apply to all business, regardless of the number of employees.

Considering discrimination against the disabled includes applicants and those employees who could be promoted, what if the job requires certain physical abilities? If an applicant is considered "disabled" how can she be also qualified for a job position? According to the law, a qualified employee or applicant with a disability is an individual who, with or without reasonable accommodation, can perform the essential functions of the job in question. So it is not a question of having to hire someone who could not physically perform in a job, the question is, *what is a reasonable accommodation*? Reasonable accommodations are defined as adjustments or modifications provided by an employer to enable people with disabilities to enjoy equal employment opportunities. Accommodations vary depending upon the needs of the individual applicant or employee. Based on case law interpreting the ADA, reasonable accommodations include:

- Making existing facilities used by employees readily accessible.
- Job restructuring.
- Modifying work schedules.
- Reassignment to a vacant position.
- Acquiring or modifying equipment or devices.
- Adjusting or modifying examinations, training materials or policies.
- Providing qualified readers or interpreters.

This list is not exhaustive and does not help to further the understanding of what reasonableness is with regard to accommodations. Another way to consider the question of reasonableness is that the employer is not required to make an accommodation if it would not impose an "undue hardship" on the operation of the employer's business.

Which leads us to a new inquiry, what is "undue hardship"? This is defined as an action requiring significant difficulty or expense when considered in light of factors such as an employer's size, financial resources, and the nature and structure of its operation. This is not a definitive explanation but better than merely "reasonableness". Also, an employer is not required to lower quality or production standards to make an accommodation; nor is an employer obligated to provide personal use items such as glasses or hearing aids.

Finally, an employer does not have to provide an accommodation unless an individual with a disability has asked for one.

One way to understand reasonable accommodations is to categorize the potential accommodations into three areas: modifications or adjustments to a job application process; or modifications or adjustments to the work environment, or to the manner or circumstances under which the position held or desired is customarily performed; or modifications or adjustments that enable an employee with a disability to enjoy equal benefits and privileges of employment, as are enjoyed by its other similarly situated employees without disabilities.

Additional best practices for Facility Managers to know include navigating through the ADA's expectations on medical examinations and inquiring about the employee's disability. You may not ask job applicants about the existence, nature or severity of their disability. On the other hand, applicants may be asked about their ability to perform specific job functions. Also, if the job offer is conditioned on the results of a medical examination, the same type of medical examination must be required for all entering employees in similar positions, and must be job related and consistent with the employer's business practices. Since medical records are confidential, employers must keep confidential any medical information they have about an applicant or employee, even the record does not contain treatments or medical diagnoses. Thus, an employee's request for a reasonable accommodation would be considered medical information subject to confidentiality requirements.

Employers who accommodate disabled applicants and employees may qualify for the Small Business Tax Credit, Work Opportunity Tax Credit or an Architectural Tax Deduction for providing accessible parking spaces, ramps, sidewalk curb cuts, walkways at least 48 inches wide and converting existing entrances to those that are more accessible.

5.3.1 Federal enforcement of ADA

Because of our dual court systems of both federal and state courts, it is possible for a building to meet state law regulations, but be out of compliance with federal ADA requirements. It should be noted that all older buildings not up to ADA standards are not "grandfathered" under the ADA. Existing buildings, even those not undertaking remodeling, are still required to be brought into compliance with ADA according to the Department of Justice (DOJ).

The Department of Justice has initiated a priority list for required barrier removal in five main areas. The priorities are:

- Priority 1: Accessible approach and entrance.
- Priority 2: Access to goods and services.

- Priority 3: Access to rest rooms.
- Priority 4: Any other measures necessary.

As indicated, the highest priority is that building owners must ensure that there is compliant parking and a compliant path of travel to a building entrance. The next priorities cover access to drinking fountains, telephones and restrooms. Finally any other additional measures required can be considered. This priority list is a recent action on the part of the DOJ. Because of this, many Facility Managers are not aware of the obligation for barrier removal under the federal law.

In addition, each state has its own regulations regarding accessibility. Compliance with all codes can get confusing. The Facility Manager must know the state and local codes because the state code may be required if it is a more stringent technical requirement. If the state requirement is less stringent, the new barrier removal requirement for existing facilities will supersede the less stringent local or state codes. This resolution to the clash of competing laws is unique to federal systems and falls under the legal concept of "pre-emption". Generally, federal pre-emption refers to the invalidation of a US state law when it conflicts with federal law.

5.4 Chapter summary

Under US law there are an overwhelming number of diverse responsibilities imposed on property owners. As a representative of the property owner, the Facility Manager can cause great harm to her employer if she lacks a basic understanding of the property law, associated rights and responsibilities. Other responsibilities of the property owner will also be mentioned in Chapter 7 on tort law.

5.5 Questions

1. Which areas of property law will a Facility Manager most likely encounter in her practice?
2. Does the Facility Manager have responsibility for injuries to disabled persons occurring on her company's property? Explain your answer.
3. What is covered under the ADA?
4. What should the Facility Manager do if a "reasonable accommodation" cannot be made?
5. At what point in the hiring process does the ADA apply to a disabled person?

6. Give an example of an unreasonable accommodation under ADA.
7. Give an example of a reasonable accommodation under ADA.
8. What if the reasonable accommodation is prohibitively expensive for a small business owner; must she still provide the accommodation?
9. In your opinion, is the ADA requirement of accommodation fair? Explain your answer.
10. Conduct a quick Internet search; list two other countries that have similar requirements to the US law.

6

Environmental Law

They were universally a thirsty race. Might not the basket, stable-broom, mat-making, corn-parching, linen-spinning, and pottery business have thrived here, making the wilderness to blossom like the rose, and a numerous posterity have inherited the land of their fathers? The sterile soil would at least have been proof against a lowland degeneracy. Alas! how little does the memory of these human inhabitants enhance the beauty of the landscape!

In: *Walden*, Henry David Thoreau (1817–1862)

6.1 Introduction

In the modern sense, the constitution is silent on the matter of the environment. Some scholars have argued that the preamble sets the stage for environmental stewardship, but it is safe to say that most environmental regulations relevant to Facility Managers come from statutes and administrative laws (Ogle 1998).

One best practice in facility management is to keep abreast of federal and state environmental laws. Effective methods include periodically checking the US Environmental Protection Agency's website and joining local community organizations that collectively keep up with additions and changes in the law. Examples of these organizations include the International Facility Management Association (IFMA) and the National Association of Environmental Professionals (NAEP). This chapter does not address all major statutes regulating the environment, but instead offers a framework for the Facility Manager to utilize when organizing legal information. A short historical perspective is included, and typical violations are discussed to present a rudimentary understanding of environmental stewardship for the built environment professional.

Legal Concepts for Facility Managers, First Edition. Linda Thomas-Mobley.
© 2014 John Wiley & Sons, Ltd. Published 2014 by John Wiley & Sons, Ltd.

At the close of this chapter, the following student learning outcomes are expected:

- Describe the basic types of environmental regulations.
- Demonstrate an understanding of the historical perspective of conservation as it began in the USA.
- Identify common environmental violations in the built environment.
- Locate up-to-date environmental regulations.

6.2 Historical perspective

Environmental law, as we know it today, began with the notion that natural resources must be respected and preserved. Conservation in the USA can be traced back to the nineteenth century with the formation of Yellowstone National Park. The early conservation movement supported the preservation of government lands so that future generations could enjoy the lands well into future.

In the USA the conservation movement is associated with early environmentalists John Muir and Henry David Thoreau. Muir is credited with speaking out for worker safety. As a carriage worker Muir was almost blinded by an accident while working. This accident prompted Muir to have a new appreciation of natural beauty and caused him to set out on a journey to see "America's natural wonders" (Schweikart and Allen 2004). The famous author and poet, Henry David Thoreau also appreciated nature and is noted for leading the Transcendentalist movement. He is known for once lamenting the loss of a tree when it was cut down (Bode 1982). Other conservationists got organized and soon the movement impacted upon US law.

In recent times, individual responsibility developed into a shared responsibility. To accomplish this, two environmental law categories have emerged. The first category includes laws imposing penalties for breaching environmental duties and the second includes laws offering incentives to those who protect, maintain or reclaim polluted property. Even with these distinctions, the array of laws can be overwhelming and difficult to understand. If you include state attempts to protect local environment, navigating environmental law seems to be best left to environmental attorneys and judges. So what can the Facility Manager do to avoid exposing her company or herself to liability?

6.3 Complications with environmental law

Environmental laws in the USA were adopted in a piecemeal fashion; as a result, some regulations overlap and others even contradict each other. In an attempt to help navigate the environmental law maze, this section dissects the subject into three sections: the role of regulators, the major laws and the common violations faced by Facility Managers in their normal course of business.

6.4 The role of regulators

It should be no surprise to the student that the US federal and state governments are the major protectors of the environment. Federal law is quite extensive with regard to environmental laws, but state laws also apply to many of the same issues. Because of this the Facility Manager must research both types of applicable laws, which often overlap. State standards apply in the state where the property is located. When state regulations differ from federal regulations the legal concept of pre-emption helps to determine which law applies. Under pre-emption, whichever law is the more restrictive should be followed. A good rule of thumb for the Facility Manager then, is to always follow the stricter law.

6.5 Sources of environmental law

US environmental law is a complex and interlocking body of treaties with other countries, federal and state statutes and regulations, and common law that operates to protect the natural environment from pollution.

Under common law, judges of federal and state courts have created environmental law by resolving disputes over the application of federal environmental laws. Decisions from US Supreme Court cases have had major impact on environmental regulations. As you will see in the next chapter, the common law and the law of torts are important tools for the resolution of environmental disputes that fall in gray areas. Disputes alleging nuisance, trespass, negligence and strict liability have been used to hold individuals liable for activities causing release of pollutants.

Responsibility for the administration of environmental regulations is distributed among numerous federal and state agencies often times overlapping and sometimes containing conflicting purposes. The US Environmental Protection Agency (EPA) has administrative authority over many of the country's national air, water, waste and hazardous substance programs. Other federal agencies, such as the US Fish and Wildlife Service and National Park Service have conservation missions, while the United States Forest Service and the Bureau of Land Management are focused on the beneficial use of natural resources. Some federal environmental regulations are more stringent than state regulations, but whether or not the federal environmental laws serve as a "Cap" or a "Floor" is an often-litigated issue. A federal regulation serves as a "Cap" when it prohibits states from implementing a state regulation that is stricter than the federal regulation but allows states to implement a regulation that is less strict than the federal regulation. Conversely, a federal regulation serves as a "floor" when it bars states from implementing a regulation that is less strict than the federal regulation, but allows states to enact a regulation that is stricter than the federal regulation.

In the instance of a conflict of regulations, or which law should govern, state or federal, the legal doctrine of federal preemption comes into the conversation. Basically when the federal government enacts a law the legislatures will state whether or not this area is so important and vital to the country that federal law will preempt any state law. Some times this is not clear and states will argue for their right to make laws for their citizens. This baffling and complicated area of law is argued in cases where many states have a different view on regulating a particular activity. Environmental protection is one such activity where the preemption doctrine comes into play.

The legal concept of preemption has resulted in state governments administering state law adopted under state police powers or federal law. When it is said that a state uses its "police power", we are referring to the right given by the US Constitution. Police power refers to the basic right of local governments to make laws and regulations for the benefit of their communities. Under the system of government in the United States, only states have the right to make laws based on their police power. The right of states to make laws governing safety, health, welfare, and morals is derived from the Tenth Amendment, which states, "The powers not delegated to the United States by the Constitution, nor prohibited by it to the states, are reserved to the States respectively, or to the people." State legislatures exercise their police power by enacting statutes. By the way, police power does not specifically refer to the right of state and local government to create police forces, although the police power does include that right. Thus, because preemption requires states to use the stricter law, they either follow federal law, or make up their own stricter law using their police power to make laws governing safety, health and welfare.

Statutes are regulated by federal agencies via laws recorded in the Code of Federal Regulations, especially Title 40 of the Code of Federal Regulations (CFR). Title 40 contains the regulations of the Environmental Protection Agency. Additional CFR sections include Title 10 (energy), Title 18 (Conservation of Power and Water Resources), Title 21 (Food and Drugs), Title 33 (Navigable Waters), Title 36 (Parks, Forests and Public Property), Title 43 (Public Lands: Interior) and Title 50 (Wildlife and Fisheries). Specific landmark federal statutes regulating the environment will be discussed in the next section.

Since the early 1970s the federal government has passed laws via Congress directing the US Environmental Protection Agency to regulate environmental clean-up and restoration. Many laws are designed to address specific

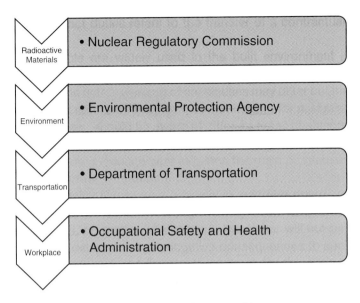

Figure 6.1   Federal agencies controlling environmental laws.

environmental issues such as wastewater, hazardous waste sites and clean water. Others address specific industries. The federal government has responsibility through federal regulatory agencies to control radioactive materials, the environment, transportation and the workplace. Federal agencies involved with this task are depicted in Figure 6.1.

6.5.1 *Selected environmental statutes*

Environmental law can be approached from the many perspectives of those concerned about Earth's sustainability and human health. Examples include ecologists, sociologists, journalists, farmers and politicians. All points of view are valid, but for the Facility Manager, one suggested perspective is to consider environmental law as a subset of land use restriction.

This section presents an overview of environmental law from the perspective of those with interests in land, such as property owners and estate holders, as discussed previously under property law.

Environmental laws have far-reaching consequences for property owners, potential buyers, developers, tenants and Facility Managers. It is essential to assess a property's environmental status prior to purchasing or leasing the property and to continually monitor environmental conditions throughout possession, and even thereafter. The scope of environmental laws are such that the environmental condition of a property can cause potential financial exposure for anyone with a former, current and/or future interest in the property.

In the past, the main focus for a property owner was whether the buyer or tenant could meet financial obligations. As a direct result of today's broad reaching environmental laws, all possessors of real estate can now cause unwanted liability for environmental contamination to the owner, landlord, tenants, lenders, and future sellers and owners.

Modern environmental law has also given birth to the Potentially Responsible Party (PRP). The definition of a PRP is alarmingly broad; defined as a "possible polluter" who may eventually be held liable under environmental statutes for the contamination of a property. Currently PRPs are all of the following (Code of Federal Regulations):

- The current owner or operator of the site;
- The owner or operator of a site at the time that disposal of a hazardous substance, pollutant or contaminant occurred;
- A person who arranged for the disposal of a hazardous substance, pollutant or contaminant at a site; and
- A person who transported a hazardous substance, pollutant or contaminant to a site, who also has selected that site for the disposal of the hazardous substances, pollutants or contaminants.

It should be noted that under this description, every Facility Manager is a PRP. Thus, motivation for having a working knowledge of environmental law is obvious.

Early environmental laws were characterized as "command and control" laws where the federal government used its power to firmly regulate industries identified as polluters with the goal of reducing or eliminating exposure to hazardous materials. These laws are complex and tend to overwhelm both the government enforcement officials and Facility Managers. Furthermore, unlike other areas of the law, many of these environmental laws are both civil and criminal making serving time in prison a possibility.

Since the 1990s, Congress has adopted a new approach designed to cultivate a culture of cooperation. Incentives of various types are used to encourage industry to reduce waste. These laws also offer incentives for developers so that they are encouraged to consider developing abandoned industrial properties known as *brownfield sites*. Brownfield sites are abandoned or under-utilized industrial or commercial properties with actual or perceived environmental contamination.

As a first step for the student of facility management, environmental laws can be comprehended based upon their operation. For ease of instruction, an explanation of the regulations in this chapter will be divided into three categories: prevention, clean-up and compliance.

6.5.2 Prevention

There are numerous environmental regulations designed to protect the environment, so a sub-category of these laws would also be useful. Protecting the environment regulations can also be categorized as either laws designed for protection before or after pollution occurs. Prior to a release of hazardous materials, some laws regulate the actions of individuals in an attempt at prevention of pollution and in the alternative, at least the control of the pollution that is caused by planned industrial processes. The laws dealing with prevention of pollution often apply to a single constituent like air, water or land. In addition, prevention laws also regulate conservation and management of natural resources such as forests, mineral deposits or animal species.

Recent environmental pollution prevention statutes use economic incentives to motivate potential parties into designing processes that reduce waste, utilize recycling strategies and implement technology to reduce hazardous emissions. Examples of recent environmental prevention laws include the Pollution Prevention Act of 1990 and the 1990 Amendments to the Clean Air Act.

6.5.3 Environmental waste clean-up

After a release occurs, additional laws regulate pollution clean-up. In environmental law pollution clean-up is referred to as remediation. Remediation laws focus on the removal and disposal of contaminants accumulated through industrial development. Statutes such as the Comprehensive Environmental Response, Compensation, and Liability Act (CERCLA) operate on a theory of strict liability, forcing property owners and others who may have generated waste to clean it up, or pay for the clean-up. Since the statutes are based on the legal doctrine of strict liability, even if the parties dispose of the waste in an acceptable manner they are liable for clean-up should an unwanted release of waste occur. CERCLA is also known as the "Superfund" Act, not because there is an unlimited amount of money available from the government for remediation, but because the law operates to raise funds from responsible parties for clean-up.

6.5.4 Compliance

Compliance statutes happen to belong to the most numerous of the categories of environmental statutes. They focus on ongoing pollution and are aimed at businesses creating waste and contamination through regular operations. These laws impose civil and criminal penalties for those who pollute, be it intentional or the result of carelessness. These laws attempt to control the source of pollutants and monitor the storage and disposal of hazardous wastes for the entire lifecycle of the contaminant. Statutes falling into the compliance category include the Safe Drinking Water Act, the Resource Conservation and Recovery Act of 1976, and the Federal Water Pollution Control Acts.

It is not the intent of this book to list and define all existing environmental statutes currently used in the USA, but the following table includes the most common statutes that may be encountered by the typical Facility Manager.

One last statute often studied along with environmental law is the Occupational Safety and Health Act (OSHA). Generally, Facility Managers should be familiar with this statute and regulations disseminated by the US Department of Labor. OSHA requires employers to comply with safety and health standards covering conditions and operations in the workplace. Similar to the common law duty to keep an area safe from hazards, OSHA regulates work sites, requiring owners to maintain a workplace free of recognized hazards where no standards currently exist. Safety regulations for both general industry and specifically for the built environment industry are covered.

There are two main duties imposed on employers; the general responsibility to provide a hazard-free place of employment and a responsibility to comply with OSHA standards. Under OSHA, employers can be found guilty of willfully violating specific standards or making a false representation in required documents. As suggested by the term "guilty" this type of violation is a crime, as opposed to a civil wrongdoing. One is only found "guilty" in criminal cases, for civil lawsuits a defendant may be found "liable". Cases illustrating the application of OSHA are used in Part III.

6.6 State laws

Some state environmental laws of interest to the Facility Manager include cost recovery statutes, statutes restricting the transfer of contaminated property, lender protection laws, specific hazard laws and disclosure laws. The two most significant types of state environmental laws include the cost recovery type and the restriction of transfer for contaminated sites type.

Cost recovery laws allow the state governments to recover costs for cleaning up hazardous waste accidents. One type of cost recovery law that is considered an aggressive cost statute is called a *Superlien*. A Superlien is a lien on property that is granted to the government so that it can take action to provide compensation for environmental clean-up costs. Liens provide funds indirectly by preventing an owner from selling the property until they pay off existing liens.

Table 6.1   Compilation of environmental statutes.

Statute	Category	Synopsis
The Pollution Prevention Act	Prevention	National policy that pollution be prevented or reduced at the source, prioritizes prevention actions in this order: source reduction, closed loop recycling, recycle/reuse/reclaim, waste treatment, waste disposal
The Comprehensive Environmental Response, Compensation, and Liability Act (CERCLA)	Clean-Up (Remediation)	Sets procedures for responding to releases of hazardous substances to the environment. Requires notification of releases.
The Safe Drinking Water Act 1974	Clean-Up (Remediation)	Requires owners and managers of public water systems to comply with national drinking water standards
The Federal Insecticide, Fungicide, and Rodenticide Act 1972	Clean-Up (Remediation)	Applies to owners who use, store or dispose of pesticides. Regulates use and record keeping of chemicals.
The Rescue Conservation and Recovery Act of 1976	Compliance	Regulates the management of solid and hazardous wastes, defines those wastes and authorizes the EPA to set standards for facilities that generate or manage hazardous waste. Regulates underground storage tanks.
Federal Water Pollution Control Act 1972 and 1977	Compliance	Regulates wastewater discharges to surface water. Regulates storm-water runoff and discharges of hazardous materials to navigable waterways.
Clean Air Act 1990	Compliance	Regulates air pollution and toxins and the renovation and demolition of structures with asbestos containing material. Regulates emissions into the air of pollutants.

6.7 Common violations

Environmental law violations can be difficult for the Facility Manager to avoid, especially because of the large number of laws. This section will outline the most common violations of the law a Facility Manager may face.

Threats such as oil spills, chemical spills, radiation emergencies or biological threats apply to all industries. The list is somewhat different for Facility Managers working in office settings, but by no means is the office employee exempt from environmental disasters. A good rule of thumb to remember is if you work with air conditioning; cooling systems; any business practice that emits effluent into the air, water or soil; be very careful. The overriding rule of thumb for any Facility Manger is to inform the US Environmental Protection Agency (EPA) and the state environmental office if an environmental problem is discovered.

The EPA encourages Facility Managers to acknowledge the need for a continuously improving environmental plan and suggests that they routinely check for problems, immediately notify officials of spills or unintended emissions, and immediately take steps to locate the source, stop the spill and take measures to clean it up.

Common violations include:

- Improper renovation including the improper handling of lead based paint (LBP).
- Not checking to see if state environmental regulations are stricter than federal regulations.
- Knowing definition of hazardous waste (HW). For example, hazardous wastes exhibit characteristics of a hazardous waste; they may be listed in the regulations; or they may be a mixture of listed hazardous and non-hazardous solid waste. It is also waste derived from treatment, storage or disposal of a listed waste, or is a waste that is state regulated.
- Mismanagement of hazardous waste, such as storage, disposal record keeping and keeping forgotten storage containers.
- Mismanagement of underground storage tanks (USTs) such as a failure to provide erosion protection. The Facility Manager must also document ownership of hazardous waste and ownership of any release detection devices.
- Mismanagement of pollutants to navigable waters of the United States. This is important because most sewer pipes lead to navigable waters eventually.
- Keeping up with law changes, knowing newly named pollutants or reduced limits of known pollutants.

6.8 Chapter summary

Because of the far-reaching nature of the environmental statutes, common problems have emerged over time. The conscientious Facility Manager will follow the advice of the US Environmental Protection Agency and work to develop a comprehensive quality management plan for environmental interests, which should be updated regularly. The plan should deal with banned substances, once widely used in the built environment industry, such as asbestos, polychlorinated biphenyls (PCBs) and lead paint. Understanding the general organization of environmental regulations, how to resolve conflicts within the law and the need for a continuous plan to cover potential hazards will go a long way to keep the Facility Manager out of danger from criminal prosecution.

6.9 Questions

1. What types of potential punishment a company can face if an environmental accident occurs?
2. What type of environmental liability is the Facility Manager typically exposed to?
3. Name three common environmental violations.
4. If a state law has a stricter standard for disposing hazardous waste than the federal statutes, which law should the Facility Manager follow? Explain your answer.
5. What are the three categories of environmental laws?
6. In your opinion, which type of environmental law is most effective? Explain your answer.
7. Is the concept of holding all potentially responsible parties financially responsible for hazardous waste clean-up reasonable? Explain your answer.
8. Illustrate the overlap between the Clean Water Act, RECRA and CERCLA.
9. What is the "Superfund"?
10. In your opinion, should environmental laws be more punishment or encouragement?

References

Bode, C. *The Portable Thoreau*. New York, New York: Penguin, 1982.

Ogle, C. Preamble: Relevance to Environmental Law: Does the United States Constitution Provide Environmental Protection? In: *Constitutional Law Foundation*. Oregon: L.A.W. Public Interest Law Conference, 1998.

Schweikart, L. and M. Allen. *A Patriot's History of the United States*. Sentinel, 2004.

7

Tort Law

> Justice is the end of government. It is the end of civil society. It ever has been and ever will be pursued until it be obtained, or until liberty be lost in the pursuit. In a society under the forms of which the stronger faction can readily unite and oppress the weaker, anarchy may as truly be said to reign as in a state of nature, where the weaker individual is not secured against the violence of the stronger; and as, in the latter state, even the individuals are prompted, by the uncertainty of their condition, to submit to a government which may protect the weak as well as themselves; so, in the former state, will the more powerful factions or parties be gradually induced, by a like motive to wish for a government which will protect all parties, the weaker as well as the more powerful.
>
> **Alexander Hamilton (1755–1804)**

7.1 Introduction

As a former military officer under General George Washington during the American Revolution, Alexander Hamilton is said to have understood the importance of security as a function of government. These historical facts coupled with the above quote may lead a student to think that Hamilton was most concerned about security and how government should protect the weak therefore sacrificing justice and liberty. This notion is sometime said to have caused Hamilton to remark therefore that "justice is the end of government". Consider another interpretation of the quote substituting the word "goal" or "objective" for the word "end". This substitution is reasonable since one possible definition of the term "end" is a goal, and not a termination. In this interpretation we discover that, perhaps, Hamilton was remarking that justice

Legal Concepts for Facility Managers, First Edition. Linda Thomas-Mobley.
© 2014 John Wiley & Sons, Ltd. Published 2014 by John Wiley & Sons, Ltd.

is the goal of government and the goal of a civil society. If the government seeks to administer justice to all, making right the wrongs people impose on each other is a reasonable purpose of the law. A tort is a wrong, and one of the fundamental objectives of the law is to serve as a mechanism to redress wrongs.

This chapter introduces the law of torts. This area of law is one of the first, basic courses taken by all law students in the USA in their first term. Torts are also one of the basic areas of law that Facility Managers must understand, because this area is associated with property ownership and directly related to management.

The student learning outcomes for this chapter will allow the following:

- Define a tort.
- List several types of torts.
- Explain the legal difference between an intentional tort and an unintentional tort.
- Define negligence.
- List the elements of negligence.
- Define strict liability.
- List the major defenses to alleged torts.

7.2 What is a tort?

Tort law is an area of the law that is familiar to most of us, yet the very word "tort" causes a pause. Although difficult to fully define, a tort is basically a civil, non-contractual wrong. It is not a crime regulated by criminal law, nor is it a breach of contract regulated by contract law.

A tort is a harm, but since life is full of people harming other people and property, not all harms are torts. Additionally, other areas of the law are also concerned with harm, but are not necessarily torts. For example, crimes often result in harm to other people, breach of contracts and disregard to property rights can also result in a form of harm: what makes a tort different?

As a beginning definition, a tort is a harm that is recognized by the courts as unlawful. Put another way, a tort is basically a civil, non-contractual wrong for which the law provides a remedy. The solution that the government through law provides to those who feel they have been wronged is the opportunity to file a lawsuit and claim for damages, which are usually in the form of a cash settlement.

There are some acts that constitute both a crime and a tort. In this case there may be a civil lawsuit and a criminal lawsuit. For example, if a Facility Manager decides to take money from her employer, she may be subject to prosecution via a criminal lawsuit for theft, and subject to a civil lawsuit under tort for conversion. Conversion is any unauthorized act that deprives an owner of personal property without his or her consent (Gale and Lehman 2008). Torts can be divided into three categories: intentional torts, negligence and strict liability.

7.2.1 Intentional torts

Our actions can be intentional or unintentional. An intentional act that causes harm to others is an intentional tort if recognized by the law. If you yell at a child, who then starts to cry to the mother, you have caused harm. But since the law does not recognize yelling as a tort, you have not broken the law.

Intentional torts include those acts intentionally committed that are wrongful and that the law provides a remedy for in the form of a lawsuit for damages. It is an intentional invasion of the rights of another. Intentional torts include "torts to persons", such as assault, battery and false imprisonment. Compare "torts to persons" to "torts to property", such as trespass and conversion. There are also miscellaneous intentional wrongs the law provides remedies for that include misrepresentation, defamation, intentional interference with a contract, libel and slander. For a more detailed understanding of these torts, please see the definition in any good legal dictionary. Torts specifically related to the practice of facility management will be explained throughout this chapter and following sections.

The reason torts are important is because many of these wrongs come up in the built environment in situations where the Facility Manager acts for an employer. Of course, Facility Managers are liable for their own intentional torts, but wrongful acts by others may also be included in some instances.

Employers are liable for the intentional torts committed by their employees if they are within the scope of their employment. Most employees acting within the scope of their employment are usually not behaving in a way to harm others, but there are some circumstances harm to others can occur. What if the employee is a security guard? It is conceivable that a security guard acting within the scope of her employment can act in a way to cause assault, battery and even unlawful imprisonment. In this illustration, whomever the security guard acted for can be responsible, and in many instances security guards work for Facility Managers.

A model made up of parts called elements can be used to identify all types of torts. If all of the elements in the model exist, there is a good chance that the wronged person can avail herself to the courts to seek damages.

Intentional torts have three critical elements, which include (1) an act; (2) intended by the defendant; that, (3) caused harm. In order for the plaintiff, or person who has been wronged, to prevail in court and win the damages they seek, all three elements must be proven in court. These necessary elements are represented in Figure 7.1. During trial, each element will be explored by

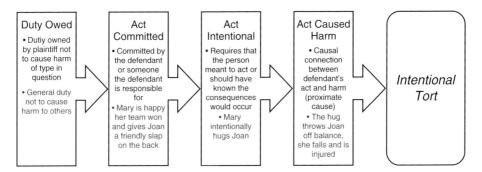

Figure 7.1   Elements of intentional torts.

the parties using testimony and other facts, subject to rules of evidence, to persuade the trier of fact to rule in their favor. In US courts, the trier of fact may be a jury or a judge.

So what are the intentional torts the Facility Manager should be aware of? The three most common intentional torts are assault, battery and false imprisonment. Assault is an act intended to cause a harmful or offensive contact with the plaintiff or a third person. Assault has also been established by the courts to include not only intent to cause harm, but intent to cause "imminent apprehension of harmful contact" or fear, causing the plaintiff to think harm is impending. The courts have not found words alone sufficient to cause an assault, but if combined with threatening movement, assault results.

The tort of *Battery* is committed when the plaintiff makes physical contact with the defendant in an undesirable manner. Elements the plaintiff must show to win a case of Battery include evidence that the defendant acted intending to cause harmful or offensive physical contact to the plaintiff against their will without justification and the plaintiff suffers the harmful or offensive contact as a result. This sounds a lot like the definition of Assault, but there is a difference. In Battery a physical contact has to actually occur. Because Battery includes offensive contact, actual physical harm to the plaintiff is not necessary. An unwanted kiss or grabbing papers from an employee in an offensive way can constitute Battery.

False imprisonment is a tort, sometimes called false arrest or wrongful detention. If a defendant acts intending to confine the plaintiff, there are no reasonable means of exit, confinement takes place and the plaintiff knows she is confined or harmed by the confinement, and the defendant may be liable for this tort. This is why you will notice that security hired to control shoplifting in a store will allow a potential thief to leave the premises prior to apprehending and detaining a suspected shoplifter.

In addition to intentional torts where harm was caused to a person, torts can also be applied to property. These torts include trespass to land, trespass to personal property and conversion. Facility Managers should be aware of their own potential liability for trespass on to the land of neighboring property owners and for the property torts committed by her employees and agents. Just as in the case of torts to persons, torts to property include some duty of the defendant to do no harm and an intentional act causing harm to property by the acts of the defendant. Also there must be some physical invasion of the plaintiff's land for trespass to occur. For additional information on the trespass to personal property, conversion or other less common intentional torts specifically, the student is referred to a good legal dictionary.

7.2.2 Libel and slander

When an employee of an owner makes a false statement about a customer, the customer may bring an action for libel or slander against the owner to redress the injury. Libel is a false, malicious and defamatory statement, expressed in print, writing, pictures or signs, intending to injure the reputation of the claimant and exposing him to public hatred, contempt or ridicule. Libel must be published to an individual other than the claimant in order to support a cause of action. Slander consists of oral defamation in (1) imputing to another a crime punishable by law; (2) charging a person with having some contagious disorder or with being guilty of some debasing act, which may exclude him from society; (3) making charges against another in reference to his trade, office or profession, calculated to injure him therein; or (4) uttering any disparaging words productive of special damage that flows naturally therefrom.

As you can see the intent to cause physical harm along with causing physical harm is not necessary for a plaintiff to prevail on a cause of action for an intentional tort, but what if the act is an accident? Is there such a thing as an unintentional tort?

7.2.3 Negligence

Until relatively recently, in order for one person to sue another person for negligence, the parties had to have some legal connection. The most common connection in business is through contract. When parties are connected via contract, they are said to be in *privity*. For example, if Mary contracted with Lucy for house painting, we can say that Mary and Lucy are in privity of contract.

In one of the most famous cases negligence cases called MacPherson (MacPherson v. Buick Motor Co. 1960), a New York Court of Appeals judge, Benjamin N. Cardozo is said to have removed the requirement of contract for duty in negligence actions. The plaintiff, Donald C. MacPherson, a stonecutter, was injured when one of the wooden wheels of his car collapsed. The defendant, Buick Motor Company, who manufactured the vehicle, did not manufacture the wheel. It had been manufactured by another party and installed by defendant.

Who was negligent? It was agreed upon by the parties that the defective wheel could have been discovered upon inspection.

As was the case in those days, the defendant denied all liability. Buick Motor Company argued that since MacPherson had purchased the automobile from a dealer and not directly from the defendant, Buick owed no duty of care to the plaintiff. Today, an argument like this seems inherently wrong but that was not the case in 1919. In writing the court's opinion for the appellate case, Judge Cardozo stated:

> *If the nature of a thing is such that it is reasonably certain to place life and limb in peril when negligently made, it is then a thing of danger. Its nature gives warning of the consequence to be expected. If to the element of danger there is added knowledge that the thing will be used by persons other than the purchaser, and used without new tests, then, irrespective of contract, the manufacturer of this thing of danger is under a duty to make it carefully* (MacPherson v. Buick Motor Co. 1960).

The failure to be careful is considered a breach of duty we have to others, a breach of the social contract that allows our society to run smoothly. Just like we assume crimes will not be committed against us, in order for society to function, we also assume others will live up to their duty of general care. For example, we assume that a licensed barber will behave like other barbers and not drift off to sleep in the middle of cutting our hair. We assume licensed drivers will follow the rules of the road and not drive into an oncoming lane after falling asleep at the wheel. We assume everyone will fulfill their role as responsible citizens in our global society and take care not to harm others by their actions or lack of action.

Negligence occurs when someone has a responsibility or duty not to cause harm; breaches that duty causing injury to another as a direct result of their actions. For the most part our caregivers teach us the general expectations required in polite society, but in the case of a professional, such as a Facility Manager, careful study of the profession must be made to gather information and understand what the professional's duty to others entails.

The elements of a case for negligence are depicted in Figure 7.2. You will notice that the elements are similar to intentional torts except for one difference. Negligence does not require that the defendant act intentionally. Within this area of law the concept of duty of care is often discussed. The duty not to harm others can be broadly defined, so exactly what duty does the defendant owe the plaintiff? The duty of care for all persons is to use care to avoid subjecting others to an unreasonable risk of injury. For the Facility Manager, care is defined as paying adequate attention to possible dangers and making all required repairs or adjustments to eliminate danger. This standard is called the *reasonable care standard*, to act as a reasonable person would. How does an average person define reasonableness? How does a Facility

IVERPOOL JOHN MOORES UNIVERSITY
LEARNING SERVICES

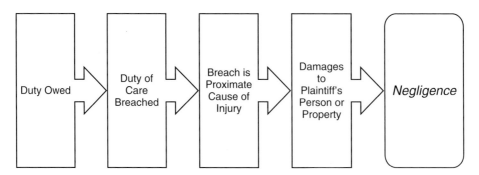

Figure 7.2   Elements of negligence.

Manager define reasonableness? Fortunately for us, both have been defined by courts over time and depend heavily upon what similar people do in similar circumstances. We will explore reasonable behavior for Facility Managers in Part III with example cases.

One additional and important element that is more prominent in the claim of negligence is the use of the term "proximate cause". To prove both intentional torts and negligence the plaintiff has to show that the actions of the defendant are the proximate cause of her injury. Proximate cause is a legal term of art and an element of a tort requiring the defendant's harmful actions to bear some reasonable causal connection to the plaintiff's injury. Although the concept of proximate cause can be difficult to understand, for the purposes of our discussion we can define it as a cause the law will recognize. Some causes are so far removed from the harm that the law will cut off legal liability. For example, if a baby cries causing someone to wake up, load a weapon next to her bed and kill someone, the law will not recognize the crying baby as a proximate cause for the killing. Under the proximate cause doctrine, which is famously perplexing throughout the legal community, the judge can limit the scope of the defendant's liability if they are deemed too remote from the eventual injury.

In a New York case, a boat was improperly moored to a dock. The boat drifted away and crashed into another boat. Both boats crashed into a bridge, which collapsed and blocked the river. Because of this blockage, wreckage flooded the land near the river and prevented any traffic from crossing the river until all had been cleared. Is the defendant who improperly moored the boat responsible for the boat crash? How about the bridge? Since the river was blocked, is the defendant responsible to the owners of the other boats unable to move? These boat owners lost money because their cargo could not make it across the river (In Kinsman Transit Co. 1964). Figure 7.3 illustrates how far the defendant's liability extended in this case. The defendant's liability stopped at the point that the judge considered reasonable.

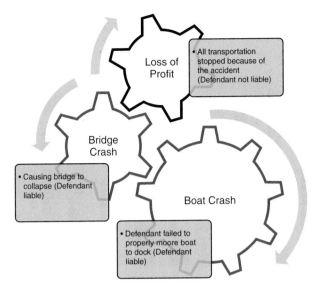

Figure 7.3   Defendant's liability in Kinsman Transit Co. case.

7.2.4 Strict liability

There are circumstances when the Facility Manager can be held liable to a plaintiff through no fault of her own. Under strict liability the defendant need not act intentionally to harm another, nor behave negligently, breaching a general duty of safety. This is because strict liability is defined as liability without fault. Strict liability is used when the circumstances or activities that have generate an injury or harm are deemed so inherently dangerous that negligence does not have to be proven for there to be a judgment against the defendant. The elements of a case for strict liability are shown in Figure 7.4.

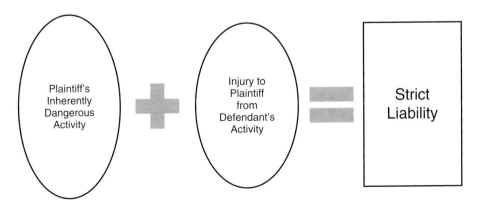

Figure 7.4   Elements of strict liability.

The elements for strict liability are simple; liability totally depends on the defendant's activity. If, according to a statute, the defendant is involved in inherently dangerous activities, and someone gets hurt because of that activity, the defendant is liable regardless of any care the defendant may have taken to prevent injury.

Currently, inherently dangerous activities are identified in state and federal statutes and include businesses involving wild animals, commercial suppliers of products and ultra-hazardous activities. Wild animals are considered all animals incapable of being fully tamed and domesticated animals that have known violent propensities. In the commercial products circumstance, the defendant must be a manufacturer or a commercial supplier and not a casual seller. Also the product must be so defective as to be unreasonably dangerous and the project must reach the ultimate user or consumer without being substantially altered.

The term "ultra-hazardous activities" sounds as though it could cover many risky activities. Also, who is the authority that will determine if an activity is risky? Under current law, an activity is considered ultra-hazardous if it is not a common activity within the particular community, also if it involves a significant risk of serious harm to persons or property regardless of the amount of care taken to prevent that harm. Examples include blasting to break up rock, pile driving, fumigating with noxious gas, and storing or handling high-tension wires, explosives or flammable liquids. Almost all of the activities listed among the examples are activities the Facility Manager may be inclined to perform over the course of her career. Thus, it is important for Facility Manager to realize that she may be strictly liable for injuries on the premises caused by these and other similar activities. Additionally, using an independent contractor to shift the liability may not always protect the Facility Manager.

7.3 Defenses to torts

Understanding the elements of the various torts is necessary but represents only one half of the law. Just because a plaintiff gets injured and decides to file a lawsuit does not mean the defendant will automatically be held liable. Defendants have various defenses available to torts, which may eliminate or at least reduce potential damages paid.

Even when all of the elements of a tort are be presented to the court and admitted into evidence at a trial, a defendant is not liable if a valid defense exists. This section will not discuss all potential defenses but the most common defenses to intentional torts are depicted in Figure 7.5. To be held not liable using one of these defenses, the party will have to produce their own evidence to show what they assert is true. The trier of fact will then have to weigh both parties' evidence and decide which version of the story is most believable.

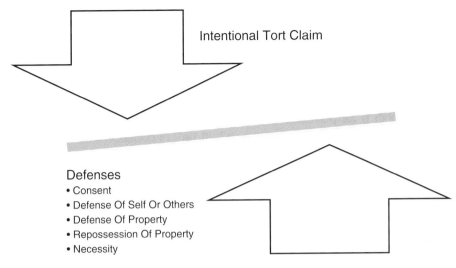

Figure 7.5 Common defenses to intentional torts.

Most of the intentional tort defenses have legal definitions that restrict their use, so the common usage of the words identified as the type of defense should be avoided. The Defense Of Consent is available to the defendant if the plaintiff voluntarily gave permission to the defendant. Defense Of Self or others is valid if the defendant reasonably believes that she is being attacked and if she uses reasonable force to protect herself or another person. The Defense Of Property is usually granted when a defendant used reasonable force to defend her land or other property. The use of deadly force can never be used to defend property, unlike self-defense claims. The Repossession Of Property defense is used when a defendant is attempting to regain property that they have demanded be returned. This defense is only available if the state has no statutory procedures for repossession. Finally the Defense Of Necessity applies to certain circumstances in which a person may, out of a basic need, use the property of another without permission. Necessity is used when the defendant would suffer more harm than would be suffered by the plaintiff.

Defenses to Negligence include contributory negligence, comparative negligence and assumption of the risk. Contributory negligence consists of negligent behavior by a plaintiff that contributed to the harm. This defense asserts that the plaintiff should not recover any damages because of her actions. If the defendant believes that both parties are at fault she can use the defense of comparative negligence. This is a legal doctrine that compares the relative fault of the plaintiff and the defendant in a negligence action and awards damages based on the defendant's percentage of fault. For example, if a plaintiff is injured by an obstruction in her path because she did not notice it while reading the newspaper, this may be a circumstance in which to use the defense of contributory negligence.

Assumption of the risk is an important defense to negligence because many times the public has a clear understanding of the risk but decides to engage in an activity anyway. Under this defense the plaintiff is barred from recovering damages for the defendant's negligent acts where she has assumed the risk of injury or damage from those acts. In order for this defense to apply, the plaintiff must have been aware of the risk and assumed it voluntarily. When this defense is used the major part of the court dispute lies in whether or not the plaintiff knew or should have known the risk. The court will want to decide what a reasonable person would do in a similar circumstance.

Defenses to strict liability are fewer than in other torts. The defense of contributory negligence cannot be used because of the definition of strict liability, that is, even if the plaintiff contributed to her injuries, the defendant business is ultra-hazardous, therefore, she will be liable. Assumption of the risk is a valid defense for a defendant in strict liability. If it were not, live animal performances and bungee jumping would be prohibited. Finally if a state has adapted the comparative negligence defense as a possibility, some of the liability could be reduced.

7.4 Premises liability

Premises Liability law lies at an intersection between property law and torts. This area of tort law is very important to Facility Managers because they often find themselves serving as the controller of property. Not only are Facility Managers legally liable for their own intentional torts and negligence, they can be liable for those injured at the buildings they manage, as you will soon see. Many premises liability cases are based on claims that a possessor of land breached a duty of care owed to others as a result of conduct on or a condition of that land. Special rules govern the duty of care owed by owners and occupiers of land. Since the owner of the property places a Facility Manager in control, she is responsible to behave as a prudent owner would. But who exactly would the Facility Manager be liable to? Everyone who enters her buildings?

7.4.1 Definition

Premises liability refers to liability for injuries occurring on property owned by another. The person liable for unsafe property may be the owner, or anyone who is in possession and control of the property.

It should be easy to understand that the person who is in possession of property and has control over that property can be any number of parties. The controller of the premises can be the titleholder, a tenant or even a third party wrongfully occupying the property in the absence of the rightful owner. The most important distinction to remember, with regard to liability for injuries on property, is that the law imposes certain duties on the person who possesses and asserts control over real property, because that is the individual in the best position to know about any dangerous conditions on the property. Control under the law is defined simply as the person who has the right to admit or exclude others from the premises.

In premises liability law the level of responsibility fluctuates depending on who is in control of the property. Additionally, the law changes depending on the legal relationship the Facility Manager has to the person who came on to the property and was injured. Just as the law recognizes different categories of people who occupy land such as an owner, tenant, third party or Facility Manager, the law also recognizes classes of people who enter onto the land that require protection.

The area of law detailing the duty a possessor of land owes those who come on the land is often ripe with rumors about how a plaintiff or attorney gained riches from "slip and fall" cases. Though these cases do exist, over time statutes have been passed by legislatures to eliminate the unfair lawsuits filed by those claiming an injury even though there was no real danger on the land. Lawsuits with no real merit are sometimes classified as "frivolous" by the courts with penalties that include holding the attorney who takes on a frivolous case financially liable.

The responsibility to pay for injuries can extend to many different categories of land possessors. This is because of the notion that responsibility should lie with the party who has control over the property. Also, an orderly community assumes that those who control property will keep the land relatively safe for others who come on to the land. This doctrine of fairness is based on the concept that the possessor holds greater knowledge about the details of the property, such as uneven flooring, and she can warn or correct any safety hazards another person may encounter. This notion that a possessor of real property must protect visitors is also a legal duty placed on private citizens by the government. This is because in addition to being the right thing to do, the possessor of the land often stands to benefit by making any profits associated with the land.

People entering the property can be invited guests, clients, social guests or even uninvited trespassers – all are owed some duty to keep the property safe. Under certain circumstances, even people who do not come on to the property may be owed a duty of care not to be injured by something on the property.

7.4.2 Duty of care to third parties on property

For most Facility Managers, the duty to protect others from harm is real and an ordinary part of the job. The duty of care is greater to those who are invited. Invited people include guests or customers. Additionally, the Facility Manager serving as a representative of the owner also owes a duty to all who enter the premises. Often the duty to protect a guest is given to the same person that has the task of maintaining the premises, frequently the Facility Manager. Keeping the premises safe and free of hazards is one of the primary responsibilities of the Facility Manager and is accomplished through mundane tasks such as keeping the premises clean, free from debris and operating in the way the space is intended to operate. The level of care required in an office setting is greater than the level owed to an inhabitant of a warehouse, but both spaces should be free from unanticipated hazards. For example, one would not expect to find a swimming pool in the middle of a grocery store, so even if the store is clean and free of debris, if a customer is not warned that a swimming pool exist in aisle three, there could be a problem. Also, the extent of the duty of care for Facility Managers employed by the building's owner is greater than the duty owed by Facility Managers employed by a tenant, since the scope is larger. This is a seemingly small difference between these two types of owners, but this distinction or extra duty could have an impact on how a case would be decided by a court. Figure 7.6 shows the most common definitions of the classes of third parties who may enter property.

Third parties entering the property of another are legally classified as an invitee, licensee or trespasser. Additionally, trespassers are sub classified as adult, "discovered" or child. Depending on the class of the party entering the land, a different duty of care is required under the law. Many states have simplified these duties by enacting statutes to control premises liability, but several jurisdictions still follow these classifications causing confusion as to the extent of liability.

A person is considered a trespasser if she intentionally and without consent or privilege enters another's property. Possessors of land owe the lowest standard of care to this type of person, with exceptions. If the owner is not aware of a trespasser and that person is an adult, no duty of care is required. If, on the other hand the owner discovers that there are trespassers on her

Invitee	An invitee is a person who is invited onto private property, whether expressed or implied, for the financial benefit of the owner.
Licensee	A licensee is a person who is invited onto land by the owner for social purposes that have no economic value to the owner.
Trespasser	In other words, a trespasser is one who enters or remains upon the land without the landowner's consent.

Figure 7.6   Common classes of third parties in property law.

land, she must exercise reasonable care. This person is called a "discovered trespasser". The owner cannot simply ignore this discovery. The duty owed to the discovered trespasser is to ensure their safety, which can be in the form of warning the discovered trespassers of hidden dangers on the land. This duty is owed only if the owner is aware of any dangers.

Children trespassing on land have protection indirectly under the doctrine of attractive nuisance. Attractive nuisance is defined as an artificial condition on the property that is both appealing and dangerous to children. Courts have held that an attractive nuisance is an object likely to draw the attention of children who are unable to understand the risk posed. Although it can be any artificial condition, the doctrine has been used to hold owners liable for injuries caused by swimming pools, abandoned cars and trampolines among other items (Bennett v. Stanley 2001). If an owner has an attractive nuisance on her land she could be held negligent simply for having the artificial condition on the land, no matter how much she tried to make the object safe and childproof.

The licensee, as used in US law, refers to any person who has been given consent to enter or remain on the land of another person. Consent does not have to be formally given; it can be implied such as the case of a parking attendant standing on the street waiving a car on to a lot for parking. The consent is the one main element of law that distinguishes the definition of a licensee from the trespasser. Another unique element of the legal definition of a licensee exists because of the benefits gained. A person is considered a licensee if the owner does not benefit from her presence. If a person has permission to be on the premises, but the owner does not charge a fee for this permission and has nothing to gain, even indirectly, from her being there; that person is considered a licensee.

The duty of care owed to an invitee is much different from that owed to others entering the property of another. The invitee is defined as a person who is permitted to enter the possessor's land for purposes connected with the possessor's industry. For example, customers in a store or bank are considered invitees. Important for Facility Managers to note is that the definition of invitee also covers people delivering goods purchased or sold by the possessor and independent contractors and others working on the premises for the possessor. Even though the presence indirectly benefits the owner, the duty of care for an invitee is still the standard. Figure 7.7 depicts how the class of third party entering the property dictates the duty of care owed by the owner, or controller, of the property.

One more element of presses liability needs to be noted, and that is, what exactly does the law consider a premises? The word "premises" refers to an owner's physical property and included the land near the property called its "approaches". The approaches are defined as the property directly contiguous, adjacent to and touching the entrance to the property of the owner. The entrance to the property in this instance has to be a rational entrance, one

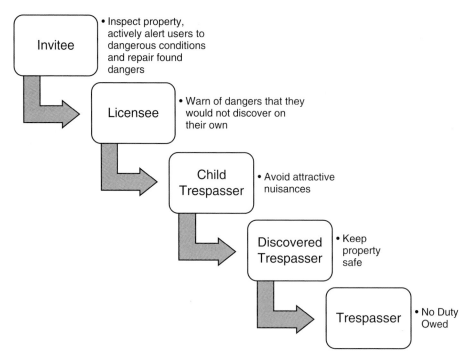

Figure 7.7   Duty of care owed to third parties.

through which the owner would think a reasonable customer would use while entering or exiting her business. If the approach is a public property, the owner must care for whatever portion someone would have to cross to reasonably enter the property, but to a limit. An owner generally has no duty to maintain traffic control devices on a public street.

The Facility Manager usually encounters the potential for premises liability exposure often. Situations typically involve a person becoming injured by some hazard existing on the premises at the time she enters. One can imagine the case of an injury occurring to a patron of a grocery store on a rainy day. The person responsible for maintaining the safety of the store has a duty to keep the floor dry and clean for customers who benefit the owner.

As in most tort cases the owner of property is not liable for a customer's injury simply by virtue of the injury occurring on the owner's premises. The claimant must prove that the owner was negligent. As you know now, proving negligence requires a breach of duty being the proximate cause of the injury suffered.

A common premises liability claim is for injuries suffered with a person slips and falls on a foreign substance on the floor of a commercial building. A foreign substance is anything on the ground that is not ordinarily present, such as a puddle of water, a grape, a piece of paper, or any other food or beverage item.

These types of cases have been given the label "slip and fall" cases. Courts have determined that a plaintiff bringing a slip and fall lawsuit must show (1) that the owner had knowledge of the foreign substance and (2) that the plaintiff was without knowledge of the substance.

It is not required by the plaintiff to inspect the building before entering as an invitee. The customer in a store just has to show the same amount of caution that any ordinary person would exercise in the same situation. An invitee's admission that she did not look at the site on which she placed her foot prior to her fall does not establish that the invitee failed to exercise ordinary care. What about the owner of the property? How extensive is the duty of care to keep the premises safe? In extreme situations, courts have held that owners have a duty to keep building occupants safe even when the occupant is the major cause of the injury. Situations exist where intoxicated employees have sued owners for their injuries. It is important to remember that the Facility Manager may be held responsible for injuries caused to, but also by, occupants, particularly if the type of injury is foreseeable. The law expects the Facility Manager to have some sort of maintenance schedule or plan to show that regular inspections for hazardous conditions are conducted. We will look at actual premises liability cases in Part III.

7.5 Damages

Damage is one of those words that can be confusing because the term is used in the legal community two different ways. One definition for damages you may be familiar with is the actual loss or harm suffered by a person. For example, damage to an automobile in an accident is one use of the word. When we say that the plaintiff in a tort case must prove she was harmed or injured, we are saying that she must show what damage was suffered.

Damages are also compensation, usually money, paid to a plaintiff to reimburse her for loss or injury. Although not particularly helpful as a teaching device, we can say that a plaintiff can get damages for her damages. The rules for the format or the amount of these types of damages can vary based on the type of claim that is presented. Damages for winning a property law claim can be different for damages in a tort or contract law claim. Also, these types of damages can either be compensatory, nominal or punitive.

Compensatory damages are awarded to offset the plaintiff for actual harm or loss suffered, and nothing more. Compensatory damages may include payment or reimbursement for medical expenses. Other compensatory damages that may seem indirect, but are still offered to reimburse the plaintiff are damages for loss of earnings for missing work, and pain and suffering. The rationale behind awarding a plaintiff compensatory damages, is to restore the injured person to the same position that the she was in prior to the injury. For example, if an apartment is flooded due to the upstairs neighbor's pipes bursting, the compensatory damages may include the cost of replacing the carpet, damaged dry wall and other injuries the plaintiff suffered because of the incident. Compensatory damages are what we traditionally think of as the amount of money necessary to correct the problem.

Compare compensatory damages to nominal damages, these damages refer to a small sum awarded to the plaintiff when the lawsuit is won, but there was no actual damage repairable by money. Nominal damages are used to show that the harm suffered was in principle rather than actual.

Punitive damages are also an award of money to the plaintiff but differ in that they are awarded when the defendant acted in an outrageous manner. Punitive damages are not given to make the plaintiff whole by compensating her; they are used to punish the defendant and to deter others from acting in the same way. Punitive damages are not usually granted for ordinary negligence cases. The action by the defendant must be intentional and malicious or extremely reckless.

A plaintiff is entitled to punitive damages in cases where it is proven that the owner's actions showed willful misconduct, malice, fraud, wantonness, oppression, or that the defendant showed deliberate indifference to the consequences. Punitive damages are usually presented in cases of intentional torts and false imprisonment. States have written statutes to limit the amount of punitive damages that can be awarded, with exceptions for cases where the defendant acted with the specific intent to cause harm or acted while under the influence of alcohol or drugs, so that her judgment was substantially impaired.

7.6 Chapter summary

Torts are one of the categories of civil law that most frequently impact the behaviors of a Facility Manager but the definition of a tort is not as exact as students may wish. If you remember a tort is a civil wrong and not a crime, understanding intentional torts, negligence and strict liability will not be difficult.

7.7 Questions

1. Give an example of a tort a Facility Manager is likely to be held liable for.
2. Is the legal definition of "intentional" the same as the common definition used outside of a legal context? Explain your answer.
3. Is an accident the same thing as negligence? Explain your answer.

4. Which of the four main elements of negligence is most difficult to prove? Why?
5. Is the legal concept of strict liability fair? Is it necessary? Explain your answers.
6. How can Facility Managers avoid premises liability claims?
7. If a plaintiff has to prove that an injury occurred in order to win a case for negligence, can a jury award nominal damages? Explain your answer.
8. Should state legislatures limit the amount of punitive damages a plaintiff can be awarded? Explain your answer.
9. Using resources available to you, find a news article about a lawsuit where the jury awarded punitive damages.
10. Do you think a Facility Manager can act in such a way that they would be liable for punitive damages? Give an example.

References

Thomson Gale and J. Lehman. *West's Encyclopedia of American Law*. *2*. Cengage Gale, 2008.

8

Contract Law

> [P]arties to a contract are free to determine for themselves what primary obligations they will accept. They may state these in express words in the contract itself and, where they do, the statement is determinative; but in practice a commercial contract never states all the primary obligations of the parties in full; many are left to be incorporated by implication of law from the legal nature of the contract into which the parties are entering. But if the parties wish to reject or modify primary obligations, which would otherwise be so incorporated, they are fully at liberty to do so by express words
>
> **(Diplock 1980). William John Kenneth Diplock, Baron, KC**

8.1 Introduction

Although Baron Diplock, a member of the Kings Court in the UK, is better known for creating the "Diplock Courts", a juryless terrorism-focused forum, his thoughts in the above quote on contracts hint to the main reason for contract disputes – unexpressed primary obligations. Parties to a contract come with expectations for performance and in most cases every single obligation cannot be expressed in writing. It is this gap between what is expected and what is delivered that lies at the heart of the legal concept of breach of contract.

A contract is much more and much less than is often thought. It is much more, in that a simple statement can carry with it wide ranging legal obligations grounded in centuries of US Jurisprudence, and much less in that an agreement can be rendered useless if the drafter fails to include a simple legal element. Facility Managers must enter into many contracts and therefore must understand the basic theory of contract law. The key to contract law is

Legal Concepts for Facility Managers, First Edition. Linda Thomas-Mobley.
© 2014 John Wiley & Sons, Ltd. Published 2014 by John Wiley & Sons, Ltd.

recognizing which agreements are actually legally binding contracts, and what rights are available for parties faced with a broken or breached contract.

One of the key motivations for the Facility Manager in using contracts is to shift the risk of performing a task to one who is more expert at this task. For example, specialized mechanical system repair is best left to qualified experts who happily take on the risk of performing the job for the agreed-upon cost. Risk considerations and the use of the contract, as a risk mitigation device, will be discussed in Part III. For now, the student should concentrate on understanding how contracts are formed and what happens if a breach occurs.

In this chapter the expected student learning outcomes are as follows:

- Define the legal term "contract".
- Describe the Facility Manager's role in the formation and operation of a contract.
- Explain the concept of breach of contract.
- Explain how conflicting terms in a contract are resolved.
- Define the term "lease".

An important consideration for a Facility Manager when providing a service is identifying who will perform the service. Is there a sufficient human resource with expertise to use in-house forces, or is the task one that requires specialized knowledge? If the decision is to use outside services, then the issues and concepts surrounding contract law emerge.

8.2 Defining contract law

Stated simply, a contract is a legally recognized agreement. Another definition is an agreement between two people with written and articulated obligations that is endorsed by the parties, through their signatures, who believe they will benefit from the obligations to be performed. Although the first definition is short and vague, while the second is more definitive, both are true. It is the area between these definitions that causes problems resulting in lawsuits. The best practice is a reasonably specific, detailed and transparent agreement.

8.3 Autonomy to contract

US law gives autonomy to contracting parties to choose the key content of their contracts. As most contracts involve economic exchanges, the law also gives parties the power to place some value on each other's performance. A legally recognized contract imposes a legal sanction by the court. This sanction is essential to obtaining the promised performance in the situation where one party fails to complete their obligations.

In US law, the courts support autonomy to contract, because individual parties are thought to be in the best position to decide the terms of their agreements. Were there no autonomy in contracting, the weight of enforcing regulations would be a heavy burden on the courts. Additionally, parties are also more likely to perform in accordance with their promises if they have participated freely in making the exchange and determining the terms. Finally, this notion of freedom of contract is consistent with the notion of a free and open society, thereby encouraging free enterprise.

The autonomy to contract assumes contracting parties have equal bargaining power, equal access to information and are operating in a free market. In some cases these assumptions may be too generous.

If equal bargaining power does not exist, there can be coercion, causing one party to agree to the terms because they feel they have no other choice. This unequal power is known as *adhesion*. An adhesive contract results when one of the parties has little or no bargaining power. Adhesive contracts are legal, but if the terms are heavily biased, the contract may be considered unconscionable and therefore be deemed unenforceable. *Black's Law Dictionary* defines unconscionable to be a contract,

> . . . so unreasonably detrimental to the interest of a contracting party as to render the contract unenforceable. . . the basic test is whether in the light of the general commercial background and the commercial needs of the particular trade or case, the clauses involved are so one-sided as to be unconscionable under the circumstances existing at the time of the making of the contract. . . a bargain so one-sided as to amount to an absence of meaningful choice on the part of one of the parties together with contract terms which are unreasonable favorable to the other party. . . (Garner 2009)

8.4 Built environment contracts

In theory, more informed parties increase the likelihood of all expectations being met. However, there exists a point of diminishing returns where too much detail may actually be detrimental, causing more disputes and a contract with less detail. The level of specificity can be placed on a continuum and plotted against the potential for disputes, as shown in Figure 8.1.

You will notice as the level of detail increases, the potential for disputes decreases – to a point. Facility Managers should avoid using overly detailed contracts because they tend to be one-sided in favor of the party drafting the agreement. No contract is "airtight". Uncontemplated situations may arise that cause a project to require revision. If the parties attempt to cover every conceivable eventuality they run the risk of limiting the contractor's ability to

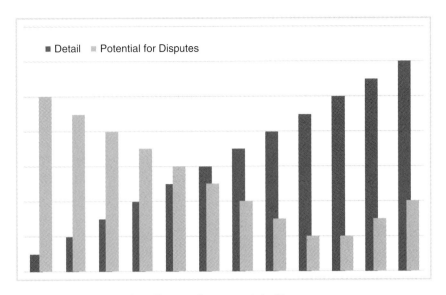

Figure 8.1   Detail related to disputes in contract drafting.

choose the "means and methods" for performing her work. The means and methods for performing work refer to the discretion experts have in deciding how to fulfill the scope requested in a contract. For example, telling an asbestos abatement contractor how to remove, bag, transport and dispose of the hazardous waste changes the relationship. It is the contractor who should choose the method of abatement and therefore take the risk of any errors made. Too much detail given to a contractor may dictate these "means and methods" of work performance and thereby eliminate the professional discretion of the contractor. When contracts eliminate the discretion of the contractor and result in a "to-do" list instead of an agreement for professional services, courts interpret the language as an employer/employee relationship. If the relationship changes from an independent contractor to an employer/employee arrangement any risk transferred to the contractor is eviscerated and the employer is responsible for all duties required under labor laws.

Consider the case of *Privette v. Superior Court* in 1993 (Privette v. Superior Court 1993). Mr Franklin Privette hired Jim Krause Roofing, Inc. (Krause) to install a new tar and gravel roof. Using a caldron to keep the tar at the proper temperature and a pumping device parked in a driveway next to the duplex, the roofing crew transported hot tar to the roof. When the gravel truck arrived, the crew moved the caldron and pump to make room for the truck. After the gravel was placed on the roof, crewmembers realized they needed several more gallons of tar to complete the job. The foreman asked his employee, Jesus Contreras, to carry 10 five-gallon buckets of hot tar up a ladder to the roof. While climbing the ladder to complete this directive, Contreras fell off the ladder and was burned by the hot tar he was carrying.

Contreras requested Workers' Compensation benefits for his injuries. He also filed a lawsuit against the owner of the duplex, Mr Privette. Notice how the legal relationship between the plaintiff and defendant is important to note in this case. According to the court, "a person who hired an independent contractor generally was not liable to third parties for injuries caused by the contractor's negligence in performing the work" (Privette v. Superior Court 1993). This was because the law in that jurisdiction was previously determined. This stated law held that a person who hired an independent contractor had "no right of control as to the mode of doing the work contracted for" (Green v. Soule 1904). The work performed was the activity of the contractor, who is better able to control the risk of the contracted work. The court in this case explained that Workers' Compensation Insurance is designed to protect an injured worker in situations like this. The court then concluded "in this case, roofing employee Contreras cannot prevail on a lawsuit against the duplex owner Privette for injuries compensable under the workers' compensation system" (Privette v. Superior Court 1993). Workers' Compensation is a type of insurance employer's purchase to pay for injuries to their employees and is used to protect employees, regardless of fault. This is another example to illustrate why a Facility Manager should not attempt to control the "mode of doing the work", in other words the means and the methods should be left up to the contractor. Since the worker was not an employer of the building owner, Privette was not responsible for the injuries suffered by the contractor's employees.

8.5 Contract elements

In the built environment industry the actions of owners, designers and constructors, sometimes referred to as contractors, have evolved through time into a common set of obligations and expectations for performance. Generally accepted components that should be included in any contract are referred to as "contract elements". Elements of a contract include an offer, acceptance, legal subject matter, consideration and competent parties.

8.5.1 Offers

The first basic element of a contract requires that one party makes an offer, or communicates a promise to do something, which the other party accepts. This offer defines the basic terms of the agreement. Within the realm of the Facility Manager, an example of an offer is a proposal by a vendor to provide a specified service at a specified cost. Common errors in offers include incorrect mathematical calculations, omission of key promises necessary for successful completion and the failure to state a time frame for which the offer is extended.

Facility Managers should be aware that requesting vendor proposals is not an offer to contract in the legal sense. Rather, it is an announcement that offers to contract are being requested from vendors who wish to supply the goods or services as described. However, the proposal drafted and given to the Facility Manager by a vendor does constitute an offer, and if all of the terms are agreed to without modifications, the parties will be bound in contract. If the Facility Manager changes any term in the vendor's proposal this technically invalidates the offer and changes the modified proposal to a counter offer that the vender may or may not accept.

8.5.2 Acceptance

The other basic element necessary for a contract to exist is acceptance. An acceptance is a clear and unambiguous acknowledgement accepting the offer and the terms as stated. Satisfying the requirement for acceptance is not as straightforward as it may seem because there are several legally recognized ways to accept an offer. Acceptance can be in the form of a signature, a verbal statement, or even the keeping the goods or services given by the person expressing the offer.

8.5.3 Legal subject matter

For the element of legal subject matter to exist the actual work being promised should be lawful. Even if there is an offer and acceptance to perform work, if the work in question is unlawful a contract has not been formed and the parties will not be obligated to execute the proposed service.

8.5.4 Consideration

The required element of consideration is usually in the form of payment for services rendered. The rationality of the amount agreed upon does not come into question for the courts, with some exceptions such as the federally mandated labor rates that must be paid to those working on federally funded projects.

8.5.5 Competent parties

This element of a contract necessitates all parties to a contract to be of legal age and of sound mind. Typically "of legal age" in most jurisdictions is 18 years but this varies by state. "Sound mind" questions are litigated when one party is mentally ill or intoxicated. This element tends not to be an issue for Facility Managers.

8.6 Statutes of fraud

There are additional requirements the law has put in place to help people wishing to enter contracts avoid differences in interpretation and, consequently, disputes. For example, the law will only enforce certain contracts if they are written and signed by the parties. This legal doctrine is called a *Statute of Fraud*. Statutes of Fraud vary from state to state but the general mandate requires contracts concerning land, debts, marriages and services not completed within one year must be in writing. Though having the agreement in written form is not always a requirement, the best way to avoid misinterpretation is to require written contracts.

8.7 Other legal issues in contract law

8.7.1 Unjust enrichment

When defining the term contract at the beginning of this chapter, the short simple definition of "a legally recognized agreement" was given. This definition is actually just as correct as the other definition, requiring that all of the elements discussed previously (offer, acceptance, legal subject matter, competent parties, etc.) must be met. This is because, in some situations, the courts will simply impose a contract upon parties. This type of court-imposed agreement can arise in many situations, the most common being to prevent "unjust enrichment". Unjust enrichment occurs when one party performs work, which benefits another party, and because of some trifle detail, all the elements of a contract are not present. For example, someone agrees to build a fence for you and after completion of the fence you find out that the builder is actually 14 years old and, therefore, not a competent party of legal age to enter into a contract. Technically, all of the elements of a contract are not met. To prevent unjust enrichment, that is, a free fence, the court will recognize the agreement with the 14 year-old as a valid contract. The rationale for this action by the court is not difficult to appreciate, a contract is imposed upon the parties because the other result is unfair. A court-imposed contract can occur under any circumstance where the judge believes injustice would occur if the agreement were not enforced. There is a difference in the operation of these court-imposed contracts, however. The court imposing the agreement must determine the consideration owed to the party who performs the service. This amount is required to be the fair market value of the work performed otherwise an unreasonable amount for the service may be requested by the builder. This would also be unfair.

8.8 Contract interpretation

A common source of disputes comes from the potential for contract language to be interpreted in multiple ways. The popular book *Eats Shoots and Leaves* illustrates how the placement of a comma can alter the entire meaning of a phrase (Truss 2006). For example, "eats shoots and leaves" can mean some animal likes to munch on bamboo shoots and green leaves. With the addition of a comma the phrase "eats, shoots and leaves" can mean someone eats lunch, shoots a gun and then exits the building.

Through the evolution of common law and by legislatures enacting statutes, the courts have developed methods to resolve differing interpretations of contracts. Knowing how a court is likely to interpret a problematic contract term is valuable information Facility Managers need in order to review a contract before signing. The five basic rules of contract interpretation are shown in Figure 8.2.

A brief explanation of these five rules is necessary for a full understanding. The requirement that the document "be read as a whole" means that all words, clauses and sections must be considered. One party cannot cut and paste certain terms while ignoring others. The contract will be "construed against

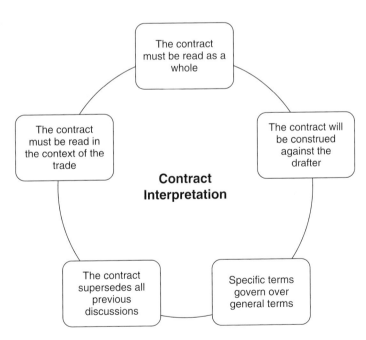

Figure 8.2 Contract interpretation.

the drafter" means that in the case of unresolvable conflicts in language, the court will give the most favorable interpretation to the person who did not draft the contract. The reason is because the drafter of the contract is in the best position to write an unambiguous contract, and if the document has conflicting terms the party without input to the contract language should not suffer.

The rule that "specific terms govern over general terms" means that, if a term is general enough to include the specific term, the stricter specific provision will govern. For example, if in one section of a contract the terms state that all change orders need to be presented to the owner within a week, and in another section the terms state that change orders must be submitted in five days, the five-day requirement, which is the more specific term, will govern since a week can also be interpreted as seven days. The contract "supersedes all previous discussions" means the court will only look at the contract language and not consider prior negotiations. This rule underscores the necessity to read every word of every contract to make sure all agreed-upon promises are in the contract.

Ejusdem generis (eh-youse-dem, generous: adj.) Latin for "of the same kind", used to interpret vague legal language. Where a list is used to note specific classes of persons or things and then refers to them in general, the general statements only apply to the same kind of persons or things specifically listed. For example, if a law refers to automobiles, trucks, tractors, motorcycles and other motor-powered vehicles, "vehicles" would not include airplanes, since the list was of land-based transportation. Finally, reading the contract "in the context of the trade" means local industry customs should be used as a guide. These rules of thumb illustrate one approach to interpreting contract language and should be used by the Facility Manager as a guide.

8.8.1 Contract drafting: assigning risk

As mentioned before, the basic reason to enter a contract is risk shifting, or moving the risk of performance or failure from the Facility Manager to the contractor. Since assigning the risk is a major aspect of contract drafting, another key to avoiding disputes lies in the basic and most commonly accepted practices of contract drafting.

The general rule of drafting a sound contract is to assign the risk to the party controlling that risk. The problem with this rule is its over generality. What if the risk is of a nature that neither party controls? Examples include natural disasters and other complications not addressed in the contract. As with any general rule, reality has a way of finding exceptions that require a judgment call.

A more detailed rule of thumb for contract drafting has emerged with three basic tenets:

- Assign the risk to the party who controls it.
- If either party cannot control the risk, assign the risk to the party who can purchase insurance for damages potentially caused by the risky situation occurring.
- If neither party has the ability to insure against the risk, assign it to the party willing to take the risk. The party willing to take on a risk is usually the party who is in the business of performing the work.

If after applying these rules any risks remain unassigned, all parties should share the resulting risks. For example, if a Facility Manager wants to contract with a janitorial service for office cleaning, it may be tempting to put additional requirements on the janitorial contractor, such as requiring them to bring their own water so the company can save on utilities. However, such a request limits the number of janitorial companies who will bid for the job, increases the cost of the contract and raises questions leading to disputes; for example, how much water, the quality or purity of the water required or what to do if the contractor's water runs out in the middle of performing a cleaning task? A one-sided agreement where one party carries all of the risk can lead to an adversarial relationship among the parties, which could lead to strained relationships. Also, Facility Managers should be mindful of anyone over eager to enter into a contract with onerous terms. The party may be desperate for work or irresponsible, such that in case of a failure to perform, they have no assets to collect upon rendering the terms of the contract useless.

Another common example in proper risk assignment is hazardous waste removal. The risk of removing the waste should be assigned to the party performing the removal, but performance risk is not the only risk involved in remediation projects. Consider the risk of improperly transporting the waste, not using appropriate equipment, vehicles or transportation procedures. Failure to properly transport hazardous waste could lead to an accident. You learnt in the environmental chapter that everyone involved in transporting waste, even the land owner contracting with an expert to remove the waste, is identified as a *Potentially Responsible Party* (PRP) under federal statute. PRPs are held "jointly and severally liable" and must pay for remediation either by themselves or by sharing the cost with other PRPs. "Joint and several liability" is a legal concept whereby two or more parties are held liable together (jointly) with each other so that they may split the damages owed, or remain individually (severally) liable for the entire amount when the other parties cannot afford to pay damages. Think of the situation where your rental agreement indicates that you are held jointly and severally liable for the rent payment for an apartment you share with two other roommates. If the roommates do not have money to pay the rent, the entire rent is still due on the first of the month and you will have to pay all of it as promised to the landlord.

What if, during a routine waste removal, the truck driver has a seizure: the truck is damaged and spills its contents into a lake? Also, what if, in this example, the risk of removal was assigned via contract to the truck driver's company? The risk of a truck accident was insured and thus assigned to the truck company, but what about the risk of contaminating the river? According to the three tenets of contract drafting, the contract drafter should have assigned the unknown risks to the profiting party who, in this example, is the truck company.

Risks are assigned to parties using artfully crafted contract clauses. The actual wording of these clauses may differ but the operation of standard clauses serves as the mechanism for assigning risks. The Facility Manager should be aware of different types of contract clauses that tend to cause disputes in a specific industry.

8.9 Contractual duty

The majority of the time both parties perform as promised. When parties perform as promised and the contractual relationship ends, the parties are said to have "discharged" their duties. Additional avenues to discharging ones duties under contract exist. The Facility Manager need not fully understand the legal details of discharging contractual duties other than to know that discharge can be completed by performing the promise, agreeing to substitute something else for performance, amending the promise or by operation of law such as bankruptcy.

If the promised service cannot be performed through no fault of a party because the obligation is prevented by matters beyond her control, the obligation is said to have been discharged by impossibility or frustration of purpose. For example, if a hotdog vendor agreed to provide snacks at an event two blocks from the World Trade Center in New York City on September 11, 2001, the vendor would be discharged by impossibility since completing performance would be impossible after the unanticipated attack on the buildings.

On the occasion a party does not perform as promised, a breach of contract may have occurred. If a breach of contract has occurred, the person injured, acting as the plaintiff, can sue in civil court. As in the law of torts, for a plaintiff to prevail on a breach of contract lawsuit, certain elements must be proven. Figure 8.3 depicts the elements the plaintiff must prove using evidence to win her case.

It should be noted that one breach of contract element is quite different from the tort elements. The plaintiff cannot be in breach of her own promise to the other party. This requirement is referred to as the *Clean Hands Doctrine*. The plaintiff must have "clean hands" before she can allege that the defendant breached her promise. In breach of contract cases the remedy sought by the

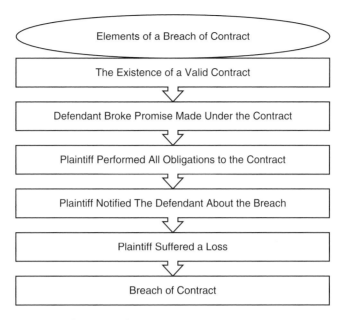

Figure 8.3   Elements of breach of contract.

plaintiff is usually a compensatory amount of money. Damages available to the plaintiff include compensatory damages and nominal damages. Punitive damages are usually not available for defaulting on a contract. Sometimes the plaintiff may ask for the promise to be performed because money may not be a good substitute. This is called *Specific Performance*. For example, if one purchases architecturally unique home built at the turn of the century, registered as a historic property, and the seller breaches the contract to sell, the court may grant specific performance because there is no amount of money that could compensate the loss of that particular home.

Another type of damages, not defined during the discussion on tort law, is called *Liquidated Damages*. Liquidated Damages are negotiated at the time the parties enter into a contract and are therefore not granted by a court. They are usually a sum of money granted in return for anticipated or common breach, such as finishing the work later than expected. In the built environment industry, construction contracts typically include Liquidated Damages Clauses. If a contractor fails to deliver a completed project on the agreed-upon date, she may have to pay liquidated damages for every day late. This is important for the Facility Manager to know when entering into construction agreements for new construction or renovation. The liquidated damages serve as an incentive for the contractor to finish as agreed upon because automatic payment to the owner will be granted without her having to file a lawsuit in the event the project completed later than promised.

The defendant to a breach of contract suit may not be liable for damages if she has a valid defense. Defenses to breach of contract fall into two categories:

- The promise cannot be performed through no fault of the defendant.
- The contract requiring performance was not a valid contract to begin with.

This second defense is the reason why it is so important to important vendor contracts are valid and enforceable at the negotiation stage.

8.10 Preserving the risk assignment

Paying careful attention to contract drafting is all for naught if the legal relationship between the parties is not maintained. The situation of third-party injuries illustrates the importance of preserving risk assignments. An owner can escape liability for a third-party injury if the owner can show that the person who injured the claimant was not an employee but an independent contractor. An individual is determined to be an employee or an independent contractor depending on the degree of control retained or exercised by the Facility Manager. When the Facility Manager can demand a certain result, but does not control the time, manner or method of the contractor's work, then the person is an independent contractor and not an employee. A person is also presumed by the court to be an independent contractor when the contract designates her in such a manner. However, if the Facility Manager retains the right to control the manner of performance, then the relationship shifts to one of employee/employer regardless of whether the employer ever actually exerts such control. Additional discussion on the line drawn between independent contractor and employee occurs in Part III.

8.11 The property lease contract

A lease is an agreement between a landlord and a tenant governing the terms of their relationship. Leases typically address rent, terms of possession and use of premises. Recalling the section on leases in Chapter 4, you know that a lease is both a conveyance of an estate and a contract. It is a conveyance of an interest in real property because it creates an estate in real property for the lease. It is a contract because it contains all of the mutual promises made by the landlord and tenant and is enforced by the courts.

Well-drafted modern leases anticipate most of the problems that have been litigated over the years by including clauses to state the terms of the lease. Language providing appropriate remedies to compensate for the defaults of

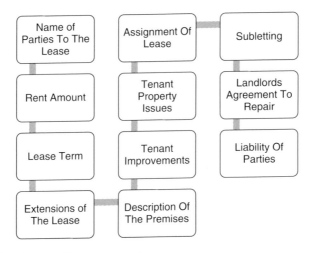

Figure 8.4   Provisions of lease contract.

either the landlord or tenant is also included. Nearly every type of commercial property lease includes provisions depicted in Figure 8.4.

8.11.1 Names of parties

Naming the landlord and tenant in a lease seems like an obvious and simple prerequisite. However, there are occasions when recognized parties are not identified and the lease as a contract becomes unenforceable. For example, if more than one party is to be a tenant, all tenants must be named and each must sign the lease. Property co-owners must also sign the lease as the landlords. As you already know there are several ways to jointly own property with varying legal consequences. If a married couple owns the property as tenants by the entirety, one spouse cannot bind the other spouse to a lease. If the ownership group is joined by owning the property through a tenancy in common or a joint tenancy, all owners must also sign the lease, no one owner can bind the others.

Complications with joint ownership can be simplified when the landlord or tenant is actually a legally recognized corporation because a president or vice president can bind a corporation. However, this type of joint ownership has its own complications. Just as it is necessary to properly identify the parties to the lease contract, it is also important to cite in the lease the full legally recognized name of the corporation, and not simply the name that the corporation is "doing business as" (or DBA). A business commonly known as "Morgan, Inc." may actually have a proper name of "The Morgan Corporation". Research with the Office of the Secretary of State may have to be conducted to verify the proper legal name. Different rules regarding the naming of a tenant or landlord to a lease apply depending on the type of business entity and its operation.

A limited liability partner in some states cannot sign a lease, while a member in a general partnership can bind the entire partnership. Care should be taken to verify the full, proper legal name of a business entity. If you were the Facility Manager renting a corner of a McDonald's parking lot for six months, what would be the full, legal name of the landlord? Would it be McDonald's, McDonald's Industries or McDonald's Corporation?

8.11.2 Exculpatory clauses

The other components of the lease follow local business practices or whatever is detailed in the lease document. One component of the lease important to the Facility Manager is party liability. The subject of liability is addressed in the lease using contract language that attempts to limit contractual liability by negotiating indemnifications, waivers and releases into the lease document. These clauses, known as exculpatory clauses, can be as elaborate or simple as the parties wish. Typical exculpatory clauses are the "As Is" clause, the "Waiver and Release" clause, and the clauses outlining "subrogation" and "indemnification".

The "As Is" clause protects landlords from harm resulting from dangerous conditions in the leased property. The clause usually states that by taking possession of the property, the tenant demonstrates that the property is in good condition. This type of clause is important because the landlord does not want to retain liability for a dangerous condition on a property that she no longer has control over.

A waiver is a clause used by the parties, usually the tenant, to give up some of their rights, such as the right to have exclusive use of the property. For example, if a tenant insists on maintaining the right to have exclusive use of the property, this may be problematic. This is because such a right may prevent the landlord from entering the property for maintenance. *Subrogation* and *indemnification* both protect the party from acts of third parties. Under subrogation, the protected party has the right to "stand in the shoes" of the other party and make use of all rights available to the second party. For example, insurance companies often ask for this right so that they can pursue a third party for losses. Compare this rather all-inclusive right to indemnification, which is an agreement by one party to act as the guarantor of another party. Indemnification operates to substitute the first party's liability for that of the second party by agreeing to reimburse the second party for any losses suffered. Indemnification is not as comprehensive as subrogation. In many leases the tenants indemnify the landlords, or agree to reimburse the landlord for harm caused by the tenant. It is important to remember that when you ask for indemnification you only get reimbursed for expenses. In contrast, subrogation allows you to assume the legal position of the person, making you eligible for any money owed to the second party.

8.11.3 Lease termination

A lease can be terminated in a number of ways. The most common include: surrender and abandonment occurring when the tenant turns over possession; operation of the law where the court orders a tenant to vacate the property; breach of lease for failing to live up to obligations in the lease and having to relinquish control of the property; or constructive eviction, which occurs when the tenant cannot occupy the property because of some problem preventing quiet enjoyment.

Let's say you are renting an apartment and the lease will expire in six months. You get an unexpected yet exciting job offer in another country that requires you to begin right away, if you move out without any intention to return, it would be an occasion of surrender and abandonment, allowing the landlord to terminate the lease. Termination by operation of law can occur if, for instance, the state has planned to construct a highway that happens to run right through the middle of your building and requests that all tenants vacate. Finally, breach of lease termination can arise if you fail to keep your apartment free from debris and your untidiness causes destruction of the property. Demanding that you move out in this case is an eviction, which thereby terminates the lease.

Constructive eviction is a complex doctrine to understand unless you realize that it is both a strategy and a remedy. The most common use of constructive eviction as a strategy occurs when the property is uninhabitable or unbearable because of noise, unsafe conditions or other circumstance. In this case the landlord is not making an affirmative statement to the tenant that she should leave, but because of the landlord's inaction, the tenant cannot reasonably stay. The remedy of constructive eviction can be a self-help remedy in some instances. The legal system recognizes the desire for private disputes to be settled using self-help remedies, and oftentimes supports actions to resolve disputes without involving the courts. In the landlord/tenant circumstance, if necessary repairs appropriately communicated to the landlord are not made, and the tenant decides to leave and not pay rent until the problem is resolved, the tenant has practiced self-help and availed herself to the constructive eviction remedy.

As in the case of breach of contract, if the terms of a lease are not followed the parties have several remedies available to them for non-compliance. Figure 8.5 lists the remedies available to both parties.

The remedy of *Distraint and Distress for Rent* available to the landlord is actually a right and a remedy. The right of *Distraint* allows the landlord to enter the tenant's property, take the tenant's personal property and sell it to recover losses incurred. The remedy of *Distress* allows the landlord to apply the proceeds of the sale to unpaid rent. This heavy-handed remedy is not popular and some states have abolished it for fear of landlord abuse. The landlord also has the ability to place a lien on the tenant's property, which is claiming a right

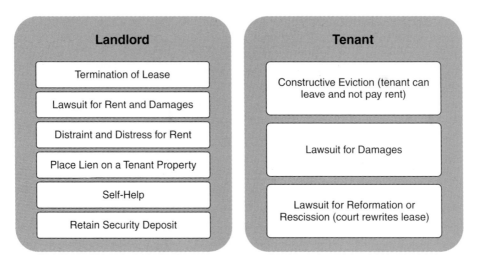

Landlord	Tenant
Termination of Lease	Constructive Eviction (tenant can leave and not pay rent)
Lawsuit for Rent and Damages	
Distraint and Distress for Rent	Lawsuit for Damages
Place Lien on a Tenant Property	
Self-Help	Lawsuit for Reformation or Rescission (court rewrites lease)
Retain Security Deposit	

Figure 8.5   Remedies available for breach of lease contract.

to any money that could be generated by the sale of the tenant's property. This is especially useful in commercial leases when the tenant has high value property, such as commercial inventory or equipment. The remedy of "self-help" includes any arrangement the landlord and tenant can agree upon, such as transferring title in a car in exchange for past due rent.

When the tenant exercises her remedy of suing for lease restructuring or rescission, if she prevails, the court may rewrite the lease to make it reflect the parties' true intentions or void the lease altogether. This remedy is rare.

8.12 Additional contract concepts

Contracts can be amended, but to be a valid amendment the new contract must have the mutual assent of both parties of some change in the contract terms. If this were not the case, why would anyone want to either pay more for a service or perform more services under an existing contract? Many times, the basic terms and elements remain the same, such as offer, acceptance, competent parties and legal subject matter, but at least one element must change. This element is usually consideration.

Additional contract law concepts Facility Managers should be aware of include third-party beneficiaries, assignment of contracts and delegation of contract duties. Third-party beneficiaries are people who are not parties to the contract but individuals who may receive some consequential benefits of the contract. For example, if a couple signs a lease then one possible third-party beneficiary to the lease would be a child living with the couple. Assignment of a contract occurs when one party gives contract rights to another person while delegation of contract duties refers to the transfer of a contractual obligation to someone else.

Standard contracts are widely used in the built environment industry. In these types of agreements risks are assigned to the parties via various standard contract clauses. The actual wording of the clauses may differ but the operation of standard clauses serves as the principal mechanism for assigning risks.

The Facility Manager should be aware of different types of standard contract clauses that are used in the industry, especially those that tend to cause disputes. For the facility management industry, the main problematic clause is the *no damage for delay* provision.

No damage for delay clauses are typically in standard contracts that favor the Facility Manager or owner. Although it may seem desirable to have a contract stating that, no matter what occurs, the owner will not pay any extra money if there is a delay, there are negative consequences to such a clause. If a Facility Manager wants an "air-tight" contract for the remodeling of an office building, once bidders realize that a no damage for delay clause is in the standard contract, few if any builders would want to win the bid. Those who do end up bidding for the contract may price the work too high, to cover any contingencies that arise.

8.13 Chapter summary

Using contracts to shift risk of all types is commonly used in the practice of facility management as an accepted business practice. Regardless of its intent, the obligations created between parties bind them until the intent of the contract is fulfilled. Knowing where the common pitfalls occur in using contracts and what actions the courts are likely to take when breached, gives the Facility Manager a deeper understanding of how she can avoid liability.

8.14 Questions

1. Why does the court uphold agreements, which are clearly missing one of the elements of a contract?
2. What is the Facility Manager's most common role regarding built environment contracts?
3. Explain the practice that in drafting contracts, risk should go to the party able to control it.
4. In your own words describe what is required in a lease.
5. Why should the landlord have more remedies for a breach of lease contract than the tenant? Is this "fair"? Explain your answer.

6. Explain the concept of self-help.
7. Can you elaborate on why the remedy of Distraint and Distress may be outdated?
8. How is the word "constructive" used in the instance of constructive eviction?
9. Are formal contracts always necessary? Explain your answer.
10. What should the Facility Manager do when terms of a contract seem to contradict each other?

References

Garner, Bryan. *Black's Law Dictionary, Deluxe 9th Edition*. West, 2009.
Truss, L. *Eats Shoots and Leaves*. Gotham, 2006.

9

Criminal Law

> There is no den in the wide world to hide a rogue. Commit a crime and the earth is made of glass. Commit a crime, and it seems as if a coat of snow fell on the ground, such as reveals in the woods the track of every partridge, and fox, and squirrel.
>
> **Ralph Waldo Emerson (1803–1882)**

9.1 Introduction

The quotation above is taken from one of Emerson's most famous essays entitled "Compensation" (Emerson 1847). He begins stating "The wings of Time are black and white; Pied with morning and with night" to illustrate his idea of balance and eloquently goes on to describe that, for each action, there is a reaction of sorts – bad and good. In this quote, appearing about two thirds of the way through the writing, nature seems to conspire against an escaping criminal. Emerson's ideals about justice expressed in "Compensation" still stand as one of the best examples of the written essay.

Most of the time, a Facility Manager's potential legal exposure falls under Civil Law. However, there are occasions where the exposure overlaps or falls squarely under Criminal Law. In contrast to civil lawsuits where private parties usually conduct the prosecution, government officers on behalf of the public bring criminal prosecutions. If convicted, a defendant can be sentenced to jail or pay economic fines and even sometimes experience both.

Legal Concepts for Facility Managers, First Edition. Linda Thomas-Mobley.
© 2014 John Wiley & Sons, Ltd. Published 2014 by John Wiley & Sons, Ltd.

Upon successful completion of this chapter the following student learning outcomes are expected:

1. Identify the major differences between civil and criminal law.
2. Describe the "beyond a reasonable doubt" standard.
3. Explain how the Facility Manager may be held liable as a result of a decision made during the management of a facility.
4. Explain the difference between the rules of civil procedure and the rules of criminal procedure.

9.2 Criminal procedure

Criminal procedure contains the relevant rules and proceedings through which the government enforces criminal law. The rules of criminal procedure are actually laws themselves. Municipalities states, and the federal government each have their own criminal codes, which define the types of conduct that constitute crimes. Title 18 of the United States Code (USC) outlines federal crimes. Typically, federal crimes deal with activities that either extend beyond state boundaries or directly impact federal interests.

The US Supreme Court is responsible for the Federal Rules of Criminal Procedure (F.R.Crim.Pro.). These provisions must be followed when working with the courts, especially during lawsuits. Simultaneously, the Federal Rules of Criminal Procedure outline the procedure for conducting federal criminal trials. States have their own rules of criminal procedure, many of which closely model the F.R.Crim.Pro. Following the Federal Rules of Criminal Procedure ensures that all of the guarantees included within the US Constitution's Bill of Rights are preserved for the accused defendant. Rights such as due process, equal protection under the laws, the right to have legal counsel present, the right to confront witnesses, the right to a jury trial and the right to not testify against oneself, are basic protections for the criminal defendant.

Due process refers to the legal requirement that the government must respect all of the legal rights that are owed to a person. These rights are particularly relevant when someone is charged with a crime. Many attorneys refer to due process when they argue that a person has the right to a hearing before any adverse condition is imposed. Saying that a person deserves due process, usually means that they have the right to be heard before an impartial evaluator before property is taken away or their liberty is revoked. The right to equal protection under the laws ensures that all people are treated the same under the law, irrespective of their position in society.

While state constitutions and procedural rules may increase the protection given to criminal defendants, the laws may not offer less protection than that guaranteed by the US Constitution.

9.2.1 Investigations and Accusations

The F.R.Crim.Pro. provides guidance and processes that police officers and other law enforcement officials must follow. Failure to follow proper procedure can result in the suppression of evidence or the release of an arrested suspect. This right of the alleged criminal defendant is often criticized because sometimes rules can be manipulated by a skilled attorney to dismiss a criminal action. In some instances, the rule that was manipulated was a mere technicality having nothing to do with the merits of a case. Police are required to make criminal defendants aware of their basic rights prior to the individual making any statements that may be used as evidence against her at trial. One famous legal requirement is that police officers must ensure that defendants understand the right to remain silent and the right to have an attorney present: the Fifth and Sixth Amendments to the US Constitution. The defendant must knowingly, intelligently and voluntarily waive those rights in order for the government to use any statements as evidence against the defendant (Miranda v. Arizona 1966). Law enforcement must also follow the Fourth Amendment, which prohibits unreasonable searches and seizures. Under criminal law a search and seizure is the inspection of a person or location searching for evidence of a crime and taking any found evidence. If this is not performed according to the rules, the court may not allow evidence to be admitted in a trial (Mapp v. Ohio 1961).

One way for law enforcement to ensure proper procedure is to obtain permission from the court to search for evidence. This is referred to as a *search warrant*. To obtain such a warrant, the police must convince a magistrate that they have good reason, or "probable cause", to believe the evidence they are looking for is in the specific location stated on the request for the warrant. Probable cause is defined as "a reasonable amount of suspicion, supported by circumstances sufficiently strong to justify a prudent and cautious person's belief that certain facts are probably true" (Handler 1994). Police must also describe the place they will search and the items they will seize. There are exceptions to the requirement of having a warrant signed before a search can begin, including searches made at or near the US borders; following a lawful arrest; stop-and-frisk arrests; when seized items are in plain view; when the articles are in an automobile; when a private individual makes the search; under emergency circumstances and when the officer has a good reason to believe she may find a crime or evidence relating to a crime. The exceptions are many but they take into consideration other individual rights granted by the Constitution.

In order to avoid convicting an innocent person, the US Constitution gives certain protective rights to criminal defendants. One crucial right is the presumption of innocence. For the prosecution to win at trial the person or people tasked with determining which presented facts are true, must find the defendant guilty "beyond a reasonable doubt". Compare this to the civil trial standard of a "preponderance of the evidence", a much easier standard to meet. Figures 9.1 and 9.2 illustrate this comparison.

Ensuring proper due process requires that all criminal defendants receive a fair trial. They have the right to bring forth their own witnesses to testify, mount their own evidence and present their own theory of the facts. The courts indirectly interpret this right to include requiring the government to turn over all evidence that will be used against the defendant before trial so that the defendant can interview all of the prosecution's witnesses.

The Sixth Amendment to the Constitution guarantees criminal defendants the right to a speedy trial. Because of this, the government cannot wait too long before filing charges. What constitutes a speedy trial has evolved over the years due to the increase in population. Speedy in some jurisdictions

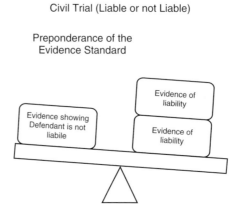

Figure 9.1   Civil trial standard.

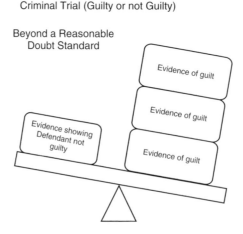

Figure 9.2   Criminal trial standard.

may be considered slow in others. The Sixth amendment also guarantees the right to a publicly held trial, an impartial jury of the defendant's peers and the right to help from an attorney during their trial. If a defendant cannot afford an attorney, the government is required to provide one free of charge. The government, through the Public Defender's Office usually provides free attorneys. The Federal Rules of Criminal Procedure stipulate that an accused shall have access to an attorney at every stage of the proceedings, beginning with the defendant's initial appearance in the courtroom after arrest. Also, if a defendant demands the presence of an attorney during a police interrogation, the officer must stop the any questioning until the defendant's attorney is present. There is a requirement that the legal help the defendant receives from an attorney must be "effective counseling". Ineffective assistance can cause the courts to issue the defendant a new trial. There is much debate over what constitutes "effective counseling". Some attorneys are better than others, if one has a mediocre attorney, is this ineffective counseling? In order to bring forth a claim for ineffective counsel, the defendant must prove to the court that the attorney representing her is not following normal professional practices and that this ineffective assistance resulted in a fundamentally unfair result.

9.2.2 Bail

After the police arrest a suspect, the court sets initial bail. Bail is a specified amount of money to be paid to the court that will allow the defendant to be released from custody following the initial arrest. If the defendant shows up for the scheduled court dates, the court refunds the bail amount. However, if the defendant fails to show up for a hearing, or some other obligation, the bail is forfeited and the court issues a warrant for the individual's arrest.

9.2.3 Arraignment

The next step in the process is arraignment. An arraignment is a court proceeding where the defendant is officially called before a court of that has jurisdiction over the case and told about the offense charged by the government. At this stage, the defendant is asked to enter a plea of guilty, not guilty or another alternative provided in the specific jurisdiction. Depending on the jurisdiction, arraignment may also be the time where the judge determines whether to set bail or release the defendant trusting her to show up for future hearings.

Understanding the nature of the crime you are charged with is a guarantee by the Sixth Amendment to US Constitution, stating defendants shall "be informed of the nature and cause of the accusation against them". The Federal Rules of Criminal Procedure, rule 10 states that, at the arraignment "federal courts must read the indictment or information to the defendant or state the substance of the charge to the defendant and ask him or her to enter a plea".

For more serious crimes the Federal Rules of Criminal Procedure require a defendant to be present at the arraignment, but the defendant may be absent if the potential punishment is a fine or the offense is considered trivial.

The court rules in some states only require that arraignments be held for felony-level charges, but not for misdemeanor-level offenses. One way to remember the difference between a felony and a misdemeanor is the amount of time potentially spent in jail. A felony is defined as an offence that may result in a year or more of confinement. Figure 9.3 depicts the questions asked and other items decided during an arraignment.

Even though it seems as though the arraignment was a preliminary hearing, the stage actually called "the preliminary hearing" follows the arraignment. At the preliminary hearing, the court determines whether enough evidence exists for the prosecution to meet the preponderance of the evidence standard. At this stage, the prosecution must convince the court that the majority of the evidence indicates that the defendant is guilty. The defense has the right to cross-examine the government witnesses during this hearing. Under federal law, a grand jury, rather than a judge, makes this determination when the defendant faces "capital or infamous crimes" pursuant to the US Constitution's Fifth Amendment. A capital crime can result in the defendant being sentenced to death, while an infamous crime is any particularly serious crime. After the preliminary hearing, the prosecution and defense argue small details by filing various motions before the judge. These motions usually deal with the evidence to be heard at trial; for example, whether the court should suppress certain evidence, whether certain individuals can testify or whether the judge should dismiss all charges for lack of evidence. These motions are generally heard by the judge at a hearing called the pre-trial hearing. This is the last hearing before the full trial.

After all these preliminary stages, the defendant finally stands trial. Both sides offer opening statements, although the defense can wait and give their opening statement after the prosecution has finished presenting all of its evidence. During the trial whenever witnesses give testimony, the defendant has the right to cross-examine the prosecution's witnesses. Cross-examination is used by both sides to ask pointed questions testing the memory or truthfulness of the witness. The defendant also has the right to remain silent and not provide testimony that could damage her chances of winning the trial. The prosecution presents its witnesses and evidence first. The defense then presents its

Figure 9.3   Arraignment inquiry.

witnesses and evidence and offers a closing argument. The prosecution offers the final closing argument, before the judge or jury (trier of fact) deliberates and returns a verdict. Figure 9.4 illustrates the process of a typical criminal trial in the USA.

For small crimes, if the defendant loses the case, the punishment decided upon by the judge is usually given immediately. Penalties may include probation, fines, incarceration, suspended sentence (in which the judge allows the defendant to serve probation first in lieu of the penalty), payment of restitution to the victim, community service or drug and alcohol rehabilitation. For more serious crimes, a sentencing trial occurs, during which the trier of fact hears evidence and arguments from the prosecution and defense regarding the appropriate sentence. The prosecution presents evidence of any existing information showing that the crime committed was particularly cruel, while the defense counters with evidence that may influence the court to pose a less severe sentence. At this stage the defendant has the right to address the judge directly without the help of her attorney. This is an opportunity for the defendant to show remorse or offer the motivations that may result in leniency.

An outline of the overall criminal procedure process is diagrammed in Figure 9.5.

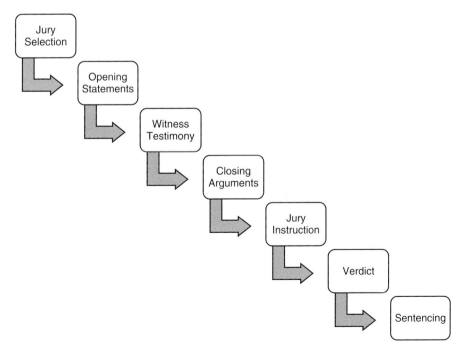

Figure 9.4   Criminal trial progression.

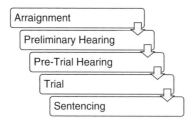

Figure 9.5   Criminal procedure process.

9.3 Facility management and crime

Understanding the criminal process is not a wasted effort for the Facility Manager. Even when carefully following all known rules and regulations, a Facility Manager will still encounter criminal law. This is because criminal behavior engaged in on managed properties is unfortunately becoming increasingly common.

9.3.1 Reducing crime

There are many ways to reduce harm suffered from criminal activity; the focus here will be on those relevant to the Facility Manager and most likely to succeed. Moving the building to a low crime area is not usually an option, and it is generally impossible to do anything about the size or function of specific facilities. However, it is relatively easy to change business practices that facilitate or encourage crime. Facility Managers are usually responsible for implementing and maintaining safe environments, and lowering the probability for criminal activity falls in this area.

A study conducted by the Police Research Group Crime Prevention Unit in the UK outlined measures proven to reduce crime and fear of crime in garages. Employing formal surveillance and patrols, using good lighting, implementing access control and maintaining a good physical appearance, are noted as important factors. Features commonly cited that raised anxiety included blind spots, shadowy areas and poor lighting in payment areas. Environmental features were also identified such as graffiti, odor and lack of maintenance or staff (Tilley 1993). Garages with high rankings by the public, lower crime levels and the positive views of the independent security advisers, tend to be particularly well managed and place a strong emphasis on customer satisfaction. These structures also have a greater level of financial investment and place greater emphasis employee training. It is always easier to build-in security during the design stage of a structure rather than modify garages at a later stage. While this study specifically addressed garages, these principles can be applied to any facility.

Facility management practices also play a crucial role in the effectiveness of security systems. For example, if exit barriers are removed at busy times to reduce waiting times, good security can be compromised and rendered useless.

9.3.2 Workplace violence

Violence in the workplace intersects legal theories of property law, criminal law, intentional torts and sometimes employment law. Hostilities directed at building occupants during the normal course of their business day is known as *Workplace Violence* (WPV) and can come from anyone with access to the facility. Facility Managers should be aware of the risks associated with any potential violence as part of their responsibility to protect building occupants from hazardous conditions. WPV has been the subject of much research, for example, the US Department of Labor (DOL) defines WPV as any act or threat of physical violence, harassment, intimidation or other threatening disruptive behavior that occurs at the work site. Workplace violence ranges from simple threats and verbal abuse to physical assaults and even homicide. It can affect employees, clients, customers or visitors.

According to the Bureau of Labor Statistics Census of Fatal Occupational Injuries (CFOI), of the 4547 fatal workplace injuries that occurred in the United States in 2010, 506 were workplace homicides. Homicide is the leading cause of death for women in the workplace. Whether it is harassment, intimidation or other behavior, WPV is a major concern for employers and employees nationwide (Occupational Safety and Health Administration 2002).

The California Occupational Safety and Health Administration (Cal/OSHA) developed a model used to describe WPV based on the offender's relationship to the victim and the place of employment. This model was amended to create a categorizing system that remains in wide use. Figure 9.6 summarizes this typology.

Facility Managers should be aware of these definitions, particularly WPV Type III.

The National Crime Victimization Survey reports data on workplace violence (Harrell 2011). Government agencies charged with protecting the safety of workers, such as the Department of Justice, Center for Disease Control and the Department of Labor, publish reports periodically, which include recommendations for reducing the occurrence of WPV. A brief analysis of data reporting on workplace violence from 1993–2009, for male and female victims, is depicted in Figures 9.7 and 9.8 (Harrell 2011).

Additional information and data for all four Cal/OSHA Types can be estimated by combining the separated data that fit into the type definition. For example, Type II Customer Client percentages can be approximated by combining the data of customer/client (31 and 42%) and patient (5 and 1%). Considering

Type I Criminal Intent

• The perpetrator has no legitimate relationship to the business or its employee, and is usually committing a crime in conjunction with the violence.

Type II Customer/Client

• The perpetrator has a legitimate relationship with the business and becomes violent while being served by the business.

Type III Worker on Worker

• The perpetrator is an employee or past employee of the business who attacks or threatens another employee, or past employees, in the workplace.

Type IV Personal Relationship

• The perpetrator usually does not have a relationship with the business but has a personal relationship with the intended victim.

Figure 9.6   California Work Place Violence types.

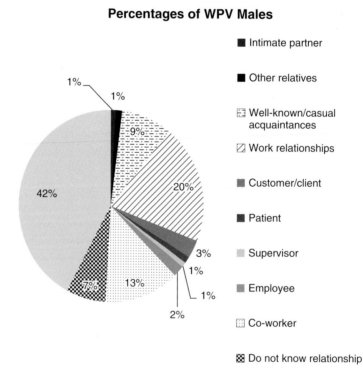

Percentages of WPV Males

- ■ Intimate partner
- ■ Other relatives
- ⊟ Well-known/casual acquaintances
- ▨ Work relationships
- ▩ Customer/client
- ■ Patient
- ▒ Supervisor
- ▦ Employee
- ⊡ Co-worker
- ⊠ Do not know relationship

Figure 9.7   Male victims of workplace violence.

Percentages of WPV Females

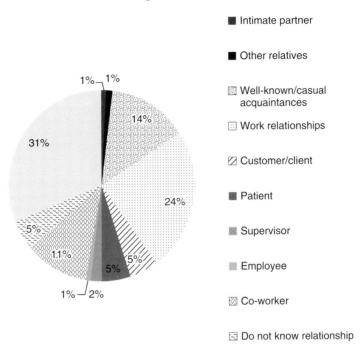

Legend:
- ■ Intimate partner
- ■ Other relatives
- ▨ Well-known/casual acquaintances
- ⬚ Work relationships
- ▨ Customer/client
- ■ Patient
- ▨ Supervisor
- ▨ Employee
- ▨ Co-worker
- ⊟ Do not know relationship

Figure 9.8   Female victims of workplace violence.

both graphs you can see that the highest percentages of violators come from the client or customer categories. The next highest categories are work relationships and acquaintances. It can be concluded that effective training in customer service and relationships with disgruntled customers, along with creating a culture of helpful customer service, has the potential to sizably reduce workplace violence. Since customer service training usually does not fall under the purview of the Facility Manager, what can she do to reduce workplace violence?

Type I WPV is prevalent in certain industries where employees interact with the public and handle cash or other valuables. According to the data, retail industry workers experience higher than average risks. Effective Facility Management strategies include classic environmental interventions, such as controlling indoor and outdoor lighting, controlling entry and exit ways, and installing mirrors and closed-circuit cameras (Hendricks and Landsittel 1999). Developing a culture of safety among employees can also be effective and can be achieved with behavioral interventions. These include training staff to use safety equipment effectively, training staff to deal with aggressive people, having an unidentified intruder protocol to follow and maintaining a good working relationship with police.

Occurrence of Type II workplace violence is reduced when sufficient staffing levels are maintained and the staff have the necessary skills to serve clients competently. Customer violence should be at the top of the list for WPV prevention strategies and this is especially important in the health care industry. Customers with needs of real or imaginary urgency, combined with a history of violence, can place employees at risk. Training specific to Type II violence includes recognition of common behaviors exhibited preceding violence, violence reduction techniques, and other interpersonal and communication skills.

Type III WPV can be mitigated if care is taken at the very beginning during the hiring process. Employers should take the necessary steps to ensure that applicants are thoroughly vetted through background checks and reference verification. Training to tackle worker-on-worker violence prevention involves creating a climate of trust so that unwanted behaviors, such as threatening, harassing, bullying or stalking, are promptly reported. Type III WPV is unique because workers who usually have a great amount of knowledge about their co-workers, physical surroundings and security measures, execute the violent actions. Because of this, observation and reporting of changes in behavior that have the potential to become a problem are critical. Facility Managers may not be able to force employees to report odd behaviors, but they can make it easier for employees to report them by implementing computer-based systems if none exist.

To prevent Type IV violence, similar interventions are necessary to those used for Type III WPV. Maintaining high standards, installing environmental controls and ensuring employees feel safe can make the Facility Manager one of the most valuable assets a company has for WPV prevention (Loomis and Marshall 2002; Workplace Violence Provention Strategies and Research Needs 2004).

9.4 Chapter summary

Facility Managers inevitably encounter situations governed by criminal law and its procedures. Understanding the legal processes and potential risk involved with workplace violence and other crimes helps Facility Managers remain proactive, and to avoid offenders and the criminal system as much as possible.

9.5 Questions

1. Why are the standards for proving a violation of criminal law different from civil law?

2. Give at least two examples of how criminal procedure is different from civil procedure.
3. Is the provision that the accused has a speedy trial necessary? Explain your answer.
4. Using your own words, explain the concept of "beyond a reasonable doubt" and compare it to the "preponderance of evidence" standard.
5. What role does the Facility Manager play in reducing workplace violence?
6. Name at least two potential locations for potential crimes in an office building.
7. Can a Facility Manager have a significant impact on reduction of WPV? Explain your answer.
8. Why is good customer service training important?
9. Give an example of Type II WPV.
10. How does WPV in the USA compare to WPV to other countries?

References

Emerson, R. W. Compensation. In: *Essays: First Series*. Prod. First Series, The Project Gutenberg EBook of Essays. (Emerson 1847), 1847.

Handler, J. G. *Ballentine's Law Dictionary: Legal Assistant Edition*. Albany Delmar, 1994.

Harrell, E. *Workplace Violence, 1993–2009*. March 29, 2011. www.ojp.usdoj.gov (accessed August 6, 2012).

Hendricks, S. A. and D. P. Landsittel. A matched case-control study of convienence store robbery risk factors. *Journal of Occupational and Environmental Medicine*, vol. 41, no. 11 (1999): 995–1004.

Loomis D. and Marshall, S. Effectiveness of safety measures recommeded for provention of workplace homicide. *Journal of the American Medical Association*, vol. 287, no. 8 (2002): 1011–1017.

Tilley, N. *Understanding Car Parks, Crime and CCTV: Evaluation Lessons from Safer Cities*. Paper No. 42, Police Research Group Crime Prevention Unit Series, London: Home Office Police Department, 1993.

Workplace Violence Provention Strategies and Research Needs. *Report from the Conference Partnering in Workplace Violence Prevention: Translating Research to Practice*. Baltimore, 2004.

10

Employment Law

> Normal is getting dressed in clothes that you buy for work and driving through traffic in a car that you are still paying for – in order to get to the job you need to pay for the clothes and the car, and the house you leave vacant all day so you can afford to live in it.
>
> **Ellen Goodman, American journalist (1941–)**

10.1 Introduction

Ellen Goodman's above quote about employment, consumption of goods and the need to consume these goods, as well as remain employed, captures emotions about work and its seemingly senseless never-ending cycle. Regardless of the rationale for working, humans spend a large amount of time in the work environment and the Facility Manager is often responsible for employment law related issues, exposing them to liability that can be avoided with a working knowledge of employment law.

Employment law governs the relationship between employers and their employees. It is derived from statutes, administrative regulations and judicial decisions. Employment law's purpose is to specify the rights and restrictions that apply to employers and employees. It is distinct from labor law. Although both areas of law address work life, labor law covers the relationship between employers and labor organizations.

Employment law in the USA regulates a wide range of issues including employee benefits, discipline, hiring, firing, leave, payroll, health and safety in the workplace, non-compete agreements, retaliation, severance, unemployment compensation, pensions, whistleblower protection, worker classification

Legal Concepts for Facility Managers, First Edition. Linda Thomas-Mobley.
© 2014 John Wiley & Sons, Ltd. Published 2014 by John Wiley & Sons, Ltd.

as independent contractor or employee, wage garnishment, work authorization for non-US citizens, workers' compensation and employee handbooks. Facility Managers are mostly concerned with safety and worker classification. Safety in the workplace covers several areas, such as the workplace violence discussed in Chapter 9, and other duties to keep the property free from dangerous conditions. Worker classification is a narrow but important area, defining an individual as an employee or independent contractor can determine injury liability.

By the end of this chapter the following student learning outcomes are expected.

- Identify areas of the law relevant to employers and employees.
- Explain why employment law is important to Facility Managers.
- Define the attributes of a worker and an independent contractor.
- Identify statutes impacting employment law.

10.2 Employment statutory law overview

The most significant sources of employment law are federal and state statutes. Relevant federal statutes include; Title VII of the Civil Rights Act of 1964, the Age Discrimination in Employment Act of 1967, the Fair Labor Standards Act of 1938, the Employee Retirement Income Security Act of 1974 (ERISA), the Occupational Safety and Health Act of 1970 (OSHA), the Americans with Disabilities Act of 1990 and the Family and Medical Leave Act of 1993 (FMLA). These statutes and additional administrative and common law will be discussed in this chapter and illustrated in the case study section of the book. Figure 10.1 indicates how these statutes relate to Employment Law, while Figure 10.2 outlines the statutes' purposes.

Employment law would not exist without employment. Therefore the first important legal theory to comprehend is the at-will relationship between the majority of employers and employees. At-will employment means that either party can terminate the relationship with no liability if no written contract existed defining the term of employment. Although there are several exceptions to this doctrine, ordinarily employers may freely discharge employees for any legal reason or even with no cause at all, and employees may leave a job for any reason at any time. The exceptions to the doctrine exist to prevent discrimination and are reflected in several employment law statutes.

In the USA, employees have certain rights, including the right not to be discriminated against or harassed because of race, national origin, skin color, gender, pregnancy, religious beliefs, disability or age. In some states, employees are also protected from discrimination on the basis of marital status, sexual orientation, gender identity or other characteristics.

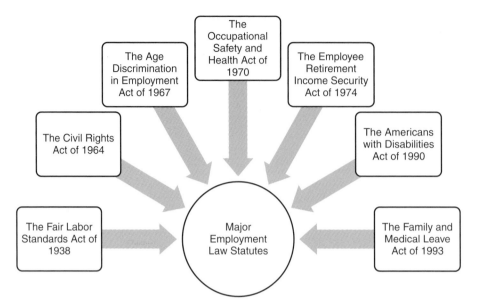

Figure 10.1   Employment rights statutes.

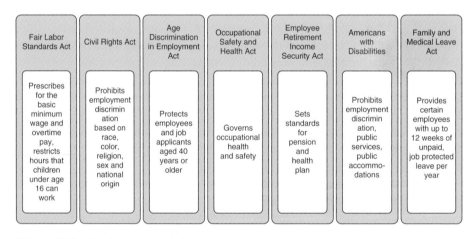

Fair Labor Standards Act	Civil Rights Act	Age Discrimination in Employment Act	Occupational Safety and Health Act	Employee Retirement Income Security Act	Americans with Disabilities	Family and Medical Leave Act
Prescribes for the basic minimum wage and overtime pay, restricts hours that children under age 16 can work	Prohibits employment discrimination based on race, color, religion, sex and national origin	Protects employees and job applicants aged 40 years or older	Governs occupational health and safety	Sets standards for pension and health plan	Prohibits employment discrimination, public services, public accommodations	Provides certain employees with up to 12 weeks of unpaid, job protected leave per year

Figure 10.2   Employment statute purposes.

Contrary to the relative flexibility provided under at-will employment, the wage an employee is paid is strictly regulated by local, state and/or federal government. Employees have the right to what government determines as "fair pay". Employees must be paid the minimum wage, as well as any overtime pay for any hours worked over 40 in one week; in some states, overtime pay is earned for hours over eight hours in one day. Federal law establishes the minimum amount that a worker can be paid per hour; currently it is $7.25 per hour. Most states and some municipalities have enacted their own minimum wage laws. For example in 2012, California's minimum wage was $8.00 per hour. Where an employee is subject to both state and federal minimum wage laws, the employer must pay the higher of the two minimum wages. This requirement is an example of the pre-emptive doctrine we've seen in Environmental Law in operation.

The Fair Labor Standards Act of 1932 was amended in 2004 and now requires all positions to be paid overtime for all hours actually worked over 40 in a week, unless those jobs meet specific requirements. Those meeting specific requirements are labeled "exempt". The test for exemption has evolved over time and now includes new job categories such as computer workers and other work not contemplated by the 1938 law. This new test continues to exempt certain classes of employees from both minimum wage and overtime pay laws. Rationale for the exemption stems from the hazardous conditions and high productivity requirements for workers at the time of the original act. Many critics of this law think this statute should be overhauled completely in light of the changing circumstances of the US laborer (Tebbe 2000).

Full time employees are often provided with a variety of benefits. A few are required under the law; however, employers decide to provide the majority of the benefits. For example, employees may be provided time off because of a family member's illness, birth or adoption. The Family Medical Leave Act of 1993 (FMLA) gives workers, who are employed in a company of 50 or more persons, a total of 12 work weeks of unpaid leave during any 12-month period for the birth and care of an employee's child; for adoption of a child; to care for an immediate family member with a serious health condition; or to take medical leave when the employee is unable to work because of a serious health condition.

As we have seen in past chapters, other employee/employer regulators like the Occupational Safety and Health Administration (OSHA), issue and enforce rules to prevent work-related injuries, illnesses and deaths. OSHA's standards apply to most private or nongovernmental workplaces. Other protections under employment law include legal restrictions on drug testing, medical screenings and lie detector tests. The Federal Employee Polygraph Protection Act (29 U.S.C. § 2001) prohibits most private employers from requiring employees to take lie detector tests and many states also ban this practice.

With any discussion on employment law, the subject of undocumented workers arises, especially in the built environment. Many reputable contractors providing services to the commercial and industrial sector utilize precautionary measures to ensure the individuals in their employ have proper documentation to work and pay taxes in the USA. In other words, their employees are "legal".

Unfortunately, some contractors, especially in the janitorial industry, do not take these precautionary measures. Those who do not follow current labor laws create an uneven playing field, putting themselves and the Facility Manager risk for heavy penalties.

Using cheaper labor, paying less than the minimum wage to earn higher profits is the main motive for not making sure all employees are legally able to work in the USA. The illegal workers usually receive a wage that is below market and they might even be paid in cash to avoid the contractor's contribution to taxes and unemployment insurance. Additionally, sometimes contractors hire a person with a valid Social Security Number and instead of treating them as a regular employee, they might treat her as a sub-contractor, allowing the company to under report for Worker's Compensation purposes. Some estimates report that these practices allow for a cost reduction of up to 30%.

The practice of using illegal labor can be widespread in some areas. Many Facility Managers are tempted to hire these contractors who are using illegal labor because of the low price offered. Since the janitorial industry is a highly competitive, low profit margin field, contractors are usually only differentiated from the competition by the quality of their cleaning and their customer service. Because of this, usually there are not large disparities in the overall costs to clean a building. If a Facility Manager notices a bid that is 30% lower than market rates, caution should be taken. This is because if a contractor is determined to be using illegal labor, the Facility Manager and building owner may also be held responsible. There are instances where the building owner is found guilty and required to spend time in jail along with other penalties. Furthermore, the Internal Revenue Service (IRS) will file for unpaid tax claims against the building owner for all the unpaid taxes on the difference between the amounts that should have been paid to legal workers.

Finally, several contractors utilizing illegal labor do not purchase Workers' Compensation Insurance. If someone gets injured and goes to the hospital, individuals without a valid social security number will be reported to the Immigration and Customs Enforcement division of the US Homeland Security Department. Facility Managers should protect themselves by requiring all contractors to regularly provide proof of legal work status for all those working in your building and a valid Workers' Compensation policy.

10.3 Independent contractors

As has been previously mentioned in earlier chapters, classifying an individual as an employee or an independent contractor is often confusing for Facility Managers. Coupled with the fact that by properly classifying a party as an independent contractor certain unwanted risks can be avoided but the pressure to make the correct determination is pronounced. Figures 10.3 and 10.4 illustrate some of the major distinguishing factors between employees and independent contractors.

Independent Contractor	Employee
• Worker supplies his or her own equipment, materials and tools • Worker can be discharged at anytime • Worker can choose whether or not to come to work without fear of losing employment • Worker controls the hours of employment • Work is temporary in nature	• Work is considered integral to the business • Worker gains a large portion of their salary from the job • Worker has lower degree of control over their work

Figure 10.3   Characteristics of an employee and an independent contractor.

Advantages	Disadvantages
• Save money, overhead can increase payroll costs by 20–30% or more • More flexibility in staffing projects, greater leeway in hiring and letting go of workers • Greater efficiency, more specialized expertise • Reduce exposure to employment lawsuits, no protection from statutes requiring minimum wage; overtime; antidiscrimination on the basis of race, national origin, color, religion, gender; right to form a union, right to take time off to care for sick family members; right to sue employer for wrongful termination (varies from state to state) • Ability to transfer risk of poor performance	• Less control over workers • Constant turnover of workers • The right to fire depends on the written agreement • May be liable for injuries you cause, not usually covered by covered by Workers' Compensation Insurance • May not own copyright in works created • Risk of government audits. State and federal agencies tend to be suspect of too many independent contractors

Figure 10.4   Advantages and disadvantages of independent contractor.

Recall the doctrine of vicarious liability from the tort law chapter (Chapter 7), employers are liable for the actions of their employees within the scope of employment, regardless of whether the employee acts negligently or intentionally. An employee acts within the scope of her employment if she is engaged in the employer's business at the time of an injury. However, just because an employee is at work during working hours, it does not mean that every act completed during this time is done within the scope of employment. If she is engaged in personal business, her actions are not considered within the scope of employment. The issue is whether the employee's actions were serving the employer. For example, an employee may be in an extremely bad mood and behaves in a rude manner toward a customer because of personal problems. Her discourteous actions toward the customer would be considered her own conduct and not within the scope of her employment. Even though a rude employee would not have to defend herself in a lawsuit for being rude, if a customer is assaulted as a result of the rude behavior during the employee's performance of her duties, the employer may be responsible and even held liable. This can be the case even if the employee's actions are intentional and she displays a personal dislike for the customer. Generalization about this type of liability is problematic because the decision to hold the employer liable in cases like this depends heavily on the particular facts of the case. Providing regular training in customer relations and rewarding employees praised by customers would help encourage a culture of customer service and minimize potential problems of this sort.

With a seemingly unfair amount of responsibility for employee actions resting on employers, hiring independent contractors would appear to be an excellent technique to shift risk. Although this is usually true, there are some statutory exceptions. For example, the duty to inspect property to make it safe for others cannot be delegated to an independent contractor. This means the duty every property owner holds for providing a safe premises cannot be completely shifted to an independent contractor, even if the contractor is hired to make the property safe. The owner retains liability for injuries. Additionally, owners are also liable for the actions of security services hired to patrol the premises, even if the service operates as an independent contractor.

Other common exceptions are listed in Figure 10.5.

The strategy of hiring independent contractors to perform work has additional ramifications. Employers do not have to pay benefits for independent contractors. This, along with the potential to shift the risk of cost and performance errors, makes an independent contractor an attractive option for employers seeking to lower costs. However, legal issues can arise if this strategy is

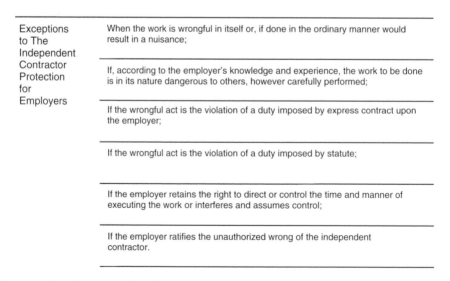

Exceptions to The Independent Contractor Protection for Employers	When the work is wrongful in itself or, if done in the ordinary manner would result in a nuisance;
	If, according to the employer's knowledge and experience, the work to be done is in its nature dangerous to others, however carefully performed;
	If the wrongful act is the violation of a duty imposed by express contract upon the employer;
	If the wrongful act is the violation of a duty imposed by statute;
	If the employer retains the right to direct or control the time and manner of executing the work or interferes and assumes control;
	If the employer ratifies the unauthorized wrong of the independent contractor.

Figure 10.5   Transfer of liability exceptions.

misused and employees are wrongly classified as independent contractors (US Department of Labor 2011). According to the US Department of Labor, mis-classification presents a serious problem for the entire economy. Operating as an independent contractor, a misclassified employee would be denied access to critical benefits and protections to which they are entitled, including family and medical leave, overtime, minimum wage and unemployment insurance. Misclassification also generates financial losses to the Treasury and the Social Security and Medicare funds, as well as to state unemployment insurance and workers' compensation funds (US Department of Labor 2011).

In an effort to remedy this situation, the Department of Labor launched a misclassification initiative, working with the United States Vice President and the Internal Revenue Service (IRS) to reduce the number of misclassified employees. If a worker or employer is unable to determine the correct status of the worker, they can request a determination from the IRS using a form entitled "Determination of Worker Status for Purposes of Federal Employment Taxes and Income Tax Withholding". The form may be filed by either the business or the worker, and sent to the IRS to review the circumstances and officially determine the worker's status.

10.4 Labor law

Labor law is distinct from employment law in that it focuses on the relationship between company management and labor unions. This area of law has a long and storied history, with the pendulum of public favor swinging back and forth for and against labor unions. Labor statutes date back to the 1930s and have evolved through time.

10.4.1 History of labor law

Prior to the late nineteenth century, the rights of working people to associate together for their mutual aid and protection were severely restricted. Until the 1890s the courts, with common law decisions, created labor relationships and unions were thought by the government to be unlawful conspiracies. The concept of legislating the relationship between industry and its workers was considered foreign. Historically, courts sided with employers and refused to assist unions against employers since no legal precedent had been set. Court injunctions were widely used to deny the traditional worker's weapons such as labor strikes, employee picketing and organized boycotts. An injunction is a remedy requested by a party asking the court to issue an order that requires a third party to refrain from doing particular actions. For example, an injunction was often requested by the management of a company to issue a court order requiring striking workers to stop their protests and go back to work. If employees refused, they would face criminal or civil penalties and may have to pay fines or accept sanctions. Failing to comply with a court injunction can be considered a serious criminal offense that merits arrest and a potential prison sentence.

The Sherman Anti-Trust Act of 1890, now officially called the Sherman Act, emerged as a way to balance management excesses (Sherman Act, [1] July 2, 1890, ch. 647, 26 Stat. 209, 15 U.S.C. §§ 1–7). This legislation provided the beginnings of a statutory basis for labor-management policy. It is a landmark federal statute aimed to limit the growth of business cartels by prohibiting certain activities that reduce competition in the marketplace. Today the act forms the basis for most antitrust litigation by the federal government. Landmark legislation and case law are new regulations that fundamentally change the way society operates with respect to groundbreaking issues.

Operation of the law in this arena continued to discriminate against labor unions until the New Deal Legislation of the early 1930s. The New Deal was a series of economic programs enacted in the United States between 1933 and 1936 that included presidential executive orders and laws passed by Congress in response to the hardships caused by the Great Depression. The aims were relief for the unemployed and poverty stricken, economic recovery for the country and financial reform to prevent the recurrence of economic depression. Today, the right of workers to form or join unions and to take action to improve their economic condition is guaranteed and several statutes that were passed subsequently protect the exercise of that right.

10.4.2 National Labor Policy

Current US labor law is controlled by the Norris–Laguardia Act of 1932, the National Labor Relations Act of 1935, the Labor Management Relations Act of 1947 (also known as the Taft–Hartley Act) and the Labor-Management Reporting and Disclosure Act of 1959. A brief explanation of these laws is given next.

The Norris–Laguardia Act is an anti-injunction act passed to limit the power of federal courts to issue injunctions against union activities in labor disputes, and to protect workers' rights to strike and peaceably picket their worksite. This was the first tool labor unions were given to stop injunctions. The National Labor Relations Act, also known as the Wagner Act, was passed as a reaction to extensive unemployment and to protect union-organizing activity. The government hoped this act would foster collective bargaining, requiring employers to bargain in good faith with the chosen representatives of the workers. Collective bargaining refers to the activity where employees collectively negotiate working conditions with their employer. The act tilted the power away from management toward unions, resulting in the power and success of labor unions increasing from the 1990s until the 1950s. In response to the growth of unions and a disproportionate number strikes, the Labor Management Relations Act of 1947 was passed. This was the first federal statute imposing comprehensive controls over the activities of organized labor. It was seen as a means of lessening the dominance of the labor movement by imposing limits on the unions' ability to call a strike (Smith 2006) and for the first time the rights of individual workers were protected. They could participate freely in union activities, but also had the freedom to refrain from participating without fear of retaliation.

The Labor Management Reporting and Disclosure Act of 1959 (LMRDA), also known as the Landrum–Griffin Act, was passed to establish a code of conduct for unions, employers and consultants, as well as to protect the rights of individual union members. Today LMRDA is administered and enforced by the Department of Labor's Office of Labor-Management Standards (OLMS). It ensures basic standards of independence and fiscal responsibility for labor organizations representing employees in private industry. Major provisions of LMRDA are:

- A "bill of rights" for union members.
- Requirements for reporting and disclosure of financial information and administrative practices by labor unions.
- Requirements for reporting and disclosure by employers, labor relations consultants, union officers and employees, and surety companies, when they engage in certain activities.
- Rules for establishing and maintaining trusteeships.
- Standards for conducting fair elections of union officers.
- Safeguards for protecting union funds and assets.

Other significant statutes and regulations affecting workers are outlined in Figure 10.6.

Today, labor unions generally represent workers in many companies in the USA. Their activities focus on collective bargaining over wages, benefits and working conditions for their members. Labor unions also represent their members in disputes with management over violations of contract provisions and many engage in lobbying activities at the state and federal levels. Figure 10.7 depicts the types of provisions included in a typical labor agreement.

Facility Managers in organizations with unionized workers may be called upon to represent management in labor negotiations. Working with labor unions requires specific expertise. Typically, usually a company employs the services of a labor lawyer or other expert to help company management navigate the sometimes delicate negotiations. Advice on negotiating labor agreements is beyond the scope of this text and will most likely to be covered in a management course. For our purposes, the Facility Manager should understand the major labor statutes and know that labor relations requires special expertise in union relationships.

The Civil Rights Act	• Gives basic individual rights and opportunities for employment
Executive Order 11246	• Contractors on federal construction projects are prohibited from discriminating
Age Discrimination In Employment Act	• Protects individuals 40 years of age older from age discrimination
Davis–Bacon Act	• Determines the wage rates that must be paid workers on all federal construction projects
Fair Labor Standards Act	• Wage and hour law
The Hobbs Act	• Ended to the use of threats of force or violence by union officials to obtain payment
Immigration Reform and Control Act	• Crime for employers who hire workers not authorized to work in the USA
The Drug-Free Workplace Act	• Requires that federal government contractors must maintain a drug-free workplace
The Americans With Disabilities Act	• Civil rights protections to the disabled

Figure 10.6   Significant employee statutes.

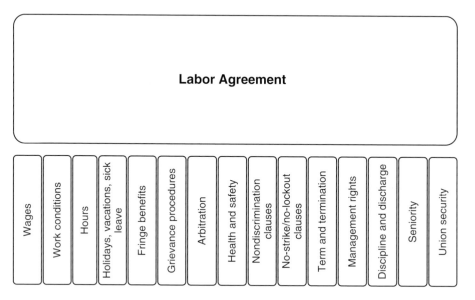

Figure 10.7   Typical labor agreement provisions.

Most unions in the USA are aligned with one of two larger umbrella organizations: the American Federation of Labor and Congress of Industrial Organization (AFL-CIO) created in 1955; and the Change to Win Federation, which split from the AFL-CIO in 2005.

The excesses of unions were of greater concern when the USA employed large numbers of manufacturing workers. Manufacturing has declined in the

USA. The important question is not, "what is the current state of US manu-facturing?" but "is the current situation temporary or part of a larger cycle?" Although the percentage of union work is dwindling in the USA, understanding employment law from the union and non-union perspectives is important because there are some pockets where unions remain dominant, and the knowledge of collective bargaining is still very necessary. If a strategic plan to embrace globalization requires a US company to expand to Sweden for example, understanding the union climate will be necessary.

10.5 Chapter summary

One of the largest operating costs in business is the expense of labor. Finding and keeping good employees can be the difference between profit or loss for a small company. Employment law regulates several issues of great importance to business and, therefore, to the Facility Manager. These include everything from employee benefits to worker's compensation.

In the USA, unions remain an important political consideration for companies. It is important for the Facility Manager to understand why they exist and how they impact business. A general understanding of how the law interacts with workers' rights is valuable.

10.6 Questions

1. What is the source of the major employment law in the USA?
2. What conclusions, if any, can you draw from the dates of the major employment law statutes? Do these dates roughly correspond to any other dates in US history?
3. Is there a limit an employer is required to pay for disability accommodations?
4. Is the operation of the law, with respect to the doctrine of vicarious liability, fair? Explain your answer.
5. Would you prefer to work as a Facility Manager in a "union shop"? Explain your answer.
6. Would you prefer to work as a laborer in a "union shop"? Explain your answer.
7. When is it advantageous to hire an independent contractor to complete work instead of using in-house labor?
8. What can the Facility Manager do to maintain the proper relationship with an independent contractor?

9. In your own words, what are the general aims of federal labor law?
10. Is the understanding of collective bargaining negotiations necessary for a Facility Manager? Explain your answer.

References

Smith, S. *Subterranean Fire: A History of Working-Class Radicalism in the United States*. Haymarket Books, 2006.

US Department of Labor. *Employee Misclassification as Independent Contractors*. 2011. www.dol.gov/whd/workers/misclassification (accessed January 19, 2013).

11

Emerging Legal Issues

Information is not knowledge. . . The only source of knowledge is experience.
Albert Einstein

11.1 Introduction

Einstein's quote is used here as a reminder that, although you have made it through 10 chapters about the law and the US legal system, we've only begun to scratch the surface. This chapter is indented to serve as a bridge between basic legal theory and the actual practice of law. Prior to the discussion on how the law is applied in typical facility management applications, a few loose ends need to be tied up.

This chapter is the last chapter in Part I. Part I was written to give the student a solid foundation in the US legal system and basic areas of law. A typical student studying the law in the USA would spend a full 17-week semester on contract law, property law, torts, civil procedure and others. The typical method of learning about these areas of the law includes reading several appellate cases, distilling procedural and substantive summaries called briefs, and then being questioned by law professors who use the Socratic Method to help the student learn the law and legal reasoning. One part of a generalized law text that summarizes the major areas with brief explanations and example cases will not make a lawyer out of the reader, but of course, that is not the purpose of this text, or a course in law for Facility Managers. If everyone interested in the law became a lawyer, society would cease to function. It is hoped that the student will understand the basic operation of the courts, the various sources of law and how this law is applied to common fact situations.

Legal Concepts for Facility Managers, First Edition. Linda Thomas-Mobley.
© 2014 John Wiley & Sons, Ltd. Published 2014 by John Wiley & Sons, Ltd.

Without the luxury of having three years of semester-long courses with plenty of practice reading case after case, the student should not worry that they are not legal research experts. With careful reading and class discussions the student who finishes Part I will be able to establish a good foundational comprehension of the legal system and how laws impact the practice of Facility Management.

This chapter is reserved for various legal concepts that did not fit well in the previous chapters. Understanding these concepts will assist the student in gaining a full appreciation of how the law operates for Facility Managers. When appropriate, examples of the concepts will be given in this chapter. Additionally, more detailed examples will be given in the last part of this text where the laws and legal concepts learned are specifically applied to the facility management profession.

The student learning outcomes for this chapter will allow the following:

- Understand Environmental Justice Issues.
- Understand how the Facility Manager interacts with the Construction Manager.
- Understand the various definitions of Construction Management.
- Explain a Project Delivery System.
- Define the term *surety*.
- Understand the impact of the Federal Rules of Evidence on Facility Management.

11.2 Environmental justice

At the crossroads of Environmental Law and Civil Rights Law is a small, very specialized legal concept that is relatively recent. This concept, known as Environmental Justice, is concerned with discrimination against protected citizen groups, and prevention of industrial plants and public roadways from ruining existing neighborhoods in the name of progress. Many in the built environment industry assume most environmental justice issues are associated with transportation or industrial pollution, but that is not necessarily the case. This brief historical background is intended to give the Facility Manager a basic understanding of this important area.

Environmental justice concerns developed as a result of the public's overexposure to hazardous waste facilities. Certain groups had more exposure than others so much so that there seemed to be a direct link between exposure and socioeconomic status. Consequences of this unequal overexposure generated debate and a strong interest in the research communities concerning environmental quality, and its relationship to race and socioeconomic status. The US General Accountability Office (GAO) commissioned studies of inhabited areas with hazardous waste sites, and found that three out of four impacted communities were African-American and all were disproportionately poor (Rodgers 2012). In 1987, other study experts examined the presence of toxins associated with hazardous waste sites and residential areas. In the research, race was the most significant variable associated with proximity to commercial hazardous waste facilities. This report also indicated that the income status of residents in close proximity to hazardous waste sites was substantially lower than the norm in that area. It has been suggested that racism plays a role in determining the location of waste sites (Rodgers 2012).

A competing theory on placement of hazardous waste sites contends that industry has simply followed the path of least resistance. Industries that produce toxic waste as a normal part of their operations choose to locate in economically poor and politically powerless African-American communities because of the lack of resistance (Rodgers 2012). These studies, and others like them, pressured federal agencies to pay attention to placement of hazardous waste sites and environmental justice law. In 1990, the EPA first publicly recognized that "environmental hazards disproportionately impact people of color" (Rodgers 2012). This research reported the likelihood of a resident being a person of color or poor increased, the closer their home was to a hazardous facility (Rodgers 2012).

While the research conclusions reported seem in favor of the race-proximity argument, many suggest that the relationship is not as clear as it seems. A variety of data problems – such as the type of waste facility, level of aggregation of the census data and the actual threat of the source facility – have limited additional research.

Environmental justice began as a movement to call attention to discrimination. By aligning social justice with popular environmental causes, and by highlighting the ethical concerns regarding civil rights of all citizens, environmental justice has become an important policy issue (Rodgers 2012).

11.3 The Construction Manager

Understanding the law and how the job of the Facility Manager intersects is one of many tools in the successful professional's toolkit. As the job of the Facility Manager is varied, sometimes the project manager function rises to the level of construction management. As has been discussed earlier, the use of contracting as a risk-shifting device is a common strategy. In addition to risk aversion, the Facility Manager usually outsources specific expertise not available in-house. Typical outsourcing contracts employed by the Facility Manager include janitorial, preventive and on-going maintenance, information technology services, and on occasion, design and construction services, among others. Even though the Facility Manager often performs project management services on small construction tasks, when the project reaches a level of complexity becoming more and more common in the twenty-first century, construction management outsourcing should be considered. Construction management services are an area of expertise growing in popularity, especially during times of major facility rehabilitation or facility acquisition.

Construction management (CM) is a confusing term because the same term refers to a job title, a series of activities and a project delivery system. Discussion is made about the Construction Management At-Risk project delivery system in this book's section on procurement of construction services, and the job of the Construction Manager is beyond the scope of this book, but the third use of the term is important to note here. The services provided by a contracted Construction Manager are required in any major facility remodel or new construction and these tasks often fall on the Facility Manager, who may not necessarily be the most efficient provider of these services.

The outsourced Construction Manager is referred to in the trade as the Agent Construction Manager. It is sometimes erroneously considered a project delivery system, but the services of a professional Construction Manager may be applied to all project delivery systems. Hiring a CM as your agent is similar to hiring an architect to provide design services, both relationships assume expert advice will be given as a component of the service contracted for. Utilizing the CM as a representative in an agency relationship affords the Facility Manager a higher degree of loyalty because hired agents have a duty to act in the Facility Manager's best interests, not their own.

An agent is a legal extension of the Facility Manager when a Principal–Agent agreement is made. The Facility Manager as Principal expands her span of control to include all activities performed by the Agent. By definition, the Agent has a fiduciary duty to supplant his own interest and serve the Principal's interest first because the nature of the relationship allows Agents to act for their Principal, including entering contracts and other obligations on the Principal's behalf.

In the arrangement of Agent Construction Management, the Facility Manager has essentially hired an expert on controlling the specific type of project being contemplated. This shifts the risk of understanding all of the intricacies involved in proper design management, planning, estimating, scheduling and managing a new project under the responsibility of the Facility Manager. This arrangement will add to the cost of the overall project, so it is best reserved for projects with higher risks for time, cost or quality failure.

The Construction Management Association of America (CMAA) is the professional association that has emerged to advocate for the use of professional construction managers in the USA. The CMAA was formed by construction industry professionals in response to the built environment industry's need to respond to dissatisfied owners. As buildings become more sophisticated and owners require projects to be completed earlier while controlling cost and maintaining quality, the traditional triad of owner-designer-constructor is inadequate. A standardized definition of Construction Management Services, along with a code of ethics and qualification standards, was formed and has been growing in size since the 1960s. Today, this organization certifies managers holding themselves out to be professional CMs by awarding the Certified Construction Manager (CCM) designation upon completion of the certification process.

As an agent solely beholden to the owner, contract arrangements and, therefore, fees for a certified construction manager, are separate from the construction cost. These fees are negotiated based on request of qualifications that help the Facility Manager to select a short list of CCMs qualified in the specific area of the specific project the Facility Manager is tasked with managing. The CCM does not actually perform the work but as a construction expert, she advises the owner on design strategies, project delivery system choice, cost control, schedule control, quality assurance and other forms of expertise not often found with an in-house Facility Manager.

The rise of the CCM's involvement in major construction or rehabilitation projects translates to instances where Facility Managers will be working more often with Construction Managers than in the past. Understanding what services are offered, what types of standard form contracts CMAA have drafted and what to expect from a good FM-CCM working relationship, will be required for the successful facility management professional.

11.4 Project delivery systems

To procure construction services, in most situations the Facility Manager will follow the path most used by what the industry calls the "owner". The owner is loosely defined as the party responsible for paying for the building.

When contemplating procurement of construction services, the most common method is via solicitation of bids. For example, when there is a need for building repair and remodeling, the Facility Manager is typically accustomed in receiving three quotations for executing the work from three experts promising to complete the work outlined in the request for bids. The Facility Manager should be careful in deciding to solicit bids and communicating the scope to potential builders. To assist the novice Facility Manager, architects and construction managers offer assistance in the form of servicing as the Facility Manager's agent in procurement of construction services. This structure adds extra costs to the total construction, but whatever means the Facility Manager chooses to procure construction, the resulting structure is what is known in the industry as the construction *project delivery system* (PDS).

Traditionally, any major modification or construction of a new building required the Facility Manager to contract with a designer for plans and specifications, which would be used in soliciting bids from builders who would take the plans and specifications, develop a cost and time schedule to be the basis of the price eventually given as the formal bid. Using an internal strategy, the Facility Manager would then choose the desired builder from amongst the bids who would then complete the project. Additional services, such as contract administration, could be requested from the architect to help guide the Facility Manager during the implementation process.

Because of the increasing complexity of building modifications or new construction, cost and scope escalation becoming more common than not, the adversarial relationship between designers and builders, and increasing litigiousness of the industry, better systems for procurement of buildings are required. Industry experts have analyzed various paths a Facility Manager can take from idea to design to construction and researchers, resulting in several project delivery systems.

A PDS defined as the process an owner takes to deliver design and construction services. A complete project delivery system contains four components: agreement type, pricing structure, a relationship scheme and a selection strategy.

11.4.1 Agreement type

An agreement type or contract is a promise that the law will enforce. In practice, parties have the choice of drafting a contract, using an industry standard contract or a hybrid solution where a standard form is modified with additional language drafted by the parties. The common standardized agreements include standard contracts drafted by the American Institute of Architects, the Construction Manager Association of America, the Associated General Contractors, the Design Build Institute of America and others. The selection of agreement type and the decision to modify it depends on the desires and goals of the parties, and is a major component of the final project delivery system.

11.4.2 Pricing structure

Typical pricing structures include lump sum, unit price, cost plus a fee, time and material or target price. Lump sum, unit price and target price are fixed amounts requiring a change in contract if the amount is changed. These arrangements shift the risk of cost over runs from the Facility Manager to the builder. The lump sum and unit price are amounts determined by the builder and included in a proposal to perform the work. The target price is a recent classification of fixed price that is determined by the owner, it refers to an allowance that reflects the maximum price the owner wishes the builder not to exceed.

Cost plus a fee and time and material require the Facility Manager to reimburse the builder for the cost of materials labor and equipment, and pay a predefined fee for services; either fixed or some percentage of the total cost of the project. This structure shifts the risk of cost from the builder to the Facility Manager. Other pricing structures referred to by different terms fall in either a pre-agreed upon price, a reimbursement arrangement or some combination of the two.

11.4.3 Relationship scheme

The relationship scheme is closely related to the contract type and represents the decision made by the Facility Manager of how the owner, designer, builder and consultants will be contractually related. In the traditional design bid build method, the owner contracts with the architect and then separately contracts with a builder for implementation of the design. Another relationship scheme includes the owner contracting with one entity that performs both design and implementation. Only the number of participants in the process limits additional combinations and choices.

11.4.4 Selection strategy

Selection strategy refers to the method the Facility Manager will use to select from among the proposals. Strategies include lowest cost, highest level of expertise, lowest cost amongst the proposers with the highest expertise, highest score based on internally determined attributes and others. Figure 11.1 illustrates how all of the elements combined constitute a complete PDS.

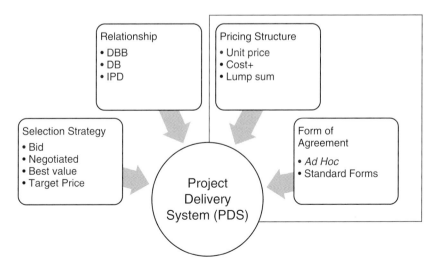

Figure 11.1   Elements of project delivery system.

11.5 Surety bonds

As an added protection in the built environment, requiring guarantees for performance or other obligations can be obtained using a form of guarantee called *surety bonds*. There are three basic types of surety bonds typically encountered in built environment arrangements. *Bid* bonds, *Performance* bonds and *Payment* bonds. Bid bonds give the Facility Manager a guarantee that the builder responding to the bid will enter into a contract and perform the work if chosen. This helps the Facility Manager because only builders with reputable companies and a history of successful projects are able to obtain bonding. If there was some problem in the chosen bidder entering into a contract, the Facility Manager would be compensated through the payment of a penalty or specific performance. Recall from the contracts chapter that specific performance means the actual performance of the original contract.

Performance bonds, required under some public works construction projects, require the bonded party to perform the tasks agreed upon, or the surety will pay a penalty or cause the job to be completed in some other way.

Payment bonds are for the protection of the suppliers and subcontractors. They ensure that the builder actually performing the work will get paid. This is crucial, otherwise a mechanics lien may be placed on a property where the subcontractor was not paid for work completed. With a lien on the property it is likely that the Facility Manager may have to pay the subcontractors directly.

To continue with the discussion of PDSs, if the Facility Manager understands that a complete PDS must contain the four components of an agreement structure, relationship, pricing structure and selection strategy, then any PDS can be analyzed for use in a given situation.

Currently the most common PDSs are Design Bid Build or the traditional method, Design/Build, Construction Manager At Risk, and Integrated Project Delivery Systems.

11.6 Design bid build

Design Bid Build (DBB) can be combined with fixed price or cost reimbursable pricing structures and most standard forms to deliver a specific project. To choose among the bidders, the selection strategy can either be low bidder, negotiated bidder or a strategy that includes only considering prices of a selected few qualified contractors, called *Best Value*. For example, the DBB relationship can be executed with the American Institute of Architects (AIA) standard contract between an architect and an owner, and this is used during the design phase. Selection of the architect will most likely be via qualifications alone or the best value of the qualified designers for the purpose of gathering the owner's needs, and designing a project that meets these needs and falls within a targeted budget. Once the construction documents are 100% complete, they are then used as a basis for soliciting bids. The owner can use the low bid selection strategy to select the lowest bidder to perform the work.

Assuming the design is actually 100% complete and any conflicts can be worked out prior to the beginning of construction or during construction, then an owner should have the desired facility constructed with the lowest cost.

As an alternative, the owner could use a different standard form and the Best Value selection strategy, and use proposals to construct a short-list of qualified constructors from which to choose the lowest bidder. The short-list of qualified constructors in the Best Value strategy is based on factors such as past experience with successfully building a similar size and type of project. Finally, the negotiated selection strategy for a contractor can be used if the owner is satisfied with the quality of the potential builder, and the parties meet and come to a common agreement on the price, time and quality of the final building.

11.7 Design/build

The Design/Build (DB) relationship is characterized by the owner having only one contract with the entity that will both design and build the project. This entity may be a designer who has hired a construction firm to manage the building portion internally. It can be a construction firm that acquires or joint-ventures with a design firm for the same purpose. Finally the DB may be an actual firm started for the purpose of working with owners who want to contract with one firm from the design through the end of the construction phase. Just like the DBB relationship, selection of a contract form can be from among standardized contracts such as the AIA ones, or an *ad hoc* contract. Selection strategies may also be chosen from low bid, negotiated or best value.

11.8 Construction Manager at risk

The Construction Manager at risk relationship structure is executed in two phases. In the first phase, called *pre construction*, the owner hires a construction manager who acts as an agent for the owner in all areas of the project. During the design phase the CM can help the owner decide among the various choices proposed during the design. In addition, the CM can conduct constructability analyses to correct inefficiencies during the design phase, which is a much easier and cheaper phase in which to make corrections. When the design is almost complete, the CM agent calculates a cost to build the project based on what is known about the project and the owner's needs. This price is often called the *guaranteed maximum price* and if accepted, binds the CM to construct the design for the GMP amount. Also, once accepted the CM agent/owner relationship changes from an agent/principal relationship to an owner/contractor relationship. The CM no longer owes a fiduciary duty to the owner as she did during the pre-construction phase. This change of relationship shifts the risk of completion within the budget to the CM who is now acting as a contractor. This second phase of the relationship is similar to the DBB relationship.

11.9 Construction Manager, agent

The Construction Manager, agent is often referred to as a project delivery system but in actuality the CM can be hired to assist the owner with any relationship, pricing structure, selection strategy or contract form.

11.10 Integrated Project Delivery

The Integrated Project Delivery System (IPD) is the most recent evolution of construction procurement methods. IPD's full definition and operation is yet to be fixed in the industry but, as the name implies, the purpose is to integrate the stakeholders in hopes of a cheaper, smoother, timely project result with high quality. This discussion is limited to the IPD as the American Institute of Architects defines it, without any doubt that there will be more refinement of the IPD in the future.

According to the AIA there are three levels of the IPD system, each level becoming progressively more integrated than the last. The three levels are the Transition Form, Multi-Party Agreement Form and the Single Purpose Entity Form.

The Transition Form was developed for stakeholders desiring greater integration without changing the traditional relationship of a contract between the owner and the designer, and a separate contract between the owner and constructor. What makes this level unique is the fact that both sets of agreements are linked to a new general conditions section by reference. This new general conditions document has been written to maximize integration by defining the obligations of the owner, designer, constructor and any consultants used on the project. Having the luxury of using the same general conditions tied to all contractual relationships used in a project reduces conflicts in contract forms, terms and stakeholders' expectations. Additionally the general conditions document requires the parties use Building Information Management to the fullest extent practicable, in furtherance of integration.

General conditions, also called the "boiler plate", outline the roles and responsibilities of the Facility Manager as owner, service provider and any design or specialty consultant used during the process. Having a standard set of rules, notice procedures and terminology allows contractors to feel comfortable working for new Facility Managers, since the basic obligations are already known prior to the work being completed.

In addition to the general conditions document, projects also have special conditions. These are very specific terms that tend to only apply to the project at hand regulating the specific idiosyncrasies that must be considered when performing the work. These terms change for each project. The agreement document that is part of the contract is a simple agreement stipulating the parties to the agreement, contact information and usually the cost for the completed project.

The Multi-Party Agreement form requires additional commitment from the stakeholders for integration. This level is characterized by a three-party agreement signed by the owner, designer and constructor, incorporating the integrated general conditions. As one would imagine, this multi-party agreement forces a closer relationship among the three main parties in an effort to generate mutual cooperation. Consultants and subcontractors are not party to the original agreement contracting directly with the designer or constructor.

The single purpose entity is the level of highest commitment for integration of the parties. As the name implies, the major stakeholders form a legal entity in the form of a limited liability company with the project being its sole purpose. Agreements for design are made between the single purpose entity (SPE) and the designer, who also happens to be a member of the SPE. Likewise the agreement for implementing the design is made via a separate agreement between the SPE and the constructor, who then contracts with subcontractors and suppliers to implement the design. Finally, but most importantly, the source of funding for the project is made by the SPE via separate agreement to the owner. Therefore, the three main stakeholders in a project, the owner, designer and constructor, serve in two capacities; one as a member of the SPE, which includes all of the fiduciary duties required of members of an LLC, and as separate entities holding agreements with the SPE. This arrangement is purported to assist in the ultimate integration, whereas the success or failure of the project has a direct impact on all parties. As projects are completed it will be interesting to see how this SPE succeeds in integrating parties that have traditionally been at odds.

11.11 Design services

To procure architectural design services, the Facility Manager should be aware of not only local customs but also federal mandates. Many people would be surprised to learn that, for the most part, bidding or selecting a designer on cost alone is considered unprofessional in the USA, because of long-standing ideas about what is professional and how architects should act professionally. This process begins with finding an architect who is skilled in designing the structure the owner seeks to design. Once an architect, familiar with the specific building type, has been secured, the owner usually negotiates a price for the design. If the parties agree, contracts can run from a letter describing the scope and including the designer's fee for services, to a full blown standardized contract with responsibilities of the parties clearly defined, along with fees, change provisions, time allotted for design and dispute resolution arrangements.

In negotiating for design services, the Facility Manager representing the owner must be aware of typical mindsets of many designers. Unlike other service negotiations, the architect may not be solely concerned with gaining an agreement that earns her the highest fee she can negotiate. Many designers are more interested in creative control, since the resulting structure is most likely public and will serve as a monument to their design abilities.

Of course on the owner's side, getting best value for a good price is the goal of the negotiation, so price and terms of the agreement may be of more concern. A helpful suggestion is to use the American Institute of Architects standard contract forms between and Owner and Architect. This document, written by those sympathetic to architects, also contemplates common risks associated with building design and attempts to allocate the risk to the party best able to mitigate.

For public and many municipal projects, the procurement of design is also not done by bid, but the process governed by the Brooks Act of 1972. This act was passed by Congress, and outlines the selection process of engineers and architects hired to work on federally funded projects. This process is more structured. Essentially the three most qualified designers are selected. Quality is based on a flexible list of items chosen by the specific government agency. Once the three potential designers are selected, price negotiation begins with the most qualified architect, moving on the second and third on the list, until an agreement on fees is made. This arrangement also assures the public sector that the agency will maintain its mandate to offer fair and open competition to those wanting to do business with the government.

Once a scope and fee arrangement is agreed upon the five typical stages, the design process follows with opportunities for the owner to approve the progress during each phase.

The first phase, called the conceptual phase, is set aside for owners to communicate additional design parameters to the architect. The purpose is for the designer to develop an idea of the use of the building, desires of the owner and constraints existing, such as budget, site selection and, possibly, time considerations. At the end of this phase the designer should produce an architectural program outlining the functional and organizational purposes for the structure. During this phase the designer will work closely with the owner to define the design problem clearly so that the subsequent design, or design solution, will serve to solve the basic problem.

The second phase begins with the architectural program and is called the design development phase. During this phase the architect will define the design and develop the solution, taking into account the specific and unique influences on the structure. If zoning issues arise, this is usually the time to address them. Unknown to many Facility Managers, the design development stage can be as detailed as the owner wishes and states in the contract. This development phase moves the design solution closer to a complete design and can be developed to 35 or 50% of the final design, depending on the terms of the contract. Design development is not a stage set in stone that is an industry standard in the USA, owners have the power to request as much development as necessary. Also during design development, models or other means to help the owner fully understand the developing design may be employed. This very important phase is the point at which the parties agree to an overarching design solution and the owner should be able to comprehend the designer's intent for the basic finished structure.

Once the development or general direction of the design is approved, the third phase of drafting final documents depicting the final design begins. This phase is called the *construction documents* phase. Choices are made to secure the building's elevation, floor plans and placement on the selected site. In addition engineering designers are called in to work out how the building should be detailed to ensure structural soundness. Also, designing the various systems necessary for occupant life safety and comfort is completed. The purpose of construction documents is to finalize the design so that the deliverables produced at the end of phase three are complete, and can be used to price and find financing for the resulting design.

Phases four and five involve the selecting of a builder and monitoring the implementation of the design, where the architect makes herself available to answer any questions concerning the design intent, and resolve any issues of conflict between the reality of the full-sized structure and the design as drawn. Some procurement schemes do not include any monitoring of the building process by the designer. This service is offered by the designer but not critical to the success of the project. Use of this service is dependent upon the sophistication of the owner and whether or not a Construction Manager or other advisor is available.

11.12 Evidence laws and their impact on facility management

When the Federal Rules of Evidence and the notion of procedural law were introduced, a basic explanation of how the rules of evidence impact a lawsuit was discussed. To go deeper into this subject is risky in this basic text on law, but a sophisticated understanding of how law and, more specifically, legal rules can not only impact a lawsuit, but an entire body of science, is worth a bit of discussion.

In technical fields like facility management, many times a dispute turns on which side had the more believable expert. Before expert testimony is even introduced to a jury for consideration, a silent legal battle is being waged behind the scenes.

In US courts, a trial judge may decide whether expert testimony will be heard and considered by a sitting jury. For a time, judges allowed expert-witness testimony according to common law guidelines. In 1923, with the case Frye v. United States, the Supreme Court attempted to set a standard procedure for federal courts. In Frye, the defendant, James Alphonzo Frye, attempted to illustrate his innocence by using the results of a systolic blood pressure test as a lie detector to demonstrate that he was telling the truth. The technology, and thus the testimony based on the technology, were both seen as experimental scientific claims. The court decided as follows:

> Just when a scientific principle or discovery crosses the line between the experimental and demonstrable stages is difficult to define. Somewhere in this twilight zone the evidential force of the principle must be recognized, and while courts will go a long way in admitting expert testimony deduced from a well-recognized scientific principle or discovery, the thing from which the deduction is made must be sufficiently established to have gained general acceptance in the particular field in which it belongs.
> (Frye v. United States 1923)

Many state courts for trials involving expert witnesses at the state level followed this precedent. In a legal sense, a precedent is a court decision that is cited as analogous to a similar situation that may occur later. If determined to be analogous, state courts generally follow previous precedent, even precedent of the Federal Supreme Court, to provide stability in decisions and in the entire system. This concept was previously discussed and we will visit it again, since the concept of standing by precedent is a fundamental tenet of common law systems.

Because of the Frye precedent, the "general acceptance" standard for novel scientific theories was born. This standard required the judge to determine whether a scientific theory was accepted among other academicians. This standard was criticized as too strict, since new and novel approaches in science tend to be slowly accepted. Not all states follow all federal precedents decided by the US Supreme Court. Whether a previous case is seen as a precedent hinges on the specific facts of a particular case. Changes in the state law that are based on Supreme Court decisions are, therefore, not immediately implemented, if at all.

In 1975, the Federal Rules of Evidence enacted by Congress attempted to clarify the admissibility of expert testimony. USCS Federal Rules of Evidence, Rule 702 states:

> *If scientific, technical, or other specialized knowledge will assist the trier of fact to understand the evidence or to determine a fact in issue, a witness qualified as an expert by knowledge, skill, experience, training, or education, may testify thereto in the form of an opinion or otherwise, if:*
>
> - *The testimony is based upon sufficient facts or data;*
> - *The testimony is the product of reliable principles and methods; and*
> - *The witness has applied the principles and methods reliably to the facts of the case.*

This rule also encompasses other general rules of admitting evidence, such as being relevant and more probative than prejudicial, and it does not specifically abrogate or eliminate the use of the Frye standard.

Although helpful, Rule 702 did not address how to test general acceptance, nor did it address whether the scientific community must generally accept the knowledge proffered as outlined in Frye. Because the rule committee did not expressly mention the Frye standard, Frye was still considered good law in most federal jurisdictions and state jurisdictions that adopted the precedent. General acceptance was a good standard; and although having general acceptance was not an automatic acceptance of the expert's testimony, it was highly regarded. When a trial lawyer was faced with a new or novel scientific theory in most disputes after 1975, a Frye test was used, especially in the case of novel forensic evidence for criminal cases. Over time, a general idea of whether expert witness testimony would be admitted was developed. Confusion over the relevance of the general acceptance standard in light of Federal Rule 702 existed, but most expert testimony evidence was admitted and many technical trials came down to a battle of the experts. Some in the legal community did not like this battle, or that both sides had to hire an expert to give an opinion on science, which is supposedly objective. If the opinions were scientifically based, then one expert's findings should be the same as, or at least resemble, another expert's opinion.

By the time the Supreme Court of the United States decided the landmark case of Daubert v. Merrell Dow Pharmaceuticals, Inc., civil defense attorneys were complaining about too much "junk" science being admitted into evidence (Daubert v. Merrell Dow Pharmaceuticals 1993). Daubert involved the allegation that the drug Bendectin caused birth defects. The case opinion outlined the Supreme Court's views on shoddy procedures, medical protocols, proficiency testing and, ultimately, junk science. The civil defense attorney finally had a definitive ruling in a federal court on novel scientific approaches. The majority opined that nothing in the new Federal Rules of Evidence incorporated the rigid general acceptance requirement of Frye. The court commented that the Frye standard would be contrary to the liberal thrust of the Federal Rules of Evidence and their "general approach of relaxing the traditional barriers to opinion testimony." In the dissenting opinion, the chief justice stated that the duty of the judge to ensure that scientific evidence is reliable and relevant is a "gate-keeping responsibility". This term is often used to describe the expert testimony filtering function of a trial judge.

In Daubert, the Supreme Court expressly rejected Frye's general acceptance test, but since case was not a constitutional one, its findings, and thus the new expert testimony rule, are not binding in state courts. This definitive action by the justices, although important, was and is not automatically sweeping in scope. Each state's supreme court or legislature has to decide whether or not it will follow Daubert and abandon the general acceptance standard. The court stated that the Daubert standard was to follow the more liberal rules set out by the Federal Rules of Evidence; however, as it exists today, the Daubert standard is anything but liberal in its application and effects. The Frye standard is actually now considered the liberal plaintiff-friendly standard, and the Daubert standard is the tougher defense-friendly law.

The confusing aspect of this new standard lies in its variability. Because of the separation of state and federal courts, some states continue to follow the previous Frye standard; other states have either adopted Daubert fully, or adopted some modified version. Federal courts closely follow Daubert's four-part test, as required. Other cases decided since Daubert have continued to refine the Daubert expert-witness admissibility standard, giving the judge more of an active gate-keeping role.

Present-day judges must now assess expert or opinion testimony of all sorts, both scientific and nonscientific. They must also ensure that testifying experts honor the same theories, employ the same methodologies, use the same tools and follow the same standards that they use in their ordinary, no litigation work. Finally, a trial judge's decision to exclude experts is reversed by an appellate court only on occasions in which judges abuse their discretion, which is considered only in rare cases. The way that Daubert is applied requires a judge to assess three main factors: whether a theory can be tested, the theory's error rate peer review of the theory and general acceptance within the scientific community. Contrast this to the generally accepted standard of Frye; the generally accepted standard allows the scientific community, not litigators and judges, to determine a theory's testability, error rate and theory review. Under both standards, the issue debated is the expert witness's reliability: the difference lies in who determines this reliability.

Thus, there are three approaches to expert testimony and its admission: the old general acceptance Frye test, in which judges rarely scrutinize the scientific validity of experts; the federal, or Daubert test, with its unintentionally strict standard; or some other standard unique to the states where Frye is not used and Daubert is not wholly accepted. It should be noted that, with all standards in US jurisprudence, evidence standards will continue to evolve.

With regard to admitting novel expert testimony, one could argue that predictability is uncertain. If a civil case is heavily dependent on expert testimony, potential defendants may be unable to forecast what actions open them to excessive liability.

11.13 Chapter summary

This chapter presented additional legal concepts the student will require to navigate Part III. These more advanced concepts, though specialized, are important to the Facility Manager and her practice.

11.14 Questions

1. Describe the area of law known as Environmental Justice.
2. What protected groups are most likely to be affected by the placement of hazardous waste sites? Why?
3. Using electronic resources, find and summarize a recent environmental justice case.
4. Describe the three main definitions of the term *construction management*.
5. In your opinion, is hiring a Construction Manager necessary? Explain your answer.
6. Can a Facility Manager practice construction management? Explain your answer.
7. Define the term *Project Delivery System*.
8. What are the necessary elements of a Project Delivery System?
9. If you were tasked with building the first office complex on Mars, what project delivery system would you use? What elements would you choose to make this system complete?
10. In your opinion, is it fair that a state's definition of an expert can determine the outcome of a dispute? Explain your answer.

References

Rodgers, C. *High Occupancy Toll Lanes Ignoring The Potential for a Violation of Environmental Justice*. Dissertation, Building Construction, Georgia Institute of Technology, Atlanta, 2012.

Summary of Part II

Amalgamating all of the rules, regulations, the constitution, court decisions, statutes and local mandates can seem overwhelming to the student of facility management. This is especially true since law students study these concepts over the course of a full-time, three-year curriculum. Though challenging, the task is not impossible, especially if you formulate a personal strategy for thinking through legal challenges.

As indicated in Parts I and II, law can be thought of in terms of its functions, sources and topic areas. In the very beginning we examined the three functions law serves. Recall that the law is a regulator, facilitator and dispute resolver. Therefore, a solid starting point when faced with any legal question is to determine which of the three functions is most likely in operation. With an understanding of what function the law is serving in a given situation, finding the appropriate area of law is manageable because you now know the sources of the law. You also have a basic understanding of how the different sources of law are made and where to begin searching for answers to basic questions. You know how the court system functions and that disputes are usually either civil or criminal. There are also established rules of the game, called procedure, that must be kept in mind. Knowing that the players all must operate according to rules that are themselves laws, should help lessen some of the frustration when working with lawyers and navigating the legal system as a whole. Finally, the areas of law important to the Facility Manager can be divided into torts, contracts, property law, environmental law, employment/labor law and sometimes criminal law.

Avoiding being held liable for wrongdoing is the main reason for the Facility Manager to study law. Liability usually means the Facility Manager failed to do the right thing with regard to keeping the premises free from hazards, breaching a contract, acting in a negligent way, working in abnormally dangerous situations exposing oneself to strict liability or improper handling, storage or disposal of hazardous materials.

The most basic legal duty that the Facility Manager is expected to uphold is her duty to perform as a professional. This means being held to the same standard as the typical Facility Manager in the community, which includes legal, moral and ethical standards.

Legal Concepts for Facility Managers, First Edition. Linda Thomas-Mobley.
© 2014 John Wiley & Sons, Ltd. Published 2014 by John Wiley & Sons, Ltd.

Part III

Application

Introduction

By now students will have gathered that there are several facets to the law. One facet is having a basic knowledge of the rules, another is an understanding that law is constantly evolving, and yet another facet to understand includes the various sources of the rules and how the source impacts its implementation. Once the concept that the law has many facets is grasped, students must then understand which of the many rules apply to a situation and what to do should those rules contradict each other.

Students might instinctively begin by compiling lists of potentially applicable rules for a given situation. However, law evolves so rapidly that such a list must be updated too frequently to be practical. It is important to remember that rules and procedures are evolving. What may have been true 10 years ago is now no longer the case. For example, our notions of privacy have drastically changed as our relationship with information has changed and now physical possession of your credit card is not necessary for a thief to use your line of credit without permission.

Instead, students are better served by compiling a list of concepts. Examples include the notion that the law seeks to protect the rights given by the US Constitution, or that a property owner should keep the premises safe for those who enter. Students, as well as all citizens, must understand the procedure for requesting and obtaining a remedy for a wrong. Knowing that the procedural rules are dependent upon the type of wrongdoing, the location of the person who is accused of the wrong and the legal relationship between the plaintiff and the defendant, is also important.

Elementary legal reasoning is dependent on a mastery of the above concepts. Rule basics like the definitions of Property, Contract, Environmental, Tort, Criminal and Employment law have been laid out in this text. Additional topics covered include knowing where the law is found, how the courts have interpreted the law and how statutes intersect. Students should also know that written legislation often overlaps and even conflicts with judge-made law or common law, and that sources of rules other than the common law and statutes exist. Additionally, to help with understanding the process of legal reasoning, students need to know how the business of government is conducted. This is especially important in jurisdictions such as the USA, since the whole legal system is based on the idea that the USA is a "government of laws and not of men", according to the Massachusetts State Constitution written in 1780.

So, at this point in the course, you may feel pretty smart and comfortable with the laws of the USA. If you do, you need to go back and begin at Chapter 1 again, because no one, not even a Supreme Court Justice, feels smart and comfortable with the law. Lawyers, judges, justices, clerks and even law professors hope at best to be competent: but comfortable? Never.

With your fundamental knowledge of rules and procedure, and remembering that being uncomfortable is par for the course, let's go on to see how understanding the law assists with the practice of Facility Management.

12

Responsibilities of the Facility Manager

The skilfull employer of men will employ the wise man, the brave man, the covetous man, and the stupid man.

Sun Tzu

12.1 Introduction

Organizing law as it applies to facilities management can be accomplished by examining specific job responsibilities. Most Facility Managers will have some involvement in human resources, engineering analysis, operations management, procurement, project management and leadership.

Using actual legal case decisions, in this chapter we will focus on potential areas of liability as applied to the professional. By the end of this chapter the following learning outcomes are expected:

- List major causes of action for negligent behavior of a Facility Manager.
- Discuss the legally required standards for due diligence in hiring.
- Define negligent hiring, training, retention and supervision.
- Define negligent entrustment.

12.2 Professional services

Determining that a workplace is safe and free from hazards requires the Facility Manager to use professional judgment. However, these types of decisions occur frequently for Facility Managers. Whether or not the Facility Manager

Legal Concepts for Facility Managers, First Edition. Linda Thomas-Mobley.
© 2014 John Wiley & Sons, Ltd. Published 2014 by John Wiley & Sons, Ltd.

fulfills her basic professional duty in a particular situation is not always clear. What are these questionable areas where the correct decision can mean the difference between being found liable or not liable for the Facility Manager?

If we look at the overall duties of the Facility Manager, we can identify the key abilities distinguishing the discipline from other professions. Unfortunately, rather than offering clarification, these definitions have contributed to the unclear characterization of the profession. In the early 1980s, The Facility Management Institute drafted a definition and registered it with the US Library of Congress. Now known as the International Facility Management Association (IFMA), the institute defines facility management as:

> *The practice of coordinating the physical workplace with the people and work of an organization. It integrates the principles of business administration, architecture, and behavioral and engineering sciences.*

This model requires Facility Managers to integrate the people, work and facilities of an organization (Cotts 1999). A simple graphical representation of a Facility Manager's roles is depicted in Figure 12.1.

Working with business functions from human resources to financial modeling, Facility Managers are responsible for a wide range of tasks. Each task can be broken down into smaller tasks, most of which have a legal component attached to them. Competing resources must be balanced against each other, and the responsibilities of the Facility Manager may exceed the available budget and human capital. This highlights an important fact in facilities management: namely that the resources to do the job as comprehensively necessary may be, and often are, very limited. It is the creative management of resources that separate the successful Facility Manager from those not so successful.

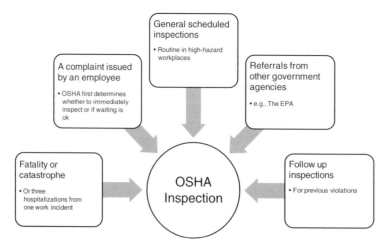

Figure 12.1   The role of the Facility Manager.

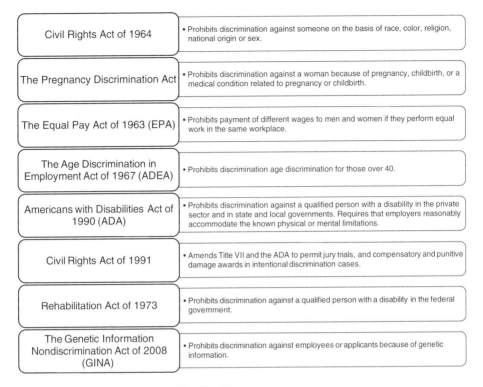

Figure 12.2   Ultimate goals of Facility Manager.

Figure 12.2 depicts the ultimate goal of the Facility Manager and demonstrates that achieving this goal requires every skill in the Facility Manager's toolbox.

The Facility Manager is responsible for an interdisciplinary mixture of skills. The services rendered should be in accordance with all of the laws governing facilities enforced by state, federal and local laws. These laws concern several areas such as reporting of income, zoning, sound employment practices and operations management. Consequently there can be a range of legal challenges related to these obstacles Facility Managers must face to achieve fully functional, safe and healthy buildings.

12.2.1 Human resources

Laws associated with human resource operations come from common law, statutory law and administrative law. At the federal level, the Department of Justice enforces employment rights using two main statutes; the amended Civil Rights Act of 1964, and the Uniformed Services Employment and Reemployment Rights Act of 1994. Chapter 10 provides an employment law overview but looking at an actual case brings this important area into focus.

Consider the case of *Staub v. Proctor Hospital*, a recent Supreme Court of the United States case (Staub v. Proctor Hospital 2009). Here, the court considered the circumstances under which an employer may be held liable for employment discrimination. The plaintiff sued the defendant because of perceived discriminatory hostility by an employee who influenced, but did not make, the ultimate employment decision.

Plaintiff Vincent Staub worked as a technician for the defendant employer, Proctor Hospital, until 2004, when he was fired. While employed by Proctor, Staub was a member of the United States Army Reserve, which required him to attend reserve drills one weekend per month and to train full time for two to three weeks a year. Both Janice Mulally, Staub's immediate supervisor, and Michael Korenchuk, Mulally's supervisor, were hostile to Staub because of his military obligations. There were times when Staub's immediate supervisor scheduled him for additional shifts without notice so that he would "pa[y] back the department for everyone else having to bend over backwards to cover [his] schedule for the Reserves" (Staub v. Proctor Hospital 2009). "She also informed Staub's co-worker, Leslie Sweborg, that Staub's "military duty had been a strain on th[e] department", and asked Sweborg to help her "get rid of him" (Staub v. Proctor Hospital 2009). Korenchuk referred to Staub's military obligations as, "a b[u]nch of smoking and joking and [a] waste of taxpayers['] money" (Staub v. Proctor Hospital 2009). He was also aware that Mulally was "out to get" Staub. In January 2004, Mulally issued Staub a disciplinary warning for allegedly violating a company rule requiring him to stay in his work area.

On April 2, 2004, Angie Day, Staub's co-worker, complained to Linda Buck, Proctor's Vice President of Human Resources, and Garrett McGowan, Proctor's chief operating officer, about Staub's frequent unavailability and abruptness. McGowan directed Korenchuk and Buck to create a plan that would solve Staub's "'availability' problems". But before they had time to do so, Korenchuk informed Buck that Staub had left his desk without informing a supervisor. Staub now argues that this accusation was false: he had left Korenchuk a voice mail notification that he was leaving his desk. Buck fired Staub. Staub sued Proctor under the Uniformed Services Employment and Reemployment Rights Act of 1994, 38 U. S. C. §4301 et seq., claiming that his discharge was motivated by hostility to his obligations as a military reservist. The plaintiff claimed that Mulally and Korenchuk influenced Buck's ultimate employment decision. A jury found that Staub's "military status was a motivating factor in [Proctor's] decision to discharge him" and awarded $57 640 in damages. The Seventh Circuit Appellate Court reversed the trial court's decision. The case was then appealed to the Supreme Court of the United States.

According the Court, The Uniformed Services Employment and Reemployment Rights Act (USERRA) provides the following:

> *A person who is a member of . . . or has an obligation to perform service in a uniformed service shall not be denied initial employment, reemployment, retention in employment, promotion, or any benefit of employment by an employer on the basis of that membership, . . . or obligation (USERRA, 38 U. S. C. §4311(a)).*
>
> *An employer shall be considered to have engaged in actions prohibited . . . under subsection (a), if the person's membership. . . is a motivating factor in the employer's action, unless the employer can prove that the action would have been taken in the absence of such membership (USERRA 38 U. S. C. §4311(c)).*

The difficulty in this case for the court was determining whether the supervisor's hostility toward the plaintiff's military service was a "motivating factor" in his dismissal. When a decision to fire is made without hostility on the part of the person doing the firing (Buck), but partly on the basis of a report prompted by discrimination, discrimination might perhaps be called "a motivating factor", Applying this analysis to the facts, the court reversed the appeals court judgment agreeing with the original jury verdict finding that Staub's military status was a motivating factor in Proctor's decision to discharge.

The Facility Manager is often in the position to control the employment of many diverse populations including reservists. Requiring professional behavior is not only required but also an important part of sound risk management. We will see more about risk management in Chapter 14.

12.2.2 Operations

Aside from keeping property and occupants safe, another major responsibility of the Facility Manager is employee management. There are four basic areas of negligence in employee management that can be a source of liability; hiring, retention, supervision and training. These overlap with the potentially more serious tort of negligent entrustment and vicarious liability. Vicarious liability has been previously discussed but not in the context of employment negligence.

Negligent hiring typically occurs when an employee hired by the Facility Manager has a reputation for exploiting her authority, and this reputation would have been easily discoverable by the Facility Manager, had she exercised due diligence when hiring. Under this legal theory, a victim of an employee's tortious conduct can sue the employer for failing to take reasonable care in hiring or retaining the employee. Negligent retention is a related theory where an employer breached her duty to council a rogue employee, and failed to take corrective action through coaching, reassignment or termination.

There are four basic causes of action in under this doctrine:

1. Negligent hiring,
2. Negligent retention,
3. Negligent supervision, and
4. Negligent training.

Consider the 2003 case of *Saine v. Comcast Cablevision of Ark, Inc.*, a case in Arkansas in which Comcast Cablevision (Comcast) was sued under the theory of negligent hiring (Saine v. Comcast Cablevision of Arkansas, Inc. 2003).

Natasha Saine arrived home and found a Comcast truck at her house and a man by the name of Ceotis Franks (Franks), dressed in a Comcast uniform, climbing down the cable pole in her yard. Ms Saine allowed Franks to enter her home to adjust her cable reception. After making the adjustments, Franks stepped outside. When he returned he pulled a knife on Ms Saine forcing her into a bedroom and raped her. Afterward, Franks hit Ms Saine in the head with a blowtorch canister, and then bound her hands behind her back, tied her feet together, and dropped her into a bathtub filled with water. After Ms Saine was thrown in the tub, he slit her throat with a knife and then he plugged a lamp into an electrical socket and tossed it into the tub to electrocute her.

Finding Ms Saine still alive, Franks held her head under water for more than a minute to drown her. When all other attempts to kill her had failed, he forced her, bound, into a closet and set fire to her carpet with his blowtorch. Even after all of Franks' efforts, Ms Saine lived, and Franks was convicted of rape, kidnapping, arson and attempted murder.

Almost a year later, Ms Saine filed a lawsuit against Comcast alleging negligent hiring, negligent retention and negligent supervision. Comcast then filed a motion for summary judgment asking the trial judge to rule in their favor arguing that there was no information available to Comcast before or after Franks was hired to warn them Franks might commit violent acts against customers. The trial court granted Comcast's motion for summary judgment. The judge found that Franks was not acting within the scope of his employment when he assaulted Ms Saine, and that they did not and could not have known that Franks had a proclivity for rape.

The trial court entered an order dismissing with prejudice other pending claims against Comcast. When an order is dismissed with prejudice, the plaintiff cannot bring the same lawsuit against the same defendants at a later date.

Ms Saine appealed the trial court's decision. She argued that the trial court made an error by granting summary judgment on her claims of negligent hiring, and negligent supervision and retention. The appellate court wrote:

Arkansas recognizes the torts of negligent supervision and negligent retention. Under both theories of recovery, employers are subject to direct liability for their negligent supervision or negligent retention of employees when third parties are injured as a result of the tortious acts of those employees. (Saine v. Comcast Cablevision of Arkansas, Inc. 2003)

According to the appellate court under these theories of negligence, the plaintiff must prove that the employer knew or through the exercise of ordinary care, should have known that the employee's conduct would subject third parties to an unreasonable risk of harm.

It should be noted that, it is not necessary that the employer be able to anticipate the particular injury that occurred but only that the employer could reasonably foresee some risk of harm to others.

During the trial, Ms Saine's attorney offered evidence through the testimony of Jeanie Leonard, a Comcast customer for whom Ceotis Franks installed cable prior to the assault on Ms Saine. Ms Leonard stated that when Franks installed her cable, he made inappropriate comments about her attractiveness, saying she had beautiful hair and eyes and "some fine-looking legs". Ms Leonard stated she was frightened and called Comcast the following morning, complaining first to a woman who answered the phone, then to a supervisor, finally to a manager who put her on hold and never returned to the phone.

The Court considered this testimony during the appeal. Comcast disputed Ms Leonard's testimony, attempting to show inconsistencies and contradictions in her two deposition sessions. The court reversed the trial court's summary judgment on the negligent-supervision and negligent-retention claims. To decide this case, the court had to believe in the testimony of Ms Leonard, the former customer. With this evidence Ms Saine was able to show that Comcast knew how dangerous Franks was.

The tort of negligent training is exemplified by the 1985 case of *Carroll Cutter v. Town of Farmington* (Carroll Cutter v. Town of Farmington 1985). One evening in 1980, a Farmington police car followed a truck into the parking lot of Luneau's Restaurant on Route 11 in Rochester, NH. The truck had earlier crossed the centerline of the highway, nearly crashing into the police car. The car contained two Farmington police officers, John Burbine and William Stawecki, a special officer hired approximately two weeks previously. Officer Burbine was giving Officer Stawecki on-the-job training, but prior to this evening had not previously worked with him. Officer Stawecki was on his third or fourth night patrol, even though he had received no formal police training.

Once in the restaurant parking lot, the truck pulled into a space. Both officers exited their car and Officer Burbine approached the driver's side of the vehicle while Officer Stawecki approached the passenger's side. Mr Cutter got out of the truck. Officer Stawecki told him to put his hands against the truck. Mr Cutter did not respond immediately, instead asking what he had done. According to

Officer Stawecki, Mr Cutter attempted to swing at him with his left hand. Cutter denied this and testified that Stawecki came running up to him, told him to put his hands on the truck and, in response to his inquiry about what he had done, shoved him hard against the car.

Officer Stawecki pushed Cutter to the ground, got on top of him and tried to handcuff him. Officer Burbine heard something hit the side of the truck and went over to investigate. He found Officer Stawecki attempting to handcuff the plaintiff and assisted him in the task. In the meantime the other occupant of the truck, Mr Bickford, got out of the vehicle. At this point back-up police officers arrived and Officer Burbine told them to arrest Bickford. Cutter claimed that he was unnecessarily roughed-up prior to being handcuffed but the Rochester police denied this allegation.

The two men, Cutter and Bickford, were taken to the Rochester police station where they were placed in custody. According to Cutter, Officer Stawecki improperly applied the handcuffs to his wrists by failing to double-lock them. As a result of the failure to double-lock the handcuffs, they continued to tighten. Cutter claimed the pressure of the handcuff on his left wrist caused permanent damage to the radial nerve, resulting in a partial disability that made him unfit for his employment as a logger or for other physical labor. Cutter also claimed to lack any work experience outside of logging and was illiterate. He further declared he had requested Officer Stawecki to loosen the handcuffs at least twice, but they were not loosened.

Cutter and Bickford brought suit against the police officers and the Town of Farmington. At the trial, the jury returned a verdict in favor of Cutter only and awarded him damages to the amount of $55 000. The appellate court agreed with the trial court and affirmed the verdict for Cutter.

In a tragic Massachusetts case of *Heng Or, administrator, v. Lawrence C. Edwards, individually and as trustee* (Heng Or, administrator v. Lawrence C. Edwards 2004), negligent hiring was alleged in a wrongful death action brought by a father on behalf of his minor daughter. Mr Or asserted that the negligent conduct of the defendant landlords in hiring or retaining a custodian, and entrusting him indiscriminately with the keys to the landlords' apartments resulted in the murder of his daughter by the custodian. At trial the jury found that the defendants' knowledge that the custodian was a jobless, homeless drifter with a drinking problem and a criminal record, was enough knowledge to find for the plaintiff. The custodian also had an order requiring him to appear repeatedly in court and to submit to a mental competency examination. The jury determined that the landlords were negligent in entrusting the keys to such a person and that entrustment of the keys to the custodian caused the wrongful death. The defendants' failure to make inquiries about the unfit custodian, especially when combined with entrusting him with the keys, created a likelihood of types of harm to others, which came about in the custodian's violent attack on the decedent. The jury's verdict was affirmed.

In a 1998 Wisconsin case arguing negligent supervision, *Miller v. Wal-Mart Stores Inc.*, the plaintiff claimed improper training of loss prevention personnel (Stanley K. Miller and Deborah D. Miller v. Wal-Mart Stores, Inc. 1998). When the plaintiffs, Mr and Mrs Stanley and Deborah Miller, left the Wal-Mart store in Superior, WI, three Wal-Mart employees approached Mr Stanley Miller in the store's parking lot. According to the employees, a loss prevention employee, Mr Richard Maness (Maness) believed Miller had stolen a swimsuit. After approaching Miller, Maness asked for the swimsuit. The exact exchange that took place between the parties is disputed, but all agree that Maness did not find the swimsuit on Miller. Miller filed an action against Wal-Mart Stores, Inc., alleging that the Wal-Mart employees unlawfully stopped, detained, searched and interrogated him. After a four-day jury trial, the jury determined that Wal-Mart was negligent in hiring, training or supervising its employees, and this negligence was a cause of injury to Miller. The jury awarded Miller $20 000 in compensatory damages for past mental pain and suffering and $30 000 in punitive damages. Wal-Mart appealed the judgment. The appellate court questioned whether the state of Wisconsin had identified the tort of negligent hiring, training or supervision, and if the elements of that tort were satisfied in this case. Wisconsin's common law of negligence states, "In order to maintain a cause of action for negligence in this state, there must exist: (1) A duty of care on the part of the defendant; (2) a breach of that duty; (3) a causal connection between the conduct and the injury; and (4) an actual loss or damage as a result of the injury" (Stanley K. Miller and Deborah D. Miller v. Wal-Mart Stores, Inc. 1998).

The first thing the court had to determine was whether Wal-Mart had a duty of care to Miller. In an unexpected statement, the court stated,

In Wisconsin, everyone has a duty of care to the whole world and the duty of any person is the obligation of due care to refrain from any act which will cause foreseeable harm to others even though the nature of that harm and the identity of the harmed person or harmed interest is unknown at the time of the act. (Stanley K. Miller and Deborah D. Miller v. Wal-Mart Stores, Inc. 1998)

Miller argues that Wal-Mart failed to properly train its loss prevention employee, Maness. Miller also argued that loss prevention employees are entrusted with special duties and given authority to stop individuals suspected of shoplifting. If not properly trained, a loss prevention employee could cause harm.

The next question the court addressed was, did Wal-Mart breach its duty of care toward Miller? According to the court,

A person fails to exercise ordinary care, when, without intending to do any harm, he or she does something or fails to do something under circumstances in which a reasonable person would foresee that by his or her action or failure to act, he or

she will subject a person or property to an unreasonable risk or injury or damage.
(Stanley K. Miller and Deborah D. Miller v. Wal-Mart Stores, Inc. 1998)

The court concluded that it is conceivable that failing to properly train or supervise a loss prevention employee would subject shoppers to unreasonable risk, injury or damage. Also, if all the necessary elements are proven, Wal-Mart should be liable for its negligent act or omission. This court did not resolve this case but the availability of the negligent training tort was available to Miller after all.

How does this case apply to the Facility Manager? Typically, engineering or facility management programs tend to not expose students to the requirements for proper supervision and just assume this information will be related to students on the job. Understanding the basic duties required by a supervisor in hiring, training and retaining employees will help the Facility Manager to reduce her risk to her employer and herself.

12.2.3 Procurement

Let's look at the potential liabilities an owner may be exposed to when procuring a commercial building. Consider the case of *Laukkanen v. Jewel Tea Co., Inc.* (1966). Tahiko Laukkanen became a paraplegic when part of a building designed by the defendants fell on her during a severe thunderstorm in 1962 (Laukkanen v. Jewel Tea Co. Inc. 1966). The defendants were licensed engineers. Defendant Cordes, who was an employee of defendant Debes, drew the plans and prepared the project specifications. The plaintiff sued both of the engineers, the store and its owner.

Laukkanen stated that in 1958 the engineers prepared drawings and specifications for the construction of a building that they knew was for public use as a grocery store. The building was later constructed according to the design. The design consisted of a hollow concrete block pylon with brick facing as a part of the west wall. This wall also contained the customers' entrance and exit doors. The pylon extended 38 feet into the air from the ground level. The top of it was approximately 21 feet higher than the top of the perimeter walls. The plaintiff also alleged that the engineers knew the concrete block pylon they designed would be located directly above the entrance to the grocery store, and that any defects in the structure would not be visible to the public. The plaintiff stated that the defendants failed to exercise the care expected of professional engineers, and that they failed to design a structurally sound pylon because its unique shape made it incapable of withstanding the wind force reasonably expected in the area.

The defendants stated the following:

- The collapse was an act of God for which the defendants were not responsible;

- The plaintiff's lawsuit was filed too late and therefore prohibited by the statute of limitations; and
- The defendants' only duty was to prepare the design and check it for structural stability, and they did not supervise the construction of the store.

The contractor testified that the pylon was built in the manner and with the materials called for by the design furnished by the engineers. An employee of another local contracting firm testified that lightweight concrete blocks were in the design documents. After the engineers designed the store they had nothing more to do with the project. The engineers approved the plans on May 5, 1958. Defendant Cordes' seal as a registered structural engineer and defendant Debes' seal as a registered professional engineer both appear on the pages of the plans relating to the method of constructing the pylon (Laukkanen v. Jewel Tea Co. Inc. 1966).

The evidence presented during the trial included weather records for April 30, 1962, which showed that the wind was recorded at 87.4 mph. An expert testified at trial that the wind was more intense than any other wind recorded by the Weather Bureau since records were kept; it was still within the range of winds to be expected in the area. The jury found that the defendants' failure to specify that a standard heavy concrete block be used in constructing the pylon, instead of the lightweight concrete blocks that were specified for use in other portions of the building, resulted in the pylon having insufficient strength to withstand the severe winds. They also determined that the defendants did not use the degree of skill ordinarily and customarily used by members of the defendants' profession under similar circumstances. The skill level or professional duties of professional engineers, is just like the skill level of professional Facility Managers. Courts often describe this duty as the "degree of skill ordinarily and customarily used by members of the profession under similar circumstances". This is the standard required in this case, and in all cases where a professional's level of expertise and duty of care is called into question.

At the trial, the defendants argued that their duty extended only to the party who contracted for their services, and since the store customer was neither a party to the contract nor in contractual privity with someone who was, she could not file a lawsuit for her damages directly against them. The defendants also noted that they were not hired to supervise the construction, and had they been on the construction site during the building process, they would have objected to the use of lightweight blocks for the pylon. Finally, they testified that the contracted-for services were completed when six sets of the plans were turned over to the owner on May 5, 1958. This date is important because the statute of limitations argument by the defendants relates to the limit of time an injured person has to file a lawsuit. If the court considers the engineer's contract completed on May 5, 1958, there may be a problem for the plaintiff.

After the trial court made a decision and the case was appealed, the appellate court had to decide if the defendants' arguments were valid, and therefore if the trial court had made the correct decision to find for the plaintiff. The appellate court stated that privity of contract is not a prerequisite to liability. Privity of contract is defined as a formal contractual relationship between the parties, if both have signed a contract, it is said they are "in privity". For many years this requirement of privity was necessary for anyone to recover damages for injuries. In modern times, this is no longer the circumstance.

At the appellate level, the central issue in this case was the defendants' failure to exercise the degree of care in the performance of professional duties as members of a licensed profession. The defendants "owed a duty to those members of the general public who can be reasonably anticipated to be present in the structure they designed" (Laukkanen v. Jewel Tea Co. Inc. 1966). Negligent behavior that is the actual (proximate) cause of a defendant's injury will require the defendant to pay damages for the injury suffered. This is true, according to the appellate court anytime the injury is conceivable, even if there is no formal relationship between parties. In the jurisdiction of the Laukkanen case, the relevant statute states:

> *No action to recover damages . . . for injury to the person, or bodily injury . . . arising out of the defective and unsafe condition of an improvement to real estate, . . . shall be brought against any person performing or furnishing the design, [or] planning, . . . of such improvement to real property, unless such cause of action shall have accrued within four years after the performance or furnishing of such services.* (Illinois Rev Stats 1963, c 83, § 24f)

The appellate court's decision affirmed the trial court's judgment for the plaintiff and against the defendants in the amount of $205 000.

As you can see, the *Laukkanen* case contained several issues of interest to the Facility Manager. The most important being whether or not a contract between an injured building occupant, a store patron in this case, and the engineers who designed the building, was required for the designer to be liable for the injuries. The trial court and the appellate court both agreed that the designers owed a duty of care not to injure anyone who would ever use the store and no contract was necessary. This makes sense because building occupants rarely, if ever, have a contractual relationship with the people who design the building they occupy. This requirement for privity of contract would essentially mean that building designers would only be liable for mistakes if the owner who hired them became injured.

Another issue was the time limit for filing a suit for injury in Illinois, or the statute of limitations. A statute of limitations is an amount of time a potential plaintiff has to file a lawsuit after an injury is discovered. Even if the defendant was at fault, if this time runs out, the plaintiff will not be able to bring a lawsuit.

This is referred to as being "barred" from filing an action against the defendant. Statute of limitations is necessary, otherwise potential lawsuits for a dispute occurring way in the past would always be open, long after the evidence and people's memories about the event could fade away. Some offenses do not have a finite statute of limitations, such as murder; this is because these offenses are so grave, society is served whenever law enforcement is able to take a killer off the streets, even if 20 years have passed after the murder. In the *Laukkanen* case the statute of limitations was four years and the injury occurred one month shy of four years.

So, the question remains, why should the Facility Manager care about any of this? This is why we hire attorneys, is it not? Well, consider that, even if your company pays for legal representation or insurance to protect your ignorance, all forms of punishment under the law are available for some offenses, not just financial. There are occasions when failing to behave professionally results in jail time, and your company cannot guarantee that their attorney will win your criminal case. Also, some environmental regulations have criminal penalties and your failure to exercise your duty of care can rise to the level of a criminal violation punishable by incarceration.

Consider cases alleging "criminal knowing endangerment", a term used by the federal government to describe entities that violate environmental regulations and release harmful substances into the environment or knowingly place employees in dangerous conditions without training or notice.

In the case of *United States v. Elias*, The owner of a fertilizer company ordered his employees to clean out a 25 000-gallon tank so that he could use it to store sulfuric acid (United States v. Elias 2001). The tank contained a large amount, over a foot, of hardened cyanide-laced sludge from a cyanide leaching process the company had patented. Cyanide is a dangerous substance and if it is inhaled it can cause a coma with seizures, cardiac arrest and death within of minutes of exposure. If the dose is low, a person may experience loss of consciousness after feeling weak and giddy. The lower dose exposure may also produce headaches, vertigo and confusion. Cyanide-exposed individuals also have a supposed difficulty with breathing.

On two occasions the fertilizer company ordered their employees into the tank. Entrance into the tank was down through a small, 22-inch hole, covered with a manhole cover at the top. Respirators and other personal protective equipment were not provided for the employees to use while performing this task. The second time one of the employees entered the tank, he collapsed. When emergency responders were finally able to get to the employee, he had severe shortness of breath and either could not breathe or felt he could not breathe. When asked about the incident by the emergency responders at the plant, and the treating physician, the owner maintained that as far as he knew only water and mud were in the tank. Sometime after the incident, the owner or someone in the company had the sludge in the tank removed.

After some time, the employee was given a cyanide antidote, but by the time it was finally administered, the employee had suffered irreversible brain damage. The owner was arrested and charged with several crimes. At the criminal proceeding, the owner was tried and convicted under the Resource Conservation and Recovery Act (RCRA) for his failure to protect his employees; the illegal disposal of hazardous waste after the accident; and a giving a false statement for creating a confined-space permit after the accident and resending it to the Occupational Safety and Health Administration (OSHA).

Later, the owner was sentenced to 17 years in prison and ordered to pay a fine of $6.3 million in restitution and $400 000 in environmental cleanup costs. In many plants, just like this fertilizer plant, the Facility Manager acts on behalf of the owner, representing the owner's interests. What would you do if you were told the tank contained water and mud, and you ordered the employee into the tank to clean it up twice?

12.2.4 Professionalism

One very essential trait of a successful Facility Manager is her ability to act as a professional, at all times. As a professional, the Facility Manager is held to a higher standard than others because she has specialized training. Also, in many instances, she is called to exercise her discretion and make a judgment on a technical matter. One very good method to help the new professional understand the areas that are potentially troublesome for any professional Facility Manager is to make a list of the specific tasks where a judgment call is likely to be made. One such discretionary task is the task of project manager.

Project management
When the Facility Manager takes on the role of project manager or construction manager, the Facility Manager owes very specific duties to others. In 2004, *EH Construction, LLC v. Delor Design Group, Inc.*, EH Construction appealed from a trial court's decision, the Jefferson Circuit Court, to dismiss the plaintiffs complaint for damages against Presnell Construction Managers, Inc. (Presnell). The original complaint was filed for breach of contract and negligence (EH Construction, LLC v. Delor Design Group, Inc. 2004). This appeal focused on the action for negligence, and not breach of contract, so the main issue in this summary is whether Kentucky Courts should allow negligence claims by contractors against construction managers.

Generally, as in this case, the construction manager contracts are strictly between the owner of the project and the construction manager. In May of 1996, the Delor Design Group, Inc. (Delor) initiated a project to renovate a commercial building into office space. Delor hired an architect and after the design was completed the structure was demolished. At this stage the owner hired Presnell as a construction manager to oversee the rest of the project. In January 1997, a general contractor by the name of EH Construction (EH) submitted a bid for the general trades to the owner. This proposal was accepted by the owner, Delor, and EH became a contractor for the project. The work turned out to be very difficult and there were several disputes relating to the timing, quality of the work and payment of outstanding invoices.

A year later, in February of 1998, the general contractor, EH filed a lawsuit against Delor, the owner; Presnell the construction manager; and other lien holders, seeking payment of $268 218. The suit also sought damages from the construction manager, Presnell, for breach of contract and negligence. The general contractor claimed that they were required to repeat much of the work already completed because of changes to the contract and faulty scheduling by Presnell. This caused other contractors and subcontractors to destroy work that EH had already finished. EH's theory for the case was that Presnell negligently supplied information that the general contractor relied on and that information caused misrepresentations in the implementation of their work which caused them to consequently suffer financial loss. EH also alleged that Presnell was negligent in its coordination and supervision of the contractors. This is significant since the main reason for hiring a construction manager is because of their proficiency for construction scheduling and coordination of labor.

In response to the general contractor's claim of negligence, Presnell filed a motion to dismiss EH's complaint against it, arguing that the claim for breach of contract was barred (prohibited) for lack of privity (no contractual relationship) and that the claim for negligence was barred for lack of any duty owed to EH. In essence the construction manager is stating that she has no duty of care to the general contractor since they do not have a contract with each other and also, there is no general duty of care in this case.

The trial court agreed with the construction manager and granted Presnell's motion to dismiss. The general contractor filed an appeal. In this appeal, EH argued that there did not have to be privity between EH and Presnell in order for a duty to arise. Recall a previous case where the designer for the grocery store argued the same thing, no contractual relationship between the engineer and the customer of the completed store. The general contractor also urged the court to impose liability for professionals, like construction managers who, in the course of business, carelessly gather and distribute information intended for use by others like general contractors. The state of Kentucky had never been asked to solve a case like this in the past. Cases with a new previously undecided type of dispute are called cases with an "issue of first impression".

The appellate court stated that Kentucky courts had in the past recognized that privity is not a prerequisite for tort actions in the case of Tabler, but not in construction cases (Tabler v. Wallace 1985). The court decided to follow the approach taken by the Tennessee Supreme Court in a similar case. Even though Tennessee is a different state from Kentucky, courts will often borrow law if it seems appropriate. The court also stated that in this case the

.IVERPOOL JOHN MOORES UNIVERSITY
LEARNING SERVICES

construction manager's liability is not just any professional duty, but an "an independent duty to avoid misstatements intended to induce reliance" (Tabler v. Wallace 1985).

In order to win its claim against the construction manager, Presnell for negligent misrepresentation, the general contractor had to prove the following:

- Presnell was acting in the course of its business, profession, or employment, or in a transaction in which it had a financial, and not volunteer interest;
- Presnell supplied incorrect information that was intended to guide others in their business transactions;
- Presnell failed to use reasonable care in obtaining or communicating the information; and
- EH reasonably relied upon the information and thereby incurred a financial loss.

The court disagreed with the trial court and reversed the order of the Jefferson Circuit Court. The appellate court then returned or remanded this case to the trial court for proceedings consistent with the new law. This means that in the state of Kentucky, a contractor may make a claim in tort against a construction manager based upon negligent misrepresentation, despite a lack of privity of contract. This case not only illustrates a new opening for liability for construction managers in Kentucky but also represents the more modern view that injured parties do not need to have a formal contract with other professionals whose work they rely on. This is significant, since more and more construction and renovation projects utilize several different classes of professionals to improve quality and time to delivery. What if the professional the general contractor relied on was the three-dimensional model builder?

The Tennessee case referred to in *EH Construction, LLC v. Delor Design Group*, is *John Martin Co. v. Morse/Diesel, Inc*. In this case the question of negligent misrepresentation was also an issue of first impression for the state of Tennessee (John Martin Co. v. Morse/Diesel, Inc. 1991). John Martin Company, a subcontractor sued Morse/Diesel, a construction manager for damages due to negligent misrepresentations made by the construction manager.

Provident Insurance Company hired Morse/Diesel as a construction manager to act on its behalf to hire subcontractors, coordinate their schedules and supervise their work. Provident later employed the John Martin Corporation (John Martin) as a subcontractor to provide concrete and rough carpentry. Morse/Diesel was not a party to the contract between Provident and John Martin, but Morse/Diesel acting as construction manager was directed to supervise John Martin's work.

During the construction of the building, an argument dispute started over the amount of concrete necessary for the subcontractor to complete its work.

John Martin filed suit against Morse/Diesel, alleging negligent misrepresentation upon which it relied causing the subcontractor to suffer damages. The appellate court stated that since Tennessee previously decided privity of contract was not a prerequisite for negligent misrepresentation against other types of professionals, such as title examiners, surveyors and attorneys; the same rule must extend to all professions whose business is to supply technical information for the guidance and use by others.

Consider *Kuhn Construction Company v. Ocean and Coastal Consultants Inc. and Robert Waite*. On August 20, 2009, the plaintiff Kuhn Construction Company filed suit for negligent misrepresentation against Ocean and Coastal Consultants, Inc. (OCC), and Robert F. Waite, P.E., P.C. (Waite) (Khun Construction Company Ocean v. Coastal Consultants and Robert Waite, PE, PC v. 2012). Prior to February 2007, an owner, Diamond State Port Corporation (DSPC) retained OCC as a construction manager in connection with the rehabilitation of Wharf Unit 2, Berth 4 (the project). In anticipation of contractors bidding on the project, OCC prepared (and DSPC distributed) bid documents, which included all of the drawings and specifications for the project.

These bid documents, containing the words "FOR BID PURPOSES ONLY", were meant to provide prospective bidders with the information they would need to submit their bids. The plaintiff alleged it reasonably relied on these documents when calculating its bid. As the lowest responsive and responsible bidder, plaintiff was hired by DSPC to be the general contractor on the project. DSPC and plaintiff entered into a $10 750 000 contract for plaintiff's services. DSPC also hired OCC to assist with the construction. Three events occurred which the plaintiff alleges is the basis of this lawsuit. Undisclosed changes to the bid documents were made after the award of the contract, unknown subsurface conditions were uncovered and there were problems with the welding. In May of 2007, OCC prepared and provided plaintiff with "Issued For Construction" drawings. These drawings, which indicated that no revisions existed, were meant to be the drawings that plaintiff relied on in the construction of the project. Because there was no indication of any marked up changes on the plans, the plaintiff requested that OCC mark any changes between the bid documents and the construction drawings. The plaintiff alleged that OCC purposefully covered significant changes in the design. One such change related to welding requirements. According to plaintiff, the bid documents indicated that welding would only be required to connect the lower sections of the steel pipe pile; the upper connection would not require welding. The plaintiff claimed that OCC lied on purpose telling them that there was language in the bid documents that required welding of the upper sections of the steel pipe piles. This is a common circumstance, where the drawings contradict the specifications. In the field it is much easier to read the plans than search through the specifications book. Another significant change that was allegedly concealed concerned datum and elevation changes.

According to plaintiff, there were numerous changes that were not disclosed, and were concealed, by OCC. The plaintiff also claimed these changes had a serious impact on their ability to work, since these changes meant much of the construction work would be impacted by the tides. Neither OCC nor DSPC would address the issue with the plaintiff.

Prior to preparing the bid documents, OCC reviewed the subsurface conditions. The plaintiff alleged that OCC misrepresented, in the bid documents, the effect that the subsurface conditions would have on the cost and duration of the project; the plaintiff also stated that it relied on these misrepresentations in calculating its bid. According to the plaintiff, several piles were damaged when they tried to drive them in areas designated by OCC in their drawings and the pile driving plan had to be altered.

In light of these alleged misrepresentations, the plaintiff claimed to have incurred additional labor and equipment expenses. The plaintiff also alleged that DSPC and OCC failed to address these issues despite the plaintiff's requests. Although the contract between the owner and the welder did not contain any specific welding requirements, or the requirement that the plaintiff use American Welding Society (AWS) prequalified base metals, OCC developed weld acceptance criteria to test the plaintiff's work for quality. Waite was hired by OCC to examine and report to OCC and DSPC about the quality of plaintiff's welds.

In accordance with OCC's plan, Waite examined the welds on 110 of the 360 steel pile pipes and issued several reports on the quality of those welds. In an August 15, 2008 report to OCC, Waite concluded that 27 of the 110 welds were problematic. The dislodgment rate should have been 0% but it was 25%. This indicated a severe problem with the weld quality in the top welds. The report ultimately concluded that there was a more than adequate justification for the rejection of all the top and extension welds due to gross non-conformance to the contract. Although the welds were rejected, Waite's engineering judgment could have been used to determine whether the welds were sufficient based on the anticipated service loading.

The only claim made against Waite in the plaintiff's complaint was one of negligent misrepresentation. In order to prove negligent misrepresentation under Delaware law, a plaintiff must show:

- the existence of a financial duty to provide accurate information;
- the supplying of false information;
- that the defendant failed to exercise reasonable care in obtaining or communicating the information; and
- that the plaintiff suffered a financial loss caused by reliance upon the false information.

A financial or pecuniary duty is not dependent on contractual privity just like the duty of care seen in previous cases. Pecuniary duty occurs when the parties are in a business relationship, from which they expect financial benefits. The engineer hired to monitor the welds (Waite), filed a motion to dismiss because he argued that the plaintiff could not prove false information was supplied. Waite argued that the lawsuit did allege any false statements, only statements based upon Waite's professional judgment.

On the other hand, the plaintiff argued that the "engineering conclusions and recommendations by [Waite] were not supported by industry standards and were erroneous" (Khun Construction Company Ocean v. Coastal Consultants and Robert Waite, P.E., PC v. 2012).

The court denied defendant Waite's motion to dismiss and upheld the trial court's decision.

12.2.5 Leadership

Facility Managers often find themselves in a position to exercise leadership. Understanding leadership techniques and strategies is best left to a course leadership theory, but it is helpful for students of the built environment to be aware of the various styles in use, especially their own styles. Facility Managers must adapt their leadership style not only to produce desired outcomes but also to avoid liability for negligence. The abusive, overzealous supervisor taking the "get it done at all costs" approach may not be the best professional model. One theory on leadership is Robert K. Greenleaf's theory of "Servant Leadership". The Servant Leadership organization is a not-for-profit organization that promotes this theory as an alternative to an authoritarian model. Additional information on servant leadership and can be found at www.greenleaf.org; and www.leadershiparlington.org/pdf/TheServantasLeader.pdf.

Since Facility Managers often supervise employees, the situation arises where the employee will have to be entrusted with potentially harmful equipment or products. If this trust is misplaced, employers and supervisors can be held liable for the tort of negligent entrustment. Negligent entrustment is usually associated with the leadership function of the Facility Manager because knowing when to trust an employee with a dangerous situation that could potentially harm her and others is one aspect of leadership. The leader is assumed by the courts to have superior knowledge about the employee, the dangerous object and the potential harm it can cause. Recall the torts of negligent hiring, supervision, retention and training discussed earlier. These torts are available as a cause of action for plaintiffs injured because the employer did not conduct a proper background check or did not notice an employee's poor performance. Negligent entrustment is a different type of tort in order to bring a lawsuit against an employer the situation must involve a dangerous object used by an employee to cause injury to a third party.

Negligent entrustment occurs when the "entrustor" is held liable because they negligently furnished another party, the "entrustee" with a dangerous object, and the entrusted party caused injury to a third party with that object. Typically, the dangerous object in these disputes is an automobile. Thus, if you negligently let an unsafe driver use the company van and injury occurs to a third party, you can be liable for the injuries.

One of the earliest reported cases under negligent entrustment is the 1915 Mississippi case of *Winn v. Haliday*. A father allegedly entrusted an automobile to his son who was known to be negligent (Winn v. Haliday 1915). The following quote from the court summarized that the key allegation that the plaintiff had to prove was:

> [W]whether the owner knew, or had reasonable cause to know, that he was entrusting his car to an unfit driver likely to cause injury to others. Furthermore, in order to impose liability upon the owner, the plaintiff must prove that the negligent entrustment of the motor vehicle to the tortfeasor was a proximate cause of the accident. (Winn v. Haliday 1915)

A *tortfeasor* is defined as one who commits a tort. According to the court, when a claim is brought against an employer, the employer will be held liable if the entrustee's record was known to the employer or would have been easily discoverable by that employer, had a diligent search been conducted. This means that the court will not only hold the employer liable for a reckless employee but also they must do a background check to make sure they know about the employee's reckless behavior in the past.

The "object" referred to in negligent entrustment cases is not restricted to automobiles and recently expanded to include all tangible items. The legal system refers to these tangible items as "chattels". Consider the 2010 case of *Shirley v. Glass*, in 2003 Elizabeth Shirley's ex-husband, Russell Graham who shared custody of their 8 year-old son, Zeus, asked his 77 year-old grandmother to drive him to purchase a shotgun (Shirly v. Glass 2010). Graham told his grandmother that he wanted to use to take his son dove hunting. But, because of a previous felony conviction, Graham was legally prohibited from buying a firearm so his grandmother had to make the purchase.

Graham and his grandmother completed the necessary paperwork for the gun purchase and, after completing the form, Graham paid for the gun and then carried it, the ammunition and cleaning kit to the grandmother's car.

The day after purchasing the gun, Russell Graham told Elizabeth Shirley he was going to commit suicide. Russell and Elizabeth's previous marriage ended after it developed into a dysfunctional relationship. According to the court, the issue was the doctrine of negligent entrustment and whether or not the doctrine could be expanded.

In Kansas, the doctrine of negligent entrustment imposes a duty on suppliers of goods not to supply goods to someone they know to be incompetent to safely use it. The question for the court was, whether or not the supplying of goods, referred to as "chattels", was the same as selling a gun.

The court expanded the definition in this case and imposed a liability on merchants under the doctrine of negligent entrustment for the first time in Kansas. The court further concluded that there was sufficient evidence for imposing liability on the firearm dealer. The court described the rationale for its decision by stating that a reasonable person would have anticipated that Graham would harm Zeus or others with the firearm. This doctrine is applied in most other states as well.

The elements necessary to establish liability under a theory of negligent entrustment include the following:

One who supplies directly or through a third person a chattel for the use of another, whom the supplier knows or has reason to know, in a manner involving unreasonable risk of physical harm to himself and others, whom the supplier should expect to share in or be endangered by its use, is subject to liability for physical harm resulting to them. The duty of the entrustor "runs directly to those who might be put at risk as a result of the negligent entrustment" (Johnson v. Johnson 2000). Negligence in entrusting a chattel to someone who is incompetent creates only the potential for liability; however, in order for liability to actually be found by a court, the supplier must also be found to be the legal cause of the harm (Axelson v. Williamson 1982).

Another example of negligent entrustment can be found in the 1989 case of *Lim v. Interstate System Steel Division, Inc.*, a car with six people in collided with an 18-wheel truck killing five of those six people in (Lim v. Interstate System Steel Division, Inc. 1989). The truck was leased from a company called Gaylon Mills, who employed the driver and received a percentage of the revenue from each load delivered. The truck driver tested positive for four stimulants after the crash. The trial court admitted evidence that the truck driver had been arrested four months earlier for possession of a controlled substance while driving as an employee of Gaylon Mills. The court indicated that the employer Gaylon Mills could be held independently liable for negligent entrustment under the doctrine of negligent entrustment.

12.3 Chapter summary

Carelessness or negligence is the common theme running through most cases of exposure to liability. The examples cases outlined in this chapter show that defendants either failed to exercise reasonable care, or failed to recognize that care was required. This chapter provides a summary of some of the legal ramifications associated with the profession of Facility Management. The student should remember that, in the most general terms, behaving like a professional and recognizing a professional duty not to injure others, is fundamental.

12.4 Questions

1. Define the tort of negligent hiring.
2. Define the tort of negligent entrustment.
3. Is it possible for an employer to be liable for both negligent hiring and negligent entrustment?
4. Would you say that, after reading this chapter, it seems as though employers are held strictly liable for the actions of their employees? Explain your answer.
5. Based on what you already know about defenses to negligence, what is a plausible defense for *Lim v. Interstate System Steel Division, Inc.* (1989)?
6. What advice would you give a new Facility Manager for a truck rental company with regard to negligent entrustment?
7. In your opinion, should an employer be held liable for entrusting a car to an employee who has been reckless in the past? Explain your answer.
8. In your opinion, should a firearms dealer be held liable for selling a gun to the friend of a convicted felon like Russell Graham? Explain your answer.
9. How far should an employer go to make sure she is not hiring a reckless employee?
10. Would it be fair to extend the legal doctrine of negligent entrustment to volunteer workers?

References

Cotts, D. *The Facility Management Handbook*. 2nd Edition. New York: American Management Association, 1999.

13

The Professional Facility Manager and the Law

> *Laws may be unjust, may be unwise, may be dangerous, may be destructive; and yet not be so unconstitutional as to justify the Judges in refusing to give them effect.*
>
> **James Wilson**

13.1 Introduction

The above quote by James Wilson, made during the Philadelphia Convention in 1787, is an example of a "legal formalist" point of view. This view essentially dictates that the law must be upheld because it is the law. In US jurisprudence, there are roughly two philosophies for the rule of law; a formalist sometimes called the *thin definition*, and a substantive also called the *thick definition*. Formalists like Wilson take the law at its face and try not to read too much into the rule. They do not judge the fairness of the rule and pay more attention to the procedures used to apply the law. Compare this view to the substantive definition. This viewpoint goes deeper and assumes the law contains notions of justice within the rules. Both viewpoints are valid because both viewpoints are represented in scholarly literature on the law. Whether you agree with the formalist or the substantive definition, the application of the law is usually the most relevant in our day-to-day lives.

Learning about the law and its operation in a vacuum is almost useless to the Facility Manager. Knowledge about the law without understanding how this knowledge is applied in practical terms is not the aim of this book. The underlying question to the study of the law for the Facility Manager should be

Legal Concepts for Facility Managers, First Edition. Linda Thomas-Mobley.
© 2014 John Wiley & Sons, Ltd. Published 2014 by John Wiley & Sons, Ltd.

"How do I avoid liability?" The simple answer is to perform the required duties of a professional Facility Manager.

The trouble with this simple answer is that generally, a Facility Manager's legal duty is much easier to understand after an accident happens. It is difficult to proactively define the law in every instance. It is much easier to give an example of a legal duty, such as "keep the parking lot safe", than it is to define and list the activities required to achieve safe a parking lot. No matter how long the list is, there will always be some task left off that might not have been contemplated before being faced with the problem. This challenge is present in most jobs requiring discretion and judgment. That's just the way it is.

Since the Facility Manager's job requires professional discretion the best way we have to define this professional duty is to do what the law requires. Because the law requires a Facility Manager to take the actions that would be taken by a reasonable Facility Manager under similar circumstances, and failure to take reasonable actions results in liability, there seems to be no definitive answer and our inquiry devolves into a never-ending cycle.

What is reasonable is not readily apparent but definitely answerable. Reasonable is whatever a reasonable, competent Facility Manager would do. To know the answer to this question, you only need to look as far as your industry association; to be a reasonable Facility Manager you must remain current in the field.

In addition to reasonableness, the Facility Manager has specifically defined duties. For example, if the building just had a new escalator installed, all of the manufacturer's instructions to maintain the warranty should be followed in case service is needed. Otherwise the Facility Manager can inadvertently void the warranty and cost her company unnecessary expenditures. The specifically defined duties are easier to follow because the extent of what must be done is expressly spelled out and can be scheduled. It is the professional duties and responsibilities that are not so well-defined, or even anticipated, which can cause problems.

What is a "reasonably" safe parking lot? It depends on the lot, the environment and what other Facility Managers in the community consider safe. Therefore, we say that the Facility Manager must operate as others operate, in a safe manner that is relatively defined so that risk can be mitigated. The more advanced our buildings become, the more will be required of Facility Managers. Responsibilities and skills essential to the Facility Manager in the twenty-first century are most likely way above expectations for the seventeenth century building caretaker.

This chapter includes specific examples of how the legal theory you've just learned about connects with the function of a professional Facility Manager. It is hoped that you will become more aware of the types of obligations required of the modern Facility Manager and how the courts have decided what is considered reasonable. By the end of this chapter, the following student learning outcomes are expected:

- Discuss the connection between the Facility Manager's function and the law.
- Define the function of OSHA, ADA and other statutes enacted to protect the employee.

13.2 Health and safety management

One of the many responsibilities of the Facility Manager rests with her function as the administrator of health and safety issues. Most Facility Managers are charged with protecting the physical assets and the occupants from injury. As you know, from the discussion of property law, the owner or controller of property has a legal duty to keep the premises safe and warn occupants of dangerous conditions. This common law duty applies to all jurisdictions, even if a safety statute does not exist.

You will also recall the owner or controller of the property has to protect not only invited guests, such as customers, but also other occupants she expects to be on the premises, including some trespassers. With the exception of adult trespassers, the duty to keep the premises free from dangerous conditions even extends to uninvited children.

Included with the responsibility for health and safety, the Facility Manager is accountable for workplace safety, the physical security of the occupants and any visitors, and the physical plant. The federal statute enacted to protect the health of workers is known as the Occupational Safety and Health Act of 1970 (OSHA 29 USC Chapter 15). The Department of Labor (DOL) website states:

> With the Occupational Safety and Health Act of 1970, Congress created the Occupational Safety and Health Administration (OSHA) to assure safe and healthful working conditions for working men and women by setting and enforcing standards and by providing training, outreach, education and assistance (Department of Labor n.d.).

The OSHA section of the DOL website is updated regularly, and is great source of detailed information on all workplace health and safety issues along with training information and statistics.

13.2.1 OSHA litigation

The OSHA cases illustrate the seriousness health and safety issues. The Facility Manager must strive to be knowledgeable and responsible for updating her knowledge annually. Some of the cases that follow may contain legal terms you are not familiar with. It is suggested that secure access to a legal dictionary or the Internet to find definitions for these terms; you will see them again in later cases.

In the first case, of *Whirlpool Corp. v. Marshall*, The defendant company (Whirlpool) maintained a manufacturing plant in Marion, Ohio, for the production of household appliances (Whirlpool Corp. v. Marshall 1980). Overhead conveyors move various appliance components used to build the machines throughout the plant. Whirlpool installed a horizontal wire-mesh screen approximately 20 feet above the plant floor to protect employees from objects that occasionally fall from the conveyors. Testimony was given that employees spend several hours each week removing objects from the screen, replacing paper lining the screen to catch grease drippings from the material on the conveyors, and performing occasional maintenance work on the conveyors themselves. Maintenance employees are usually able to stand on the iron frames to service the conveyors. To complete the service, sometimes employees find it necessary to step onto the steel mesh screen itself (Whirlpool Corp. v. Marshall 1980).

In 1973, the company began to install heavier wire in the screen because of safety complaints. Several employees fell partly through the old screen, and one employee fell completely through to the plant floor below and survived the fall. A number of maintenance employees brought the unsafe screen conditions to the attention of their foremen. Also, according to testimony, Whirlpool's safety procedures instruct employees to only step on the iron frames and not the mesh.

On June 28, 1974, a maintenance employee fell to his death through the guard screen in an area where the newer, stronger mesh had not yet been installed. Following this the company repaired the screen and issued an order strictly forbidding maintenance employees from stepping on either the screens or the iron frames supporting structure. An alternative method was developed for removing objects from the screen.

On July 7, 1974, two maintenance employees, Virgil Deemer and Thomas Cornwell, met with the plant maintenance superintendent to voice their concern about the safety of the screen. The superintendent disagreed with the workers, but permitted them to inspect the screen with their foreman with the goal of identifying dangerous areas needing repair. On July 9, Deemer and Cornwell met with the plant safety director. At that meeting, they requested the name, address and telephone number of a representative of the local office of the Occupational Safety and Health Administration (OSHA). Although the safety director told the men that they "had better stop and think about what [they] were doing" (Whirlpool Corp. v. Marshall 1980), he furnished the men with the information they requested. Later that same day, Deemer contacted an official of the regional OSHA office and discussed the guard screen.

The next day, their foreman, after himself walking on some of the angle-iron frames, directed Deemer and Cornwell to perform their usual maintenance duties on a section of the old screen. The two employees refused, claiming that the screen was unsafe. The foreman sent them to the personnel office, where they were ordered to stop working and told they would not be paid for the remaining six hours of the shift. Later, Deemer and Cornwell received written reprimands, which were placed in their employment files.

The head of OSHA, referred to as "the secretary" filed suit in the United States District Court, claiming that Whirlpool's actions against Deemer and Cornwell constituted discrimination under OSHA. The suit asked the court to order Whirlpool to remove from its personnel files all references to the reprimands issued to the two employees, and requested that the company compensate the two employees for the six hours of pay they lost. Following the trial, the District Court denied relief, stating that such relief is not available under OSHA statutes.

After appealing twice and ending up in front of the Supreme Court of the United States, the employees finally won their case. The court held that the "Occupational Safety and Health Act of 1970 (Act) prohibits an employer from discharging or discriminating against any employee who exercises 'any right afforded by'" the Act (Whirlpool Corp. v. Marshall 1980). This included the right to refuse work where an employee has a reasonable fear of death or serious injury or an illness occurring. Is this finding a surprise? How does this decision line up with the notion of employees working in an at-will situation that requires no cause to be stated for dismissal?

Automobile Workers v. Johnson Controls, Inc., decided in 1991, is especially useful to the Facility Manager because it involves issues of OSHA, discrimination under the Civil Rights Act of 1964 and environmental law, all in one case (Automobile Workers v. Johnson Controls, Inc. 1991). In this situation, a group of female workers sued Johnson Controls claiming discrimination.

The element lead is a primary ingredient in Johnson Controls' battery manufacturing process. Excessive exposure to lead poses health risks, including the risk of harm to any fetus carried by a female employee. According to testimony, eight employees became pregnant while maintaining blood lead levels exceeding that sited by OSHA as too high for a female worker planning to have a family. At some point after the employees became pregnant, Johnson Controls issued a policy barring all women of childbearing age, except those whose infertility was documented, from jobs involving potential lead exposure exceeding the OSHA standard (Automobile Workers v. Johnson Controls, Inc. 1991).

The group, including employees impacted by this policy, filed a class action lawsuit in the District Court, claiming that the policy constituted sex discrimination, which was a violation of Title VII of the Civil Rights Act of 1964. A class action lawsuit is a legal procedure by which large groups of plaintiffs with similar disputes can join together and sue a defendant.

The Supreme Court of the United States held in favor of the employees giving the reason that Title VII, as amended by the Pregnancy Discrimination Act (PDA), forbids sex-specific fetal-protection policies. By excluding women with childbearing capacity from jobs where they would be exposed to lead, the company explicitly discriminates against women on the basis of their sex. The court went on to explain,

> . . . an employer's potential tort liability for potential fetal injuries and its increased costs due to fertile women in the workplace do not require a different result. Moreover, the incremental cost of employing members of one sex cannot justify a discriminatory refusal to hire members of that gender. (Automobile Workers v. Johnson Controls, Inc. 1991)

Do you agree with this decision? Does it seem as though the employer was attempting to protect its female employees, keeping them out of harm's way? What modifications can Johnson Controls make to its policy to avoid discriminating?

In some circumstances, several statutes and different legal systems can overlap yet apply to one set of facts. Even though the Supreme Court decided *Whirlpool* after an appeal from lower trial and intermediate appellate courts, the agency also has the authority to hear disputes as long as they relate to health and safety statutes. OSHA citation disputes, which are available on their website, can be very informative. The administrative court charged with hearing OSHA cases is supplementary to the Occupational Safety and Health Review Commission (OSHRC). OSHRC is an independent federal agency, providing administrative trials and appellate hearings. It was specifically created to hear disputes involving OSHA citations or penalties. The court is called the Review Commission and consists of a two-tiered administrative court, for conducting hearings, receiving evidence and rendering decisions by its Administrative Law Judges (ALJs) and, second review (similar to an appeal) of ALJ decisions by a panel of Commissioners.

In a proceeding before the Occupational Safety and Health Review Commission, the ALJ determined if one of two citations made by OSHA inspectors was proper. According to the facts reported in a decision made in 2011, OSHA inspected a Taunton, Massachusetts work site, where 21st Century Roofing Systems, Inc. was engaged in roofing work. As a result of the inspection, on June 1, 2010, OSHA issued to a one-item "serious" citation and a one-item "repeat" citation. The serious citation alleged a violation "for failure to erect a warning line at least 6 feet from the roof edge". The repeat citation alleged a violation for "failure to protect employees engaged in roofing activities on a low-sloped roof from falls" (29 C.F.R. § 1926.502(f)(1)(i)). 21st Century Roofing Systems, Inc. disputed the violations. After hearing the testimony, the commission made a decision, which is reported on the commission's website. An excerpt from the reported case follows.

The Commission has the discretion to assess the penalties it finds appropriate. In assessing penalties, the Commission gives due consideration to the gravity of the cited condition and to the employer's size, history and good faith. . . . The [official] who conducted the inspection testified about the proposed penalties for the violations. He determined that both violations had high severity, in that falling from the roof would have resulted in serious injury or death. The serious violation had lesser probability, as there was a warning line erected on the roof. The repeat violation had greater probability, as several employees were working outside of the warning line and inches from the roof edge. OSHA applied a 60 percent reduction to the gravity-based penalties, due to the employer's size. No reductions were given for history or good faith. The employer had received a serious OSHA citation within the past three years, and its safety program was not being enforced at the site.

As set out supra, the Court assessed the gravity-based penalties without providing any reduction for company size. The Court finds a higher penalty is appropriate in light of the high severity of the violations and Respondent's overall lack of concern for employee safety and health evident by its recent past and current violations of the same standard. It is well settled that the Commission has the authority to assess a higher penalty than that proposed by the Secretary. . . . When an employer contests the Secretary's proposed penalty, the Secretary's assessment becomes "purely advisory" and the judge is required to independently arrive at an appropriate penalty. . . Under the circumstances of this case and the Commission's precedent, the Court finds the gravity-based penalties appropriate. A penalty of $2500 is therefore assessed for Item 1 of Citation 1, and a penalty of $14 000 is assessed for Item 1 of Citation 2. (Phillips 2011)

Navigating the OSHA regulations is not too difficult with some basic training and an understanding of the overall intent of the act, which is simply worker safety. Also understanding why and when an OSHA inspector would visit your property is helpful. The OSHA compliance officer will arrive at your facility to conduct an inspection if one of the situations depicted in Figure 13.1 occurs.

The legal cases applying the Occupational Safety and Health Act are the most thorough way to understand how the courts have decided these issues. The most prudent strategy is to leave case interpretation to the attorneys. Although you can access to all of the Commission's decisions, reading case after case is an arduous way to learn what is required under the Act. As a professional Facility Manager, OSHA training is required for your ongoing success and the success of those reporting to you.

13.3 Physical security issues

In this next section, we will look at the law regarding harms to people and property by third parties. Ensuring a safe workplace is but one component of the health and safety function. What are the legal ramifications of protecting

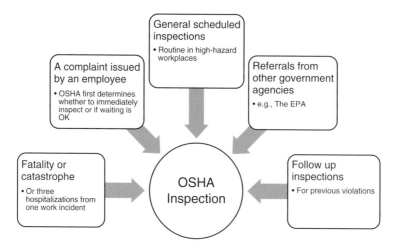

Figure 13.1   Situations generating an OSHA inspector visit.

building occupants and property from harm? What laws oversee a Facility Manager's discretion? Can a security guard use the same approaches to protect property that are used to protect a person?

13.3.1 *Protecting property*

A legal doctrine known as the "Castle Doctrine" designates an individual's home as a place in which the person has certain protections and immunities. The person may, in certain circumstances, use force, including deadly force, to defend against an intruder without being later guilty of a crime. The more recent legal doctrine of "Stand Your Ground" (SYG) employs similar legal theory and states that a person may use force in self-defense when there is reasonable belief of a threat, without an obligation to retreat first. We can say the SYG Doctrine is the Castle Doctrine without the need for a castle: both stating that force is justifiable under the law if a reasonable belief of a threat exists. Both doctrines are considered defenses available to the defendant choosing to use the force, but not considered legal immunity. Some are under the impression that these doctrines make a defendant immune to prosecution. What then, is the difference between having a defense and having immunity?

The difference between immunity and a defense is that immunity prevents an arrest, being charged with a crime, detained and subjected to a lawsuit. A defense, like the Castle or SYG Doctrines, permits a plaintiff or the state to sue but the defendant can use SYG or the Castle Doctrine as a mitigating circumstance to justify conduct. It is reasonable to think that the law expects people to defend their property, or hire a security guard to defend property. But can the action taken to defend the property be justified if the trespasser is killed? Can you kill an intruder in defense of property? Also, can the Castle

Doctrine be used in states without a SYG law to defend against a fatality resulting from the protection of commercial property?

The debate over how far an owner can go to protect her property is as old as the concept of property ownership itself. In *Phelps v. Hamlett*, the question was put to the court. In May of 1917, the defendant, Hamlett, was the renter of a vacant open-air theater building in the city of Abilene (Phelps v. Hamlett 1918). Even though the property was vacant, it still attracted children. The defendant was aware that many people frequented the theater and used it as an informal social center. Sometime near the beginning of May, Hamlett placed an iron pipe bomb under the floor of the stage and loaded it with a dangerous explosive. The bomb was placed out of sight and designed to explode when the door was opened.

Milton Phelps, without knowledge of the bomb or any danger, entered the building setting off an explosion. A large jagged piece of iron was blown through the upper portion of his right thigh, causing a serious wound and much pain. According to the plaintiff, the bomb was intended to stop unauthorized persons from entering the building. During the trial, the court found for the defendant, Hamlett, and the plaintiff, Phelps, appealed this decision. The appellate court found that:

> *While the law authorizes an owner to protect his property by such reasonable means as he may find to be necessary, yet considerations of humanity preclude him from setting out, even on his own property, traps and devices dangerous to the life and limb of those whose appearance and presence may be reasonably anticipated, even though they may be trespassers. We conclude that the judgment must be reversed and the cause remanded, because of error in the court's charge.* (Phelps v. Hamlett 1918)

The court's language at the end of the excerpt indicates the appellate court did not decide for or against the plaintiff, it simply reversed the decision for the defendant and remanded (sent back) the case to be retried. Does this case tell us how the trial court should decide who wins? The relevant "law" of this case is in the court's quote. To paraphrase, an owner can protect her property but not set harmful traps, not even for known trespassers.

In *Phelps* the harm caused was grave but not fatal: consider the case of *The People v. Silver*. The defendant, aged 22, was the son-in-law of Mrs Shook, the owner of a mine operating under the name of Temescal Clay Company (The People v. Silver 1940). The mine consisted of two open areas cut into the side of a mountain from which the mineral silica was taken. Above the open areas and right next to the property was a 640-gallon gasoline storage tank, with an unlocked, open gasoline pump located near a road. The gasoline was for the operation of the mine. Previously, gasoline had been stolen from the tank. On November 24 and 25, 1939, the defendant was stationed as a watchman on the property. On the night of November 25, 1939 the watchman walked to a point 84 feet above the gasoline pump. The watchman saw an automobile driving on the property without lights. He picked up a rifle and then saw the car back up to the gasoline pump. The defendant testified that he called out "What do you want?"; and after receiving no answer he called, "If you don't get out I will shoot". After this the watchman then shot, waited a few moments, called again, and then fired two more shots. After the second shot he heard a sound and thought someone was coming up the hill toward him. He fired another shot and ran back over the hill. The defendant called the deputy sheriff at Barstow and went to a friend's home, and then a doctor administered morphine for his nerves. He later found out that Lee Hartman had been shot and killed. Also Hartman, with his two younger brothers, Walter and Ernest, were the ones who had driven to the mining property to steal gasoline. Evidence at the trial showed that the three brothers had been to the mine before to steal gas (The People v. Silver 1940).

A different set of facts emerged at trial by Hartman's brothers. The brothers testified that, on the night in question, they arrived on the property in their automobile, turned out the lights and backed up the hill to the gasoline pump. All three boys got out of the car. While Lee and Ernest were draining the hose, a shot was fired from the hill. Lee was struck by a bullet through the chest, fell backward and apparently died immediately. The same shot entered the leg of the other brother. The boys all stated that no words of warning were given by defendant before the first shot. The brothers also testified that Ernest then started up the hill toward defendant and shouted "Stop shooting, mister!" He claims that he then heard a voice that said "Get the hell out of there or I will shoot you" and "If you don't get out I will fill you all full of lead." A second shot followed as Ernest was trying to put Lee in the back seat of the car. He testified that he again called to defendant and said, "Don't shoot any more . . . one of my brothers is shot" (The People v. Silver 1940). The brother claimed that the watchman said, "I told you guys to get out." Before they left for their home, a third shot was fired over the car. Lee was taken to the mortuary and Walter received medical aid at the hospital (The People v. Silver 1940). The defendant watchman was charged with murder. After a plea of not guilty, he was tried before a jury, which returned a guilty verdict for manslaughter. The defendant appealed. At the appellate court the defendant claims that the homicide was justifiable. The court stated the statute in California at that time:

> *Homicide is. . . justifiable. . . 1. When resisting any attempt. . . to commit a felony. . . or, 2. When committed in defense of habitation, property, or person against one who manifestly intends or endeavors by violence, or surprise, to commit a felony. . .*

It is defendant's position that the Hartmans, who according to their own testimony entered upon the property that defendant was guarding, with intent to and from which they did steal gasoline, were guilty of the felony of burglary.

In this connection reference is made to the code definition of burglary (Penal Code, sec. 459), namely, "Every person who enters any. . . mine, or any underground portion thereof, with intent to commit grand or petit larceny or any felony is guilty of burglary" (The People v. Silver 1940). The appellate court reversed the lower courts verdict of manslaughter and sent the trial back down to be retried. The relevant law of *People v. Silver* is that homicide is justifiable in some cases, these include for defense of property or person from someone who intends to commit a felony. This seems to be the opposite from the Phelps case. Is it because Phelps was a Texas case and this case followed California law? Does that mean that one can kill to protect property in California but not in Texas?

After reading these two cases you can see how the law differs and that there is no definitive rule regarding the use of deadly force to protect property. At best we can say the law is in flux, but you would think that by now the matter would have been solved. What can be said is that, in situations where an owner kills a trespasser in protection of her property, whether or not the owner will be charged with homicide depends on the facts of the particular case. Among legal scholars, the debate in this arena boils down to what one believes to be the purpose of the law. Is it to compensate for wrongs suffered? Which is the substantive philosophy? Or is it to shape the conduct of people in a society? This is the philosophy that falls under the formalist view. If your opinion falls under the substantive/compensation view, you would conclude that killing a human being in defense of property is always wrong. On the other hand, if you ascribe to the formalist/shaping view, then as long as the letter of the law was followed, killing in defense of property is justified (Posner 1972).

In these cases, the defendants were potentially liable because they themselves decided to act and someone was injured. What happens when an employer or Facility Manager is held responsible for the wrongs committed by security guards?

Under common law, employers can be liable for employees' torts committed within the course of their employment. We have seen how this operates in a former case. Understanding that torts are different from crimes, employers are at risk when the wrongs of their employees arise while employees are performing their jobs.

The key to understanding when the Facility Manager will be liable for the wrongs of her employees is strongly related to the degree of control she exercises over the employees' actions. Let's see how that plays out in the cases that follow.

In *Fifth Club, Inc. v. Ramirez*, Officer West, a certified peace officer, worked for a nightclub as an independent contractor to provide security (Fifth Club v. Ramirez 2006). This is a common situation and law enforcement officers often have second jobs providing security while they are off duty. Late one evening, Roberto Ramirez was denied admission to the club allegedly because he was intoxicated. The club doorman asked Officer West to escort Ramirez away from the entrance. West allegedly then grabbed Ramirez and slammed his head against a wall, knocking him unconscious. Ramirez sued both Officer West and the Fifth Club. At trial a jury found Fifth Club vicariously liable for West's conduct and for negligently hiring him. After the intermediate appellate court agreed with the trial court, the Fifth Club appealed to the Texas Supreme Court. In the court's opinion, they noted that employers generally don't have a duty to ensure that their independent contractors perform work in a safe manner, but employers can be held vicariously liable for an independent contractor's actions if they retain control over the manner in which the contractor performs the work. In this case, the doorman directed West to remove Ramirez from the entrance, but did not tell Ramirez how to remove him. According to the Texas Supreme Court, by not telling the officer how to do his security job, the owner of the club was not held vicariously liable for West's actions

13.4 Vicarious liability

There is something aberrant about being held liable for the acts of others. It seems only fair that we are only liable for our own acts of negligence. Entirely opposite to this way of thinking lies the artificial legal notion of vicarious liability. The courts have long recognized vicarious liability. The New York case in 1871 of *Higgins v. Watervliet Turnpike Co.* is a relevant example. In this case, a train conductor by the name of Mr Higgins removed a passenger from a train for misconduct (Higgins v. Watervliet Turnpike Co. 1871). The defendant's testimony stated that the passenger was noisy and acting disorderly refusing to obey orders. According to the passenger who was ejected, unnecessary force was used in ejecting him resulting in an injury.

   The court attributed the conductor's actions to his employer, the railroad. The railroad was held liable because the court stated it could not act except through its agents and employees. Ejecting passengers who misbehaved was completely within the authority of the conductor performing his job as the railroad's agent. The decision to impose vicarious liability was founded on public policy and convenience. The court noted "[e]very person is bound to use due care in the conduct of his business. If the business is committed to an agent or servant, the obligation is not changed." The court also stated "the negligence of the agent is the negligence of the principal". The court found for the passenger and against the railroad company (Higgins v. Watervliet Turnpike Co. 1871).

   What if the employee harms someone because she acted in a way that is prohibited by her employer? Would the employer still be liable? A South Dakota court was faced with this very question in *Thompson v. United States*. On July 12, 1975, Benjamin Kitteaux was a trainee employed by the Crow Creek Sioux

Tribe as a police officer (Thompson v. United States 1980). While Kitteaux was on duty, he arrived at the police station of the Bureau of Indian Affairs, United States Department of the Interior, where the tribal police were headquartered. Inside the building, Kitteaux drew his gun, and pointed it at Tommy Thompson. According to testimony Kitteaux then brought the gun down alongside his leg, and pretending to perform a "fast draw", pulled the gun up again. Kitteaux frequently practiced his "fast draw". This time, however, the gun fired, the bullet struck Thompson in the chest, and Thompson died.

Using the Federal Tort Claims Act as governing law, his surviving mother filed a suit against the United States for the wrongful death of her son. In an independent criminal trial, Kitteaux plead guilty and the court convicted him of involuntary manslaughter. This lawsuit was filed against the United States under the Federal Tort Claims Act.

Among others, a major issue for the court to decide was whether Benjamin Kitteaux was an "employee of the government". The government argued that tribal policemen were officially hired by the Tribal Council, paid by the Tribe, and could be fired by the Tribal Council. Because of this, the government insists that Kitteaux was not one of its employees. Also the government argued that even though Kitteaux's wages ultimately comes from the federal government, he is not considered a federal employee.

The court stated that the crucial question to be answered was not the source of wages used to pay Kitteaux, "but whether [the employee's] day-to-day operations are supervised by the Federal Government" (Thompson v. United States 1980). In this situation, the government is responsible for the day-to-day supervision of all tribal policemen, including Kitteaux. Thus he classifies as government employee. In addition to proving that Kitteaux was an employee of the government at the time an accident occurred the plaintiff (Kitteaux's mother) must also prove that at the time of the injury, the employee was acting within the scope of his office or employment. To determine this, the court looked at the state law that governs employee classification. In South Dakota the court followed the law of a previous case called Skow v. Steele. In that case the employer is liable for "the acts of the servant, within the general scope of his employment, while engaged in his master's business, and done [with] a view to the furtherance of that business and the master's interest . . . even though the acts be done wantonly and willfully" (Skow v. Steele 1951).

Was Kitteaux acting within the scope of his employment when Thompson was killed? The facts of the case state that:

- Kitteaux was on duty at the time,
- Within the confines of the police station,
- Armed with his officially issued gun.

Is this enough? Not quite, one more element must be shown according to South Dakota. It must be determined if the police trainee was "engaged in his master's business". The court determined this by looking at the employee's motive. What was Kitteaux's motive in leveling his gun at Thompson? Was it to shoot Thompson? The court determined from the trial records that Kitteaux was a recently hired police trainee and, as a part of his training as a policeman, he was given firearms training by a Special Agent of the FBI, David Powers. His training included extensive instruction of "quick draw". The Court determined, though tragically misconceived, Kitteaux's motive in pulling up his gun and pointing it at Thompson was to practice and perfect his weapon technique. Kitteaux intended to improve himself as a policeman so he could carry out his employer's business.

The defendant, who in this case is the federal government, complained that such behavior was strictly forbidden. The court stated that whether it was forbidden or not does not allow defendant to escape liability, for the law is plain that an "act may be within the scope of employment even though forbidden or done in a forbidden manner" (Alberts v. Mutual Service Casualty Insurance Co. 1963).

The court ruled that the act that killed Thompson occurred in the scope of Benjamin Kitteaux's office as a federal employee. At the end of the appeal, the court found the following:

- That the person responsible for the Thompson's death was a government employee,
- That the killing took place within that employee's scope of office, and
- That the death was the result of that employee's negligent act.

If nothing else, this case should convince you to be very careful who you hire as an employee. What if you hire an independent contractor instead? Will you be able to shift your risk to the independent contractor? Maybe.

Consider the case of *Becker v. Poling Transportation Corp.* Mr Becker and Mr Jurgens were employees of Poling Transportation Corporation ("Poling"). In August of 1995, they both were severely burned in a fire that happened while they were moving petroleum from a canal boat to a truck that was parked at the dockside (Becker v. Poling Transportantion Corp. 2004). The canal boat was a decrepit barge that was about to be sold but before the sale could take place, water and unused petroleum in the holds of the barge had to be removed. Poling's dispatcher, Rick Carment, was instructed to clean out the barge.

Poling's dispatcher called Joseph Squadritto, the Director of Marketing at Metro, to see if they wanted the petroleum in exchange for arranging to have it picked up. Poling told Metro that a vacuum truck was needed to move the product because the pump on the canal boat was broken.

Metro agreed to the deal but could not perform the work itself. Metro then asked another company called Ultimate to pick up the petroleum, even though they knew that Ultimate did not have a vacuum truck. To recap, a supervisor told the employee to clean out petroleum from a boat; the employee asked another company if they wanted the petroleum for free if they removed it; in order to remove the petroleum, a vacuum truck was needed. The other company, Metro agreed to remove the petroleum and asked someone else (Ultimate) to pick it up, knowing that they did not have the proper equipment for moving the substance.

On the day Ultimate was scheduled to remove the oil, Becker and Jurgens were assigned to assist. Becker and Jurgens used a portable pump to successfully remove the water and the supervisor was told that a vacuum truck would be coming to remove the petroleum later that afternoon. He was told that he was to supervise the petroleum transfer. Neither Jurgens, Becker or Ultimate's employee seem to ever have transferred petroleum from ship to truck. Furthermore, they had never received training on how to do so. At about 5:30 pm, the Ultimate truck, which was not a vacuum truck, arrived at the Poling yard. Also, according to testimony, the Ultimate employee informed them that Ultimate did not have vacuum trucks. Jurgens, Becker, and the Ultimate driver decided to use the portable pump that had been used earlier that day to transfer the water.

At this point in the case, it should be obvious that mistakes in judgment were made and an accident was waiting to happen. The portable pump was used to fill the first load of petroleum with no problem. The pump was then shut down to prepare for the second load. When the pump was restarted, a fire broke out on the canal boat burning both Becker and Jurgens. Becker and Jurgens sued Poling, Ultimate and Metro for their injuries.

Ultimate, the company without the vacuum truck, settled out of court paying Becker and Jurgens $250 000. Poling filed for bankruptcy, making Metro the only defendant left to appear at trial.

The court had to decide if Metro was also liable for Ultimate's negligence. The three theories of law that would make Metro liable were:

- Agency, did Ultimate act as an agent for Metro, making Metro responsible for negligence of its agents?
- Vicarious liability, since Ultimate was an independent contractor if the work was inherently dangerous, did Metro try to contract away liability for inherently dangerous activities?
- Negligent hiring, Was Metro at fault for hiring someone who could not perform the task?

A jury trial determined Ultimate was 100% at fault and found Metro liable for Ultimate's negligence under two of the three previous theories. First, although Ultimate was an independent contractor, the work contracted for was "inherently dangerous", thus creating vicarious liability for Metro. When a task is considered inherently dangerous, one cannot use a contract to shift the risk. Second, Metro was liable for negligently selecting Ultimate, a carrier without a vacuum truck.

The judge entered judgment against Metro for the amount of the verdict, subtracting the money already paid by Ultimate. The resulting judgment was in the amount of $535 000–255 000 for Becker and $280 000 for Jurgens.

13.4.1 Americans with Disabilities Act

The Americans with Disabilities Act (ADA) is just one of the laws prohibiting discrimination, enforced by the federal government. The agency responsible for enforcing these laws is the Equal Opportunity Employment Commission (EEOC). Several statutes enforced by the EEOC have previously been mentioned, Figure 13.2 depicts the entire list of statutes enforced by the EEOC.

Although the ADA is just one of the anti-discrimination laws enforced by the EEOC, it is an important law, significant for the Facility Manager. Failing to adhere to the intent of ADA is not only a building concern; it may also expose responsible parties to compensatory and putative damages for discrimination. According to the US Census, 36 million people have a disability. This represents 12% of the civilian non-institutionalized population (US Census 2011). Since becoming law on July 26, 1990 the Americans with Disabilities Act (ADA), has changed buildings and the entire construction industry. Offices are now required to be built so that individuals with disabilities who are qualified to perform a job can be accommodated, as long as the

Statute	Purpose
The Fair Labor Standards Act of 1938	Prescribes for the basic minimum wage and overtime pay, affects most private and public employment also restricts hours that children under age 16 can work
The Civil Rights Act of 1964	Prohibits employment discrimination based on race, color, religion, sex and national origin
The Age Discrimination in Employment Act of 1967	Protects employees and job applicants aged 40 years or older from employment discrimination based on age
The Occupational Safety and Health Act of 1970	Primary federal law governing occupational health and safety in the private sector and federal government
The Employee Retirement Income Security Act of 1974	Sets minimum standards for most voluntarily established pension and health plans in private industry to provide protection for individuals in these plans
The Americans with Disabilities Act of 1990	Protects people with disabilities, prohibiting discrimination in employment, public services, public accommodations and telecommunications
The Family and Medical Leave Act of 1993	Provides certain employees with up to 12 weeks of unpaid, job-protected leave per year. It also requires that their group health benefits be maintained during the leave

Figure 13.2   Statutes enforced by the EEOC.

accommodation is reasonable. But what is a disability? An accommodation? Or even the definition of reasonable under this statute?

Consider *Rodriguez v. ConAgra Grocery Products Co.* Rodriguez was diagnosed with Type II diabetes in 1997 (Rodriguez v. Conagra Grocery Products Co. 2006). A person with Type II diabetes suffers from a reduced ability to produce insulin and a reduced ability to actually use the insulin that his body does produce. As a result, sugar builds up in the blood stream, leading to hyperglycemia, which develops gradually over time.

ConAgra owns a plant in Texas. In January 2002, a temporary agency placed Rodriguez to perform heavy manual labor, including unloading delivery trucks and lifting heavy sacks. Because of the quality of Rodriguez's work, a supervisor recommended that ConAgra offer Rodriguez a permanent position. In late February 2002, ConAgra offered Rodriguez a job as a "Production Utility" employee in the plant's production area. The offer was contingent on Rodriguez's passing a background check, a drug screen and a physical exam.

A month later, with offer in hand, Rodriguez visited a private clinic with which ConAgra had an arrangement to perform all of its pre-employment physical exams. Dr Jerry Morris performed Rodriguez's physical exam. Dr Morris concluded that Rodriguez's diabetes was "uncontrolled". On the medical form submitted to ConAgra, the doctor wrote that Rodriguez was not qualified for medical reasons for the position at the plant because of "uncontrolled diabetes". Dr Morris also told Rodriguez that he did not believe Rodriguez was controlling his diabetes. Rodriguez's oral medical history and physical exam showed that he suffered no physical or mental problems attributable to his diabetes. And, Dr Morris said that he observed no ill effects attributable to Rodriguez's diabetes. After the exam, Rodriguez was informed that he would not be hired because he failed the physical exam and Dr Morris did not recommend him for employment. Four days after ConAgra withdrew the job offer, Rodriguez filed a charge of discrimination with the Equal Employment Opportunity Commission ("EEOC").

The Americans with Disabilities Act of 1990 (ADA) makes it unlawful for an employer to discriminate against "a qualified individual with a disability because of the disability of such individual in regard to job application procedures, the hiring, advancement, or discharge of employees, employee compensation, job training, and other terms, conditions, and privileges of employment" (42 U.S.C. § 12112(a)). The ADA defines a "qualified individual with a disability" as "an individual with a disability who, with or without reasonable accommodation, can perform the essential functions of the employment in question". The ADA also states that the term disability means:

- A physical or mental impairment that substantially limits one or more major life activities of such individual;
- A record of such an impairment; or
- Being regarded as having such an impairment.

Also, even if an employer discriminates against a "qualified individual with a disability", that employer can avoid liability by asserting a legitimate justification for its action, including that the plaintiff, if hired, would "pose a direct threat to the health or safety of other individuals in the workplace" (42 U.S.C. § 12112(a)).

According to the court, these rules required Mr Rodriguez prove three elements in order to prevail: at the time he sought employment he had a "disability" within the meaning of the ADA; he was qualified for the position for which he sought employment; and he was not hired because of his disability.

The court stated that the relevant questions were: at the time that ConAgra withdrew its offer to employ Rodriguez, did he have a disability within the meaning of the ADA? And, if so, did ConAgra withdraw the job offer because of that disability? The appellate court held that ConAgra discriminated against Rodriguez and returned the case to the district court for a determination of Rodriguez's damages.

In *EEOC v. Convergys Customer Management Group Inc.*, Convergys hired Demirelli as a call representative (EEOC v. Convergys Customer Management Group Inc. 2007). Demirelli was confined to a wheelchair because of brittle bone disease. To keep its call stations consistently attended, Convergys maintains a strict tardy policy. Convergys penalizes employees who are more than three minutes late, either reporting for work at the company's call center or returning from a 30-minute lunch break. Employees with 14 or more violations in a single year could be sanctioned. Potential sanctions range from a written warning to termination of employment.

For the first year of his employment, Demirelli often reported for work and returned from lunch late. Court records show that Demirelli was late reporting for work 37 times and late returning from lunch 65 times. This number was far over the company's 14 time-tardy allowance. Demirelli testified that his tardiness reporting to work was due to the lack of sufficient handicapped parking at Convergys's call center. The call center's large parking area only had two van-accessible, handicapped parking spaces-spaces large enough for a special-needs van to operate a ramp or motorized lift. These two spaces were usually occupied when Demirelli arrived, thus causing him to either wait for the space to become unoccupied or find an alternative parking space. Demirelli made unsuccessful efforts to reduce his tardiness for work. He tried arriving at work earlier but the two parking spots were still unavailable. Demirelli then began parking at a nearby movie theater, but traveling via wheelchair from the theater's parking lot to the call center took over 10 minutes and caused Demirelli considerable physical pain. Finally, Demirelli requested different hours hoping that one of the two special needs parking spaces might be available at a later hour. But even during a later work-shift, the two special-needs spots were still occasionally occupied.

Demirelli's condition and the layout of Convergys's call center hampered an on-time lunch return. Convergys's call center is a maze of hundreds of cubicles where individual call representatives answer customer calls.   Cubicles are not assigned to specific call representatives; when call representatives report for work or return from lunch, they claim the first cubicle that they can find. Most employees simply look over the top of the rows of cubicles to find an available workstation. However, this option was not available to the wheelchair-confined Demirelli. He was forced to examine each workstation. This time-consuming exercise was exacerbated by narrow aisles, making it difficult for Demirelli to navigate obstacles such as stray chairs or chatting colleagues. His search was further complicated by the fact that not every workstation was fully operational; occasionally, a workstation would be available but missing a headset or other necessary equipment (EEOC v. Convergys Customer Management Group Inc. 2007).

Initially, Demirelli's supervisor reserved a workstation for him. However, after a few months, Demirelli's supervisor was replaced. His new supervisor refused to reserve a workstation for him. A few months before his termination, Demirelli began seating himself at workstations reserved for training. His supervisors expressed their displeasure with him sitting there but did not require him to move. When his supervisors approached him to discuss his tardiness, Demirelli explained that he was having problems finding a parking space and a workstation. He asked that he be given "a grace period" of a few extra minutes to return from lunch to work. Convergy's denied this request. On June 27, 2002, Convergys terminated Demirelli's employment.

Demirelli filed a claim with the EEOC, which in turn brought this enforcement action. The case proceeded to trial, and a jury awarded Demirelli $14 265.22 in lost wages and $100 000 in other compensatory damages. After this trial, Convergys appealed arguing that it cannot be held liable for failure to accommodate Demirelli because he did not request a specific, reasonable accommodation. Furthermore the employer states that Demirelli's accommodations were unreasonable.

The law requires employers and employees to work together to resolve ADA accommodation requests. According to cases that have interpreted the Act, the disabled employee must initiate the accommodation-seeking process by making his employer aware of the need for an accommodation. Additionally, the employee must provide relevant details of his disability and, if not obvious, the reason that his disability requires an accommodation.

Once the employer is made aware of the legitimate need for an accommodation, they should analyze the employee's job tasks and the specific limitations imposed by the disability. After this analysis the employer and employee should identify potential effective accommodations. This shared responsibility for figuring out a solution is fair because the employee will usually know what types of accommodations would help her and the employer would know what types of accommodations would be reasonable at the workplace, and if there are any other jobs the employee can perform.

The court held that the employee properly requested an accommodation, therefore meeting the burden of initiating the request. The court also stated that there is no precise definition of "reasonable accommodation", and whether an accommodation is reasonable is a question of fact to be decided by a jury at the trial court. Additionally, the ADA already recognizes extra time as a reasonable accommodation. The court held that the employee's request for extra time was a reasonable accommodation and agreed with the trial court.

Why did the employer Convergys think that it is the responsibility of the employee to first to ask for accommodations? The case of *Kratzer v. Rockwell Collins, Inc.*, is often used to support the argument that a disabled employee must request a specific and reasonable accommodation (Kratzer v. Rockwell Collins, Inc. 2005). In Kratzer, a disabled employee needed to prove her proficiency with four different types of machines in order to receive a promotion. However, her disability prevented her from sitting in front of the machines for the full amount of time necessary to demonstrate her proficiency. Both Kratzer and her employer started the interactive process to find a reasonable accommodation that would allow her to use the machines and demonstrate her proficiency. As a part of this interactive process, Kratzer agreed to undergo a medical evaluation that would provide her employer with information necessary to fashion a proper accommodation. During this process, however, Kratzer did not provide certain medical information. After being denied the promotion, Kratzer sued, alleging that her employer failed to accommodate her disability. The court held that Kratzer failed to fulfill her responsibility in the interactive process when she failed to provide information necessary for her employer to fashion an appropriate accommodation.

The EEOC settled an ADA case against Starbucks in 2007. A barista with mental impairments (including bipolar and attention deficit disorders) performed well when she was accommodated with extra training and support, but a new manager stopped accommodating her. When her performance suffered, he cut her hours, berated her in front of customers, placed her on a performance improvement plan and discharged her. With the help of the EEOC the case settled for $75 000 in monetary relief to the barista and an additional $10 000 to the Disability Rights Legal Center. The employer was also required to remove all bad reviews and notes from the barista's employment file and post its EEO policy and a notice of the settlement at all stores in the area.

In *EEOC v. E.I. DuPont De Nemours & Co.*, *DuPont*, a chemical plant fired a lab clerk with scoliosis of the lumbar spine and lumbar disc disease because the company believed it was unsafe for her to walk anywhere at the plant (EEOC v. El DuPont De Nemours & Co. 2007). The company representative required the employee to take a physical examination due to her difficulty in walking. After the examination, the company concluded that it was unsafe for her to walk at all on the plant site because she would hinder an emergency evacuation. The company argued that evacuating in an emergency was an essential function of her job and that she was unable to perform that function.

At trial, the EEOC Commission presented testimony from an ADA accessibility expert who said that the lab clerk could safely evacuate the plant. The Commission also presented testimony from an occupational rehabilitation expert, who said that the lab clerk could perform the essential functions of her job and that evacuating a facility in an emergency was not an essential job function. The Commission called company managers who testified clerk did not pose a hazard and that the physical examination was not proper because it tested areas that were not part of the lab clerk's job. The jury returned a verdict for the Commission, awarding $91 000 in back pay, $200 000 in front pay and $1 million in punitive damages (EEOC v. El Du Pont De Nemours & Co. 2007). The employer appealed, and the Fifth Circuit affirmed the judgment with respect to liability, back pay and punitive damages. It reversed only the front pay award.

Understanding what triggers the ADA and what accommodations are reasonable is not just a matter of your judgment, it is a matter of law that may have been settled. Keeping up with the various EEOC decisions regarding ADA is paramount. Monthly updates are published at the EEOC's website.

13.5 Premises liability litigation

In *Harness v. Churchmembers Life Insurance Co. Et Al*, a lawsuit was brought by Stephen Harness' father against the defendants for the wrongful death of his 6-year-old son. The father alleged Churchmembers Life Insurance Company (CLIC) was the owner of land in Marion County, Indiana, and in September of 1951 they began the excavation of a pit for the installation of a septic tank on the land. The insurance company employed George F. Kopetsky to do the installation and Glen Ashmore to supervise construction. In November of 1951, Mr Kopetsky and Mr Ashmore completed the excavation of the pit, which was approximately 6 feet wide running north and south and 12 feet long running east and west. Around the perimeter, large steep mounds of earth sloped directly into the pit.

The pit sat unused from November 1, 1951, until after December 14, 1951. During this vacancy, 6 feet of water accumulated in the bottom. The pit was located in a residential area with a large number of children. During construction, many of the neighborhoods children often played on the lot and around the pit. By December 14, 1951 the pit, with its mounds of dirt and accumulated water, had frozen and was covered with snow. The court stated that this ice pond, although natural looking, was actually an artificial condition not found in nature. On December 14, 1951, at about 4:30 p.m. Stephen Harness left his home approximately 150 yards from the pit and went to the pit to play on the mounds of dirt around it. While playing on the mounds of dirt Stephen slipped onto the ice in the pit, which broke under his weight, and he drowned in the water.

The defendants argued the following:

1. *The facts alleged therein do not establish the artificially created pit was an attractive nuisance.*
2. *The facts alleged show that the plaintiff's decedent was a trespasser upon the land of the defendant Churchmembers Life Insurance Company.*
3. *The facts alleged do not show that the pit described therein was inherently dangerous.*
4. *The facts alleged do not show that the pit described therein created an unreasonable risk to children of tender years.*

(Harness v. Chruchmembers Life Insurance Co. 1961).

On January 9, 1958, the trial court found for the father. The appeals court stated that a business owner is usually responsible for the sidewalk in front of an establishment and the customer parking lot. Recall from the chapter on property law that the Facility Manager and owner are responsibile not only for the property where business is conducted but also the property someone would use to approach the main building. A slip and fall on naturally occurring ice is now treated no differently than a slip and fall on a foreign substance. In Dumas v. Tripps of North Carolina, Inc., the Georgia Court of Appeals went further and abandoned the traditional rule with regards to naturally occurring ice on the premises and, citing Robinson v. Kroger Co., held that the buildup of naturally occurring ice does not excuse the owner's duty to exercise care in inspecting the property to make sure it is safe for invitees.

What if the danger on the premises is not a physical obstruction, but a danger of a different kind? In the very sad case of Southstar Equity LLC. v. Lai Chau, the dangerous condition that existed was one of potential criminal activity (Southstar Equity LLC v. Lai Chau 2008). Southstar owned the property and hired Brookside Properties to operate the apartment. Both the owner and property manager were sued by Lai Chau for damages suffered due to a dangerous condition on the property.

Chau rented an apartment after she was told by employees that the complex was safe. One night around midnight when she was returning to her apartment at the Remington, Chau was carjacked and abducted by three young men. The abductors took Chau in her car to another location where they shot her in the head three times. The abductors took her car but surprisingly, Chau survived.

The trial jury found in favor of Chau on three different causes of action: negligence, negligent misrepresentation and intentional misrepresentation. Chau claimed the defendant owner and property manager failed to provide adequate security to protect against realistically conceivable criminal acts at the Remington. Also, according to Chau, the defendants had a corporate policy of misleading tenants and prospective tenants by concealing the high level of criminal activity occurring at the Remington. This practice was possibly, negligent or amounting to intentional misrepresentation according to Chau.

At trial, testimony was presented that when Chau visited the Remington to inquire about renting an apartment she was told by a leasing representative that the Remington had not experienced any problems with crime for the past couple of years. Also Chau was told that a guard would be patrolling the Remington at night. Additional testimony was presented stating numerous crimes, some even violent, had been committed at the Remington. Several former employees at the Remington testified to the management's lack of response to concerns about security on the premises, and leasing agents were instructed by management to tell prospective tenants that "there's no crime that we know of here" (Southstar Equity LLC v. Lai Chau 2008).

The trial judgment was based on a jury award of compensatory damages against the property owner and property manager for $5 677 000, and punitive damages awards against Southstar for $3 000 000 and Brookside for $7 000 000. The appellate court agreed with the trial court and affirmed this judgment.

Social guests, considered invitees under property law, are also owed some level of protection from dangerous conditions. In *Rowland v. Christian*, the plaintiff was a social guest in Miss Christian's apartment (Rowland v. Christian 1968). Miss Christian was told by the plaintiff, her guest, that he was going to use the bathroom. She had known for two weeks before the accident that the faucet handle in her bathroom was cracked. She told the property manager of the building of the condition but nothing was done to repair the condition of the handle. The plaintiff had used the bathroom on a prior occasion. Miss Christian did not say anything to plaintiff about the condition of the broken handle, and when the plaintiff turned off the faucet, the handle broke in his hands causing serious injuries by severing the tendons and medial nerve in his right hand.

At the time of the trail, California Civil Code stated:

> Everyone is responsible, not only for the result of his willful acts, but also for an injury occasioned to another by his want of ordinary care or skill in the management of his property or person, except so far as the latter has, willfully or by want of ordinary care, brought the injury upon himself. . . (Rowland v. Christian 1968)

The court held that Miss Christian should have warned Mr Rowland of the dangerous handle and decided for the plaintiff.

In the similar case of *Howard v. Howard*, the plaintiff was injured by slipping on spilled grease (Howard v. Howard 1960). The court found that the defendant was negligent because the defendant requested the plaintiff to enter the kitchen by a route which he knew would be dangerous and flawed, and that the defendant failed to warn her of the dangerous condition.

13.6 Chapter summary

The simple take-away from this chapter is that the Facility Manager has a duty to do whatever it takes to provide a safe environment for customers, employees and even unforeseen visitors to any property within their control. This is one of the most important areas for the Facility Manager, since maintaining the building and surrounding area is usually the main thrust of the job. The safe conditions must be provided for all classes of occupants, even those with disabilities. If not, the Facility Manager runs the risk of discriminating against a growing class of people. It is not difficult to imagine that many veterans with special needs will require building accommodations and at a rate higher than we have been used to in the past. Because of this and updated ADA regulations, the duty is higher in the situation of a disabled applicant or employee.

The legal rationale for such a high standard is simply because the Facility Manager is in the superior position with regards to knowledge about the premises and its hidden dangerous conditions.

Reviewing the case law and statutes, one can see that the extent of this duty has developed over time, placing more and more responsibility on the controller of the building. After ensuring the premises is safe for all who have potential to enter onto the property, the next best strategy is to be proactive and plan for repairing potential dangerous conditions that arise over time. One way to stay abreast of developments in this area, and ensure your building is up to current industry standards, is to remain active in industry associations. Facility Managers are also encouraged to seek industry endorsement by obtaining education and designations such as the Certified Facility Manager (CFM). A simple Internet tracking of "lawsuits involving building owners and Facility Managers", using the update function of a search engine, is also useful.

13.7 Questions

1. Why do you think there are so many statutes regulating safety?
2. In your opinion is the ADA fair? Explain your answer.
3. Why should the Facility Manager be concerned about a safe premises? Isn't that the responsibility of the owner of the property?
4. Why has Congress created administrative agencies responsible for adjudicating interpretation of specific federal statutes?
5. Some federal statutes mentioned in this chapter have created "commissions" responsible for enforcement. Choose one and write a brief explanation about the enforcement responsibilities of a specific commission.

6. Explain how belonging to an industry group for Facility Managers will benefit building occupants.
7. Why is it important to warn occupants of potential criminal behavior in the area?
8. What are the requirements to obtain a CFM?
9. With all the potential liability the Facility Manager could be exposed to, what areas of training beyond college should the professional seek?
10. Is there an extra duty to warn disabled occupants about potential hazards on the premises that may not pose a danger to able-bodied occupants? Explain your answer.

References

Posner, R. Killing or wounding to protect a property interest. *Journal of Law and Economics*, vol. XIV, no. 1 (April 1972): 201–232.

14

Risk Management

> With notably rare exceptions (2008, for example), the global "invisible hand" has created relatively stable exchange rates, interest rates, prices, and wage rates.
>
> **Alan Greenspan**

> Other things that are similarly true:
>   With notably rare exceptions, Newt Gingrich is a loyal and faithful husband.
>   With notably rare exceptions, Japanese nuclear reactors have been secure from earthquakes.
>   Though unredeemably [sic] opaque, Mr. Madoff's operations delivered excellent returns, with notably rare exceptions.
>   With notably rare exceptions, the levees protecting New Orleans have held fast in the face of major hurricanes.
>   With notably rare exceptions, locking all exits to the workplace is a harmless way to improve your employees' productivity.
>   With notably rare exceptions, petroleum extraction has minimal environmental impact.
>
> **Henry Farrell**

14.1 Introduction

Henry Farrell's response to Alan Greenspan is a humorous way of noting that most disasters are, in fact, rare. As you will learn in this chapter, preparing a proper risk strategy involves paying attention to the rare but very expensive catastrophe.

Legal Concepts for Facility Managers, First Edition. Linda Thomas-Mobley.
© 2014 John Wiley & Sons, Ltd. Published 2014 by John Wiley & Sons, Ltd.

The hallmark of any successful Facility Manager is the ability to manage risk well. She must understand the various ways the built environment should function and can malfunction, anticipate the most likely problems and protect the owner's interest in such a way that the building can be productive for business purposes, yet not expose the owner to additional unnecessary liability. It is in this sense that the Facility Manager must know the major concepts of risk avoidance, including how to avoid unnecessary legal obstacles.

At the end of this chapter the following learning outcomes are expected:

- List the major risk avoidance strategies.
- Define the term *underwriter*.
- Describe the difference between insurance and surety.
- Describe the basic services provided for by an insurance company.
- Describe the concepts behind workers' compensation legalities.
- Define risk.
- Describe the operation of a general liability coverage insurance policy.
- Describe the operation of an occurrence-based insurance policy.
- Describe the operation of a time-based insurance policy.
- Outline basic best practices for Facility Managers purchasing insurance.
- List the personal exposure the Facility Manager may face while performing duties.
- Define an agent.
- Describe the expectations of the insurance company of the insured.
- Describe the significance of being a "named insured".
- List the major types of insurance typically carried by a company.
- Define the term claim.
- Describe in general the claims process.
- Define the term *good faith* with regard to the operation of an insurance company.

14.2 Risk management

The job of a built environment professional constantly changes with the industry in which she finds herself. The concerns of the Facility Manager for a large university are quite different from the concerns of the Construction Manager for a hospital complex. Notwithstanding the differences, the owners and managers of all properties face a core set of similar loss exposures. Generally, risk considered in a commercial setting can be either business risk or pure risk. Figure 14.1 illustrates this concept.

Pure risk refers to accidents, or an occurrence of loss that was not anticipated. Compare pure risk to *business risk*, which is actually calculated based on known data. A business risk has the potential to increase profits or lead to financial losses. Determining whether a business risk is worth the cost of a

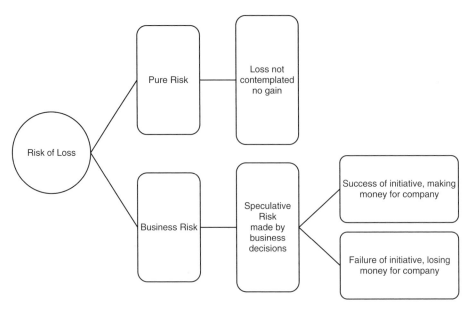

Figure 14.1   Classification of risks.

potential financial loss is a business decision. This is because, if a business loss occurs, it may be common for that specific business and is considered just the cost of being in a particular industry. Since the goal of a business is to increase the shareholder's profits, a goal of this type of analysis is to make sure successes are the result of a business risk that has been contemplated and exploited for profit.

Pure risk, which is risk that has no potential of producing revenue for a company, should be minimized. The method used for identifying and analyzing risks in order to minimize loss is called *risk management*.

In risk management the aim is to proactively prevent a loss from occurring or, at least, to minimize the costs related to a loss that cannot be prevented. In general the following steps constitute the *risk management process*:

1. Identify loss exposure;
2. Measure and analyze this loss to determine the probability of occurring, potential extent of the loss and possible frequency of the loss;
3. Choose best risk control and risk financing method;
4. Implement the chosen method or methods;
5. Monitor the risk management strategy and adjust as necessary.

This particular method was developed by the Building Owners and Managers Association Institute (BOMI) (Spock 2006). Figure 14.2 depicts a graphical representation of the steps.

The first step of identifying the potential risks requires careful attention because it is the most critical of all. The success or failure of the entire risk

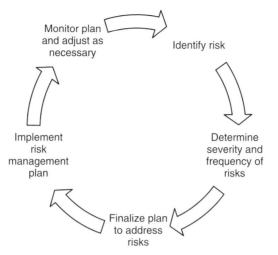

Figure 14.2   Risk management process.

management process and resulting plan depends on the correct identification of loss exposures. This list of risks must not only include those risks under the control of the Facility Manager, it must also include risks under the control of other employees of the company, and external sources like independent contractors, vendors or other potential instabilities, such as natural acts and man-made disasters. For example, consider the instance of an accounting firm located in one of the World Trade Center Towers in New York having a risk management plan formulated based solely on internal risks. On the day after the fateful terrorist attack in 2001, the accounting firm would find themselves exposed to enormous losses.

In this step you are asked to list the potential losses but what does that mean? What does the industry mean by "types" of loss exposures? There are generally three types of losses; property, liability and personnel. Property losses refer to damage to property itself, for instance, a broken computer monitor. It can also refer to real property losses like floods and earthquake damage. Additionally, the Facility Manager must also consider the indirect loss of profits related to the temporary interruption of the work, which was to be completed using that computer monitor. Other types of indirect losses associated with real property loss include rental income due to damages on the premises from a fire or other disaster.

At this point in the text, you should be very familiar with liability losses; these refer to losses from injuries caused by someone's negligence. They include physical injuries to people or property, or "personal injury" losses such as libel, slander and defamation of character. Personal injury is any injury to the body or mind. Personal injury also refers to the damage done to an individual's emotional state.

Finally, the last type of risk can be described as the risk of personnel loss. Personnel losses are those losses to the business from the disability, sickness or death of an employee. For example, the loss of an ironworker on a fast tracked construction project could have a major impact if risk mitigation strategies are not in place.

The type of loss exposure in many cases will overlap. Consider the instance where an employee is disabled because of an injury caused by another employee's negligent maintenance of the electrical system, which causes a fire. The potential resulting loss exposures include property, liability and personnel losses. The categorizing of the types of risk loss should not be strictly interpreted as having bright line subdivisions. This is more of a listing technique, in hopes that using this nomenclature to sort the risks into types will aid in the identification of all potential risks.

To classify potential losses for a specific industry, the use of published risk checklists is suggested. These are available from the Risk and Insurance Management Society (RIMS) in the United States or specialized insurance companies familiar with specific industries. The potential risk list can also be populated by making physical inspections of the property, interviewing employees working in the areas and through consultations with risk experts.

With a well-developed list of potential exposure to loss, the next step is to measure and analyze these risks. Analysis of risks is typically accomplished by estimating the potential costs and earnings lost. Additionally, a computation regarding the possible frequency of the risk will need to be completed. One of the most common mistakes at this point in risk analysis is for the company to only cover those risks that have the possibility to occur frequently. It is natural to want to address risks that occur often, especially since these tend to be the first risks that come to mind. But, as you recall in the example of the accounting agency, not analyzing the low frequency-high cost risk of a terrorist attack can be also severely detrimental to a business.

After the analysis is complete, a plan for controlling the identified risks is recommended. Controlling the risk of fire from a space heater may be as simple as prohibiting them in workspaces. A written employee handbook or safety manual clearly stating this policy may be an action item for the risk management plan. In finalizing the risk management plan, the built environment professional should make sure to include the list of risk types, the estimated frequency and severity of those risks, and an actual action plan for controlling them.

Risk management professionals suggest that the major strategies for controlling identified risks include: avoidance of the exposure in the first place; mitigation of the risk by separating hazards and other strategies to lower the cost of severity; transference of the risk by contracting with an expert willing to accept the risk for a fee; engaging in loss prevention tactics and finally, financing for those risks identified for retention (Dorfman 2007). Identification of risks for retention is often done by risk professionals who are comfortable with estimating the loss exposure. Deciding to retain certain risks is a viable and acceptable strategy, as long as the costs, severity and frequency are carefully explored.

Diligent and thorough exploration, prior to purchasing real estate, is compulsory to avoid exposure to loss from risk.

An example of the mitigation strategy of separation is used in all modern office buildings, the firewalls. Firewalls are used to separate rooms or sections of a building to limit the loss from a fire. We've seen the strategy of contracting away exposures in earlier chapters, and in our discussion on insurance we will further discuss the value of engaging in loss prevention and reduction.

Unfortunately, even with all the risk management strategies being employed, accidents still happen. It is because of these accidents that in addition to the risks being managed, potential loss must be contemplated and considered an expense of the business. The preparation for unavoidable losses includes purchasing insurance, self-insuring, contracting to a party willing to take the risk and establishing a "captive insurer". After purchasing insurance coverage, the next most widely used financing strategy is to self-insure. When a company self-insures, they determine how much is needed and they keep cash reserves on hand in case of a loss costing less than the limit established. Most adults practice this risk strategy by deciding to pay car insurance premiums that reflect a high *deductible*. The deductible is the amount of out-of-pocket expense the insured is responsible for in the event of a covered loss. For some, a low amount of self-insurance is appropriate but for others, a higher deductible, for instance $1000, will allow lower premium payments, thus saving money over time. The amount of self-insurance depends on the availability of cash reserves one can tolerate.

Establishing a captive insurer is an approach used by larger companies to finance losses. When a business entity creates a separate insurance carrier with the major customer being the entity itself, the captive insurer strategy is being used. The rule of thumb given for this arrangement to be an appropriate financing strategy necessitates that the premiums paid by a company should be in excess of several million dollars annually.

14.3 Conflict avoidance

According to Sun Tzu, (c. 500–320. B.C.E.), a name used by the unknown Chinese authors of *The Art of War*, the best battle, is the battle that is won without being fought (Tzu 1994). If we use war to represent any conflict or problem, it is easy to see why the risk management strategy of "avoidance" would be listed first and should be the first strategy employed in any loss prevention plan. Due in part to the labyrinthine nature of the built environment industry, risk and the resulting conflict is as much a part of a project as building materials and cost estimates. Seemingly small changes that may cause a significant ripple throughout a project are typically made both on the spot in haste and after careful contemplation. Yet, in the majority of projects, conflicts are resolved and the project runs smoothly enough to prevent the parties from filing formal lawsuits. Practicing active conflict avoidance is a risk management strategy that inexpensively lowers the cost of managing risks.

Conflict is a state of disharmony between apparently incompatible people, ideas or interests. Excessive disharmony in building projects is disastrous and, therefore, measures that reduce or eliminate conflicts are highly advantageous to all involved in the production of the built environment. The construction process undertaken by Facility Managers involves several diverse stakeholders with differing agendas, many of which are conflicting. The stakeholders on a project can include the owner, builder, construction manager, designer, vendors and suppliers, and the occupants. These stakeholders have to interact with each other with relative efficiency for the goal of a successful project to become a reality.

There are several successful conflict management or conflict resolution methodologies used worldwide. An overview of the various methods of conflict avoidance and conflict resolution, including the proactive and reactive, and informal to the more formal, will be discussed in this section. It should be noted that, although many of the methods are similar, different jurisdictions use them with slight modifications. Also, this discussion is designed to outline and describe conflict management concepts; your specific terminology may differ.

Six major factors define the method of conflict management (Kelleher and Lehman 2009):

1. Legal system in effect;
2. Contract or agreement language;
3. Willingness of parties to litigate;
4. Quality management systems;
5. Project delivery system;
6. Conflict resolution techniques available.

The six factors determine the likelihood of conflict occurring in a particular situation. The legal system and dispute resolution traditions of a particular jurisdiction have an effect on a party's willingness to litigate. This, along with the conflict resolution techniques available to the parties, all has a direct effect on a stakeholder's desire to communicate and resolve any potential conflicts, or allow a problem to escalate to formal litigation or other intervention if necessary. This desire to communicate can also be encouraged by the language of the contracts that are in place. Finally, the choice of project delivery system and the appropriate consideration for producing a quality project may also decrease the likelihood of litigation (Kelleher and Lehman 2009).

14.3.1 The origin of conflicts

Conflicts often start as small problems or misunderstandings, and in most cases communication amongst the essential parties will go a long way to expediting a solution. If these disagreements are ignored, or if they are unable to be resolved simply, the problem may develop into a full-blown conflict causing time delays and possible cost escalation. Since projects are by nature time-sensitive, even in jurisdictions where litigation expense is low, early informal resolution is preferred over protracted formal resolution.

There are numerous reasons for small problems to develop. Details being overlooked, a misinterpretation of a contract clause, a slight error in the estimate, unexpected weather events, delays of all sorts, changes made in the design and late payments are a few of them. Justin Sweet and Marc Schneier indicate that there are six leading causes of construction conflicts (Sweet 2009):

1. Delays with incorporating changes.
2. Owner driven changes.
3. Unintentionally ambiguous contract documents.
4. Unrealistic risk allocation.
5. Poor communication.
6. Unrealistically low bid price.

Regardless of the cause of the conflict, the focus should be on its prevention, or if that fails, its resolution. It is beneficial to the student to divide the range of the methods by which conflicts can be resolved into a series of stages for illustration. One convenient method of division used here involves the following stages:

1. Proactive stage
2. Project level stage
3. Informal stage
4. Formal stage

As the conflict advances from the proactive stage to the formal stage, the cost to the parties also tends to increase.

The proactive stage
In the proactive stage it is possible to identify, contain or resolve a conflict without major disruption. This is the most efficient stage to accomplish a consensus, and adequate attention to implementing practices and polices that reduce conflicts should be used by the prudent Facility Manager. Decisions made with prevention and cooperation as key elements prove to be most

successful. This stage encompasses all methods involving pre-planning and encouraging cooperative attitudes among the parties. Any identified incomplete or vague issues are best addressed at this stage. Ample communication and team building also mitigate possible conflicts.

Management decisions

Management decisions are not usually considered a proactive tool for conflict avoidance, yet management of the quality expected, management of the agreements among the stakeholders and sound project management are the most cost effective conflict avoidance measures. Effective leadership is an ongoing process for the Facility Manager that should be employed at the beginning of any project and throughout its duration as routine practice.

As was stated in the chapter on contract law, all parties must thoroughly read the contract documents to become familiar with the obligations required of the various parties.

In addition to savvy management and careful selection of the subcontractors or implementation team, documentation of the project's progress should not be forgotten. Several small conflicts can be resolved quickly with the aid of project photographs or detailed objectives. In the contracts for services, it is good practice to require written notice for changes, time extensions, late payments and provisions for contract termination. Schedule updates are essential, as well as cost updates and daily reports, meeting minutes and videos of progress, or other methods for updating the changing project. Documentation and frequent communication is essential to managing the project successfully and reduces the potential for conflict later, when memories start to fade.

Partnering

The manufacturing industry has used a conflict avoidance technique, referred to as partnering, since the 1980s. The United States Army pioneered partnering as an alternative measure of conflict resolution in construction in 1988. Additionally, the American Institute of Architects (AIA), American Consulting Engineers Council and the National Society of Professional Engineers have become great proponents of partnering (Cushman 1982: California Department of Transportation 2008).

Partnering is a relationship based on trust. Two organizations come together and commit, long term, to achieve mutual goals. Many organizations use this technique to foster trust and openness between parties to a large project. Partnering requires an attitude change involving the significant stakeholders of a specific project. This change requires the parties to treat each other as team members in the project, not adversarys. The team building accomplished at the very beginning of the project, through a series of meetings and workshops, is run by a facilitator with each member of the project team assembled together.

Once the decision to use this technique has been made, the commitment of company executives, as well as all the constructors, designers, owners, subcontractors and building occupants, is necessary for success.

The facilitator is a neutral person who helps the participants remain organized and focused from the outset of the process. The facilitator helps develop workshop content and leads the sessions. Generally, the workshop is held at a neutral location that enhances the partnering process. Being away from the office for the workshop is seen as a way to help participants focus on the task of team building. Typically, this process lasts from one to two days in length.

The focus of the workshop is on creating a document called the partnering charter. The partnering charter is the focal point of the relationship and the blueprint for success. In the charter, the parties set forth a series of moral commitments, general and specific, such as their mission statement, mutual goals and objectives, and finally their commitment to the partnering process. Signed by all participants and displayed at the job site and offices of the participants, the partnering charter is the codification of the agreement to working relationships based on trust and team building.

In addition to the partnering charter, the parties create an issue escalation procedure. An issue escalation procedure identifies the respective decision-makers for each party, beginning with job site personnel and ending with project executives. All parties then agree to deal with issues at the job level first, and dictate procedures and time frames that outline procedures on continuing problem solving if necessary, at the project level, without having the threat of formal litigation looming. The stakeholders also design a conflict resolution approach to be used in the event that an issue cannot be resolved via the issue escalation procedure. This process forces the participants to contemplate potential conflicts and decide prior to actual conflict how these problems will be resolved and who will be responsible.

The end of the retreat does not end the partnering process. The philosophies and procedures adopted at the workshop must be implemented and reviewed on a regular basis in order to achieve the full effect and benefit of the partnering process. Stakeholders must continue to trust each other, communicate efficiently, adhere to the partnering charter and issue escalation procedures. The parties must also recognize that having an actual conflict arise does not constitute failure, but is merely an opportunity to witness the effectiveness of the partnering process.

One drawback to the partnering methodology is that it may be difficult to achieve a sincere commitment from all stakeholders due to stubborn adherence to traditional adversarial attitudes. Some constructors may see partnering as a waste of time and would rather focus on completion of the project.

The California Department of Transportation is a strong proponent of partnering (California Department of Transportation 2008). Over time they have collected lessons learned and report that the following action items have proven to lead to success of the partnering exercise and the project as a whole. These items include:

- Follow up and measure progress
- Train and empower the field staff
- Get stakeholders to participate and buy-in
- Partner at the strategic/program level
- Ensure decision-making and risk management occurs
- Recognize and award effort

These lessons learned have been integrated into a Field Guide to Partnering on Caltrans Construction Projects available free online (California Department of Transportation 2008).

14.4 Insurance

The purchasing of insurance is another form of the risk management practice of "financing". Even with well-thought-out plans, there still exists a modicum of risk for the built environment professional. The smart professional is not only focused on mitigating and eliminating loss, she must understand how to finance the losses that will occur.

The insurance industry is somewhat of a mystery to most outside the industry. Insurance is best defined as contracting with a guarantor to finance for potential losses. The insurance contract is governed by the same legal theory other contracts follow. Parties to this contract are generally the insurance company, called the "insurer", and the purchaser of the guarantee, called the "insured". In many commercial cases the insured is usually the company and employees seeking a way to finance future losses.

14.4.1 Types of insurers

Insurance companies can be classified as a public company, a private stock company or a private mutual company. They can also be divided along geographical lines, how they set the cost of their policies, the level of risk assumed or the types of industries they specialize in.

Figure 14.3 shows the scope of government insurance programs available. The rationale is that the risks are so unpredictable that regular insurance providers would not be willing to provide coverage. In these limited situations the government has the rare occasion to compete with private insurers for business.

Private insurers cover losses usually not covered by the government, which in the judgment of private companies, make a good business case. There are two types of private insurance companies, stock and mutual. Stock insurers

The Federal Government as Insurer	Social Security Insurance Program
	Federal Deposit Insurance Corporation
	Federal Housing Administration Insurance
	National Flood Insurance Program
	Terrorism Risk Insurance
	Federal Crop Insurance Corporation
	Nuclear Regulator Commission Insurance
	Veterans Administration
	Securities Investor Protection Corporation

Figure 14.3 Government insurance programs.

are simply regular private businesses, which are typically corporations, owned by stockholders. These corporations operate for profit and provide the majority of insurance in the USA.

Private mutual insurers refer to insurance companies owned by stockholders who are also their policyholders. There, of course are other classifications as mentioned previously, which are not relevant for the purpose of this text. The point is, there are many types of entities providing insurance just as there are many types of losses to finance.

Theoretically, one can obtain an insurance contract for any risk, as long as a willing insurer exists and wishes to sell coverage. Willing insurers determine whether or not to insure a risk based on a process called *underwriting*. Underwriting is a complex decision based on historical data about the industry and specific personal information about the entity seeking insurance.

Unlike other contracts, the contracts for insurance are highly regulated and require the insurer to follow strict ethical practices so that potential purchasers of insurance can make informed decisions about the terms of the contract. Even with these regulations, insurance contracts can be difficult to navigate without the help of an agent or broker.

There are several types of insurance agents currently in practice. The type of agent will determine the type policy that the specific agent can sell for an insurance company.

Agents working exclusively with one insurance company are called bonded agents. A bonded agent is able to explain insurance contract details for their specific company. Alternatively, an agent can be non-bonded and free to sell products from a wide variety of insurance companies.

14.4.2 Types of insurance

Insurance can be divided into categories along several themes. For example, insurance products may be categorized according to what type of loss it covers, whether the loss is specific in nature or general or whether the insured is an individual, a professional or a corporation.

Typical risks Facility Managers need protection for include: *property insurance*, *commercial general liability* and *professional liability*.

Property insurance covers both physical property and business income. Claims made under this type of insurance result in the insured party being paid for replacement cost or actual cost of the property that is lost. Property insurance claims are subject to deductibles, which is the amount of money the insured must pay out of pocket before the insurance payment is made. It can be thought of as the portion of self-insurance a company is willing to fund; the higher the deductible, the lower the cost of the insurance coverage. Business income insurance covers business income loss and is not limited to physical damage of property. Business income loss refers to the loss of revenue the business suffers as a result of the damage to its buildings or personal property. This loss can be much greater than the cost of the property. Think of the loss of an ice cream maker for the month of July. The repair of the ice cream maker may only be a few dollars but the loss of income can be substantial

Commercial General Liability Insurance (CGL) is critical for protection against exposure to claims of negligence. As we learned in the previous chapters, there are vast arrays of injuries that can result from another person's negligence. They typical injuries covered under a CGL include, bodily injury, property damage and personal injury, but the damage must arise out of a negligent act. In addition to an act of negligence, the insurance claim must arise from an "occurrence" as defined by the insurance company in the policy. Generally an occurrence is an accident and not an intentional act of the insured. As a matter of practice, intentional acts committed to deliberately cause harm are excluded from CGL coverage. Unlike other types of insurance, CGL policies usually do not have deductibles, or out-of-pocket costs, which must be paid before a claim is paid.

Professional Liability Insurance, also known as Errors and Omissions Insurance (E&O), is necessary because most CGL policies exclude coverage for errors made by professionals. These insurance contracts protect the client from claims of negligence in performing professional services. The types of injuries covered under E&O are financial losses. Negligence in performance of professional services involves errors involving specialized knowledge or skills that are usually intellectual and not manual. Malpractice insurance for the negligent practice of medicine is a type of E&O insurance. Additionally, other professionals face financial exposure, such as lawyers, architects, real estate brokers, property managers, developers and Facility Managers. The basic standard causing exposure, making E&O insurance necessary, is when a professional fails to act as a competent professional should have acted in a similar circumstance.

There are many additional types of insurance available and new coverages for emerging risks are continually being created. The limit to insurance is only related to what risks insurance companies are willing to take and how much the client is willing to pay in premiums.

With an understanding of the operation of insurance policies, it should be apparent that, one simple and cheap risk management strategy is to only contract with professionals, who are themselves properly insured, and then make sure contracts for work assign risks judiciously.

14.4.3 Responsibility of the insured

Even with the purchase of adequate insurance directly related to the type of loss being managed, the insured still has obligations she must fulfill for the insurance contract to pay a claim. Figure 14.4 outlines the five basic responsibilities of the insurance client.

In addition to the insured obligations to prevent additional loss, also called the duty to "mitigate risks", some insurance companies have loss mitigation procedures that must be followed by the insured. For example, if an insurance company insures the risk of a retailer for theft, one basic risk mitigation procedure is to require insurance clients to keep the premises locked when the business is closed. Failure to employ this simple risk mitigation strategy could release the insurance company from an obligation to pay on a loss. Remembering that there are obligations on both sides of the insurance contract will help the Facility Manager to include required risk mitigation strategies in her overall management plan.

14.4.4 Surety bonds

In addition to shifting risk to an independent contractor and purchasing insurance, using surety bonds is also a financing risk management strategy common

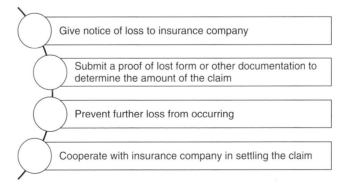

Figure 14.4   Four responsibilities of the insurance client.

in built environment projects. There exists a misconception among many that the surety bond operates the same as the insurance policy. This misconception is not only untrue, proceeding under it could be problematic for the Facility Manager.

A surety bond is a contract among three parties. The *surety company* (surety), the *principal* and the *obligee*. To illustrate the parties to a performance bond, consider the case of an owner requiring a general contractor to purchase the bond. In this case the three parties to the bond are illustrated in Figure 14.5.

Under this illustrated performance bond, the surety company guarantees that the general contractor will perform as contracted for the owner. If the promised performance does not occur, the surety company must step in to make sure the scope as promised is completed.

To fully understand the operation of the surety bond, you should understand the legal concept of "subrogation". This concept was explained as well as indemnification in an earlier chapter. The concept of subrogation can be remembered with a simple mnemonic. Subrogation refers to standing in the shoes of another. Subrogation begins with the letter "s" and so does the word shoe. In the previous example with the performance bond, requiring the contractor to grant the surety company subrogation rights means that every legal benefit the general contractor is entitled to is transferred to the surety company. But what exactly does this mean?

Suppose you grant subrogation rights to a surety company as a condition of obtaining a guarantee, or bond, that you will paint your grandmother's garage. Your grandmother requires this guarantee from you because of your past proclivity to forget promises. Since she knows that you may not perform, she has requested a performance bond to protect herself. You, wanting to make the money, ask her for half of the payment up-front and agree to comply finding a surety company that will sell you a performance bond for the job. You pay a

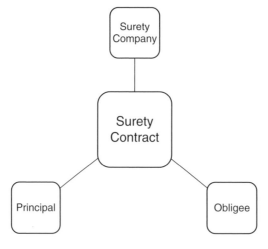

Figure 14.5   Parties to a surety bond.

small premium for this guarantee and assure the surety company that they will not have to become involved at any point in time, because you will fulfill your obligations, and paint the garage, on time and according to the agreed-upon price. Though disturbing with regard to family relations, this arrangement is a three-party agreement where the owner, your grandmother, the contractor, you, and the surety company, are all parties to a contract whereby your work is guaranteed to be completed.

On the day agreed upon for the garage painting to begin, you decide to enter a video game tournament to pass the time until work starts. As luck would have it, you keep winning and advance upward in the bracket failing to paint the garage as agreed. Not surprised, Grandma calls on the surety company to make good on their guarantee and either perform the painting or pay for someone else to do it. The surety obliges and sends a new painter to do the job. At this point, Grandma is still obligated to pay for the service but only at the originally agreed upon price. Since she previously paid you half of the total contracted price, she now only owes the other half, but the surety company must pay the full price to the new painter. All payments are made, Grandma is happy, the new painter is satisfied and you end up losing the tournament in the last round two days later.

In this example, the surety company exercises the legal concept of subrogation. The insurer now begins the process of recovering the money they paid to the new painter and any out-of-pocket costs incurred. To recover their losses, the company will come to you for payment but since you lost the tournament and never had any money to begin with, you have nothing to contribute towards their losses.

Since they have subrogation rights, they have the ability to *stand in your shoes* and recover the money you owe them. They will receive Grandma's final payment, they can recover money from your piggy bank, the few coins in your pocket, your next paycheck and any other sources available under surety law. If this does not satisfy their losses, they also have the right to stand in your shoes and file lawsuits against anyone who may owe you money. This relentless effort to recover their total costs, plus any interest owed to them, will continue until the surety company is paid in full.

Compare the guarantee and recovery efforts under subrogation of a surety company to a typical contract for insurance. After providing the agreed upon payment for your loss, the insurance company will not attempt to recover any losses. This is what you pay periodic premiums for, although this incident may increase your premiums or cause the insurer to drop you as an insurance customer, you will not have to repay any costs associated with the loss.

Many companies in the business of selling surety bonds also happen to be insurance companies. This may be one of the reasons, along with the similarity in the words "surety" and "insurance", that causes confusion but with the understanding of subrogation rights, the Facility Manager should understand these as two risk-financing strategies with very different with different consequences.

Typical surety bonds used in the built environment include, bid bonds, performance bonds, payment bonds and completion bonds. This by no means exhausts the list of potential bonds parties may decide to use for guarantees, but they are the ones most widely used.

Bid bonds are guarantees that are required by owners to ensure that the selected bidder enters into the contract as offered and provide any required performance or payment bonds. In most cases, the bid bond is used in competitive bidding, especially when the bidding is open to the public and the owner wants to make sure a qualified bidder is selected at the end of the bidding process. It is well known that preparing a bid proposal can be costly and time consuming for the service provider, in a similar vein, preparing, disseminating and reviewing bid documents is time consuming to the owner. These pre-bid tasks are generally not considered part of the project and must be absorbed as a cost of indirect overheads. The bid bond offers the owner a guarantee that if the chosen bidder is unable to enter into an acceptable contract, the surety company will pay the owner the difference between the defaulting bidder and the next lowest bidder so that the project can proceed in a timely fashion.

Performance bonds are more complicated than bid bonds, and are used as a risk avoidance strategy for the owner and a financing strategy for the builder. The example of painting your grandmother's garage is an example of a performance bond. These bonds operate to guarantee that the scope of work agreed to will be performed as required by contract or the surety company will provide compensation as agreed to in the surety contract. The most desirable compensation for the owner would be that the work agreed to by the service provider will be completed as contemplated at the start of the project. It should be noted that the surety company guaranteeing the performance bond does reserve the right to complete the contract in the way most advantageous to itself, not the principle. In the event of a breach of contract by the service provider, the surety company may choose to support the original contractor with funds and management expertise to help it complete the job. The performance bond contract can also be completed by the surety company hiring its own service provider to complete the job or simply paying for the completion based on a pre-determined cost of the project.

This means that the principal to the surety contract, which in most cases is the owner represented by the Facility Manager, may end up with a check from the surety company instead of a completed project. It should be noted that requiring a performance bond from the service provider does not actually insure a completed project but it does increase the likelihood that the project will be completed, since having a surety company come to the rescue is disadvantageous to the contractor. This is because having a principal "call" on a surety bond or requesting the surety to perform on its promise does not end the obligations of the contractor. Interestingly enough, contractors need to be bondable and provide surety bonds when required for a job, but should do everything in their power not to use the bond to complete performance.

Payment bonds operate to guarantee third parties such as subcontractors and Facility Managers that the service provider will pay for labor and supplies as used on the project. It is important for a Facility Manager to ensure all subcontractors and vendors are paid for work completed on behalf of a contractor so that filing a mechanics lien for payment is avoided. A mechanics lien operates to prevent legal transfer of any real estate until all financial obligations, such as payment to laborers, is met. It also impedes transactions such as selling the property or even obtaining loans against the property. If a general contractor is working for the Facility Manager to perform major renovations on a property, and if the general contractor gets paid for the work and does not pass payment down to the subcontractors and suppliers, then the unpaid parties can go to the courthouse and pay for a lien to be placed on the property. By requiring a payment bond, the subcontractor and vendors are protected and more likely to get paid; also the Facility Manager is protected since a laborer would have no reason to place a lien on the property.

There are other types of bonds used in the built environment industry, all for the purpose of granting guarantees that the service providers will perform as promised. These protections are relatively cheap for the service providers to obtain and give Facility Managers peace of mind in risky situations. It should be noted that being eligible to purchase a bond, or being bondable, is not easy to achieve, so if the Facility Manager insists on only working with service providers who are bondable, the pool of prospective contractors may be smaller. Do all projects need to be bonded? It will be up to the prudent Facility Manager to decide which outsourced contracts need to be bonded and if there are any situations where the bonding requirement can be abandoned. Of course, this will depend upon the specific situation, the amount of risk exposure and how comfortable the Facility Manager is with the service provider.

14.5 Chapter summary

In this chapter, basic risk management with regard to the built environment was discussed. This area is much greater than presented here. Understanding all types of risk and developing a comprehensive risk management plan are job duties of a risk management professional. Organizations like the Risk Management Society (RIMS) are a great source for researching this industry.

Risk management is an important part of planning for the Facility Manager. This process for identifying, assessing and prioritizing risks of different kinds may vary from company to company but the goal is the same: the minimization or elimination of adverse impact from negative events.

14.6 Questions

1. Why is purchasing insurance an integral part of the risk management strategy for the Facility Manager?
2. What duties should the Facility Manager perform to reduce the loss of risk?
3. Should the Facility Manager purchase insurance for personal liability?
4. What does the insurance company expect of its clients?
5. If a Facility Manager is required to protect the company's assets from exposure to asbestos claims, would they want to purchase an occurrence-based or time-based insurance policy? Explain your answer.
6. Why is risk avoidance the first step in a risk plan?
7. How can conflict management help with reducing risk?
8. Is partnering a feasible option in your area? Explain your answer.
9. Using Internet resources, find a copy of a signed Partnership Charter.
10. Could you adhere to the expectations listed on the charter you found in Q 9? Explain your answer.
11. Why does the definition of risk include two components?
12. How can the risk avoidance strategy of contracting expose the Facility Manager to risk?
13. How can the risk avoidance strategy of insurance expose the Facility Manager to risk?
14. Why is it important to consider the rare catastrophic risk?
15. Is all risk avoidable under a combination of strategies? Explain your answer.

References

California Department of Transportation. *Field Guide to Partnering on Caltrans Construction Projects*. Guide, Division of Construction, California Department of Transportation, California Department of Transportation, 2008.

Cushman, R. *Construction Litigation*. New York: Publishing Law Institute, 1982.

Dorfman, M. *Introduction to Risk Management and Insurance*. 9th Edition. Englewood Cliffs, New Jersey: Prentice Hall, 2007.

Kelleher, T, and A. Lehman. Swift, Curry and Hancock's Common Sense Construction Law. 4th Edition. New York: John Wiley & Sons, Inc., 2009.

Spock, S. Law and Risk Management. In Law and Risk Management, Spock S., pp. 8–3. Maryland: BOMI Institute International, 2006.

Tzu, S. The Art of War. (trans.) R. Sawyer. Guernsey, GY: Perseus Books Group, 1994.

Sweet, J. Legal Aspects of Architecture, Engineering and the Construction Process. 8th Edition. Edited by M. Schneier. Stamford, CT: Cengage Learning, 2009.

Summary of Part III

Part III reminds us that, at its core, Facility Management includes the practice of coordinating the physical workplace with the people and work of an organization. Behaving professionally and recognizing a professional duty not to injure others is fundamental to the success of a Facility Manager. Determining that a workplace is safe and free from hazards requires the professional judgment of the Facility Manager, which also requires a measure of professional discretion. Responsibilities and skills essential to the Facility Manager in the twenty-first century are most likely way above expectations for the seventeenth-century building caretaker. At best, they are very different obligations. Most Facility Managers are charged with protecting the physical assets and the occupants from injury. As a major component of professionalism and avoidance of conflicts and risk exposure, students and professionals are implored to stay abreast of developments in their area, and ensure buildings are up to current industry standards.

> *It was the boast of Augustus that he found Rome of brick and left it of marble. But how much nobler will be the sovereign's boast when he shall have it to say that he found law . . . a sealed book and left it a living letter; found it the patrimony of the rich and left it the inheritance of the poor; found it the two-edged sword of craft and oppression and left it the staff of honesty and the shield of innocence.*
> **Henry Brougham (1778–1868)**

Legal Concepts for Facility Managers, First Edition. Linda Thomas-Mobley.
© 2014 John Wiley & Sons, Ltd. Published 2014 by John Wiley & Sons, Ltd.

Cases

Abbot Laboratories v. Gardner. 387 US 136 (United States Supreme Court, 1967).

Alberts v. Mutual Service Casualty Insurance Co. 80 S.D. 303 (South Dakota Supreme Court, 1963).

Automobile Workers v. Johnson Controls, Inc. 499 U.S. 187 (United States Supreme Court, 1991).

Axelson v. Williamson. 324 N.W. 2d 241, 244 (Minnesota Supreme Court, 1982).

Becker v. Poling Transportantion Corp. 356 F.3d 381 (United States Court of Appeals, Second Circuit, 2004).

Bennett v. Stanley. 92 Ohio St 3d 35 (2001).

Carroll Cutter v. Town of Farmington. 126 N.H. 836 (Supreme Court of New Hampshire, 1985).

Daubert v. Merrell Dow Pharmaceuticals. 509 US 579 (United States Supreme Court, 1993).

EEOC v. Convergys Customer Management Group Inc,. 491 F3.d 790 (8th Circuit Court of Appeals, June 6, 2007).

EEOC v. El Du Pont De Nemours & Co. 480 F.3d 724 (2007).

EH Construction, LLC v. Delor Design Group, Inc. 134 S.W.3d 575 (Kentucky, 2004).

Fifth Club v. Ramirez. No. 04-0550 (Supreme Court of Texas, 2006).

Frye v. United States. 293 F. Supp. 1013 (Federal Court of Appeals, 1923).

Green v. Soule. 145 Cal. 96,99 (1904).

Harness v. Churchmembers Life Insurance Co. . 241 Ind. 672 (1961).

Heng Or, administrator v. Lawrence C. Edwards. 62 Mass Ap. Ct. 475 (Mass Appellate Court, 2004).

Higgins v. Watervliet Turnpike Co. 46 N.Y. 23 (New York Supreme Court, 1871).

Howard v. Howard. 186 Cal.App.2d 625 (1960).

John Martin Co. v. Morse/Diesel, Inc. 819 S.W.2d 428 (Tennessee Supreme Court, 1991).

Johnson v. Johnson. 611 N.W.2d 823, 827 (Minnisota Court of Appeal, 2000).

Legal Concepts for Facility Managers, First Edition. Linda Thomas-Mobley.
© 2014 John Wiley & Sons, Ltd. Published 2014 by John Wiley & Sons, Ltd.

Khun Construction Company Ocean v. Coastal Consultants and Robert Waite, PE, PC v. 844 F. Supp.2d 529 (United States District Court, February 14, 2012).

Kinsman Transit Co. 338 F.2d 708 (Second Circuit Court, New York 1964).

Kratzer v. Rockwell Collins, Inc. 398 F.3d 1040 (Eigth Circuit Court of Appeals, 2005).

Laukkanen v. Jewel Tea Co. Inc. 78 Ill. App.2d 153 (1966).

Lim v. Interstate System Steel Division, Inc. 435 N.W.2d 830 (Minnesota Appellate Court, 1989).

Lujan v. Defenders of Wildlife. 504 US 555 (United States Supreme Court, 1992).

MacPherson v. Buick Motor Co. 217 N.Y. 382; 111 N.E. 1050 (New York Court of Appeals, 1960).

Mapp v. Ohio. 367 U.S. 643 (1961).

Miranda v. Arizona. 384 U.S. 436 (1966).

Phelps v. Hamlett. No. 8936 (Court of Civil Appeals of Texas, Ft. Worth November 23, 1918).

Photo Production Ltd v. Securicor Transport Ltd. (Diplock) 1 All ER 556 (1980).

Privette v. Superior Court. 2 Cal.4th 689; 854 P.2d 721 (1993).

Rodriguez v. Conagra Grocery Products Co., 436 F.3d 468 (2006).

Rowland v. Christian. 69 Cal.2d 108 (1968).

Saine v. Comcast Cablevision of Arkansas, Inc. 354 Ark. 492 (Arkansas Supreme Court, 2003).

Shirly v. Glass. 241 P.3d 134 (Kansas Appellate Court, 2010).

Skow v. Steele. 49 N.W.2d 24 (South Dakota Supreme Court, 1951).

Southstar Equity LLC v. Lai Chau. No. 2D05-1306 (February 6, 2008).

Stanley K. Miller and Deborah D. Miller v. Wal-Mart Stores, Inc. 96-2529 (1998).

Staub v. Proctor Hospital. 560 F. 3d 647, 652 (United States Supreme Court, 2009).

Tabler v. Wallace. 704 S.W.2d 179 (Kentucky Supreme Court, 1985).

Tebbe, L. *Exempt v. Nonexempt*. 2000. http://asip.experience.com/alumnus (accessed September 9, 2012).

The People v. Silver. 16 Cal.2d 714 (California Supreme Court, December 18, 1940).

Thompson v. United States. 504 F.Supp 1087 (United States Supreme Court, 1980).

United States v. Elias. 269 F.3d 1003 (9th Circuit, 2001).

Whirlpool Corp. v. Marshall. 445 U.S. 1 (United States Supreme Court, 1980).

Winn v. Haliday. 109 Miss. 691 (Supreme Court of Missippi, 1915).

Index

Legal Concepts for Facility Managers, First Edition. Linda Thomas-Mobley.
© 2014 John Wiley & Sons, Ltd. Published 2014 by John Wiley & Sons, Ltd.